CALM:
Computer Aided Leadership
& Management

CALM: Computer Aided Leadership & Management

✦

—How Computers Can Unleash the Full Potential of Individuals and Organizations in a World of Chaos and Confusion

by Morten Middelfart

iUniverse, Inc.
New York Lincoln Shanghai

CALM: Computer Aided Leadership & Management
—How Computers Can Unleash the Full Potential of Individuals and Organizations in a World of Chaos and Confusion

Copyright © 2005 by Morten Middelfart

iUniverse books may be ordered through booksellers or by contacting:

iUniverse
2021 Pine Lake Road, Suite 100
Lincoln, NE 68512
www.iuniverse.com
1-800-Authors (1-800-288-4677)

ISBN: 0-595-32991-8

Printed in the United States of America

To my Father who has dedicated his life to helping others.

Contents

List of Illustrations ix

Introduction xiii

CHAPTER 1   How Computing Changed the World 1
  The Evolution of Computers 1
  The Hyper-Volatile World 9

CHAPTER 2   Human Potential 14
  The Potential of Human Individuals 14
  The Potential of Human Organizations 23
  The CALM Hypothesis of Unleashing Potential 27

CHAPTER 3   Eliminating Fear 33
  Acting Despite Our Inherent Human Fear 33
  Shredding the Collective Fear 44

CHAPTER 4   Computing for Wisdom 51
  Knowledge to Accept and Act 51
  Computing for the Full Organizational Potential 58
  From Knowledge to Wisdom 64

CHAPTER 5   Optimizing Individual and Organizational
             Energy 70
  Harnessing Energy and Change 70
  Energizing the Organization 76

CHAPTER 6   Computing for Energy in the Organization 87
  Organic Thinking and Computing 87
  Stopping the Bleeding 98

A State of "Being" 103

CHAPTER 7   Strategic Direction and Focus 107

Approaching Strategy. 107

Defining Leadership and Management 111

Visioning by Sending the Mind Ahead 114

Strategizing by Feeling the Environment 121

Building Core Competency on Talent. 125

Stimulating Motivation and Creativity through Objectives 130

CHAPTER 8   Mastering CALM. 133

Computing for Visions 133

Computerized Strategic Probing 136

Computing for Talent 141

Computing for Autonomous OODA. 143

The Edge of Computing 149

CHAPTER 9   CALM in the Future 152

Implementing CALM 152

The CALM Evolution 168

The Hypothesis Revisited 175

CHAPTER 10   CALM Speculations. 179

Synergic Evolution. 179

The Ghost in the Machine. 184

Life and Computers. 186

Concluding Remarks 188

Endnotes 191

List of Illustrations

Figure 2.1 Three Human Energies *19*

Figure 3.1 The Cycle of Change *42*

Figure 4.1 Example of Facts and Sentinels *53*

Figure 4.2 The Wisdom Triangle *55*

Figure 4.3 The Ambient Orb *62*

Table 4.1 Systems for Computing Against Fear *68*

Figure 5.1 Our Core Human Assets *74*

Figure 5.2 The OODA Cycle *79*

Figure 5.3 The Singular OODA Cycle Organization *80*

Figure 5.4 Organization with Multiple OODA Cycles *82*

Figure 5.5 The Strength of an Organization *84*

Figure 6.1 The Computerized OODA cycle *92*

Figure 6.2 Core Competency Assessment of OODA Cycle *93*

Figure 6.3 Core Competencies Revealed *94*

Figure 6.4 The Create vs. Maintain Equilibrium *103*

Table 6.1 Computer Systems to Energize *106*

Figure 7.1 Example of Probing *122*

Figure 7.2 The Ansoff Matrix *124*

Figure 7.3 The Theory of Finding Flow *127*

Figure 7.4 The Time Management Matrix *129*

Table 8.1 CALM for leaders and managers *150*

Figure 9.1 CALM Components and Their Ownership *164*

Figure 9.2 Three Steps to CALM *165*

Figure 9.3 Findings from the Business Intelligence in the Future Study *166*

Acknowledgments

This book has been a journey. I have had the privilege of receiving much inspiration and help from a lot of people along the way, and to all who have been willing to discuss matters of CALM as well as other aspects of life, I wish to extend my gratitude. There are a few people I wish to single out for their specific efforts, and without them this book would not have been what it is today.

Professor and author Patrick J. Robinson, MBA, PhD, has played a major role during the entire process of developing the idea as well as producing the book. Pat's willingness to meet with me for inspirational and mind-breaking dialogues while he was traveling in Denmark inspired me to develop the initial idea of CALM into a coherent concept. Pat motivated and guided me through the project from the research stage to the finished book; as explained later in this book, one could say that Pat helped me identify the "Palms in the Horizon."

Laurel Barley assisted and inspired me during her editing of the book. Her enthusiasm and help has not only provided a more readable book than I would have been able to write by myself, but her support and help has given me confidence and motivation during the final stages of the book.

Christina S. Hansen, Henrik Rosendahl, and Maria Suhr-Jessen have been kind enough to assess the book and voice their opinions, as well as to suggest areas of clarification and improvement.

From the medical faculty, Lisbeth Røhl, PhD, and neuroscientist Torben E. Lund have contributed knowledge and inspiration from their fields. Skydiving instructor Jakob Laustsen has assisted in creating experiments with skydiving and video journals, as well as in participating in discussions around the subjects related to extreme situations.

Management consultants Kim Møller Rasmussen and Ulrik Villadsen contributed their knowledge in the field of synergic cooperation.

A special thanks to my agent Penny Killebrew whose support and encouragement during the process has been invaluable.

Finally, the entire TARGIT team contributed valuable assistance throughout the whole project in terms of analytical tools, Web sites, Internet surveys, feedback, and, most importantly, faith and support.

Introduction

I have worked with computers for what seems to me to be a long time, most of my life actually. It all began while I was playing with computers at age fourteen, back in 1984; I became fascinated with user interfaces, as I saw them as the key to leveraging the potential of computers to benefit people.

Back in 1984, the private school I went to was the first in the local community to embrace computers in elementary education; during the first year the computer classes were only for students with high grades in math and English. Needless to say, a number of students felt that they were being abandoned by a technological development that they intuitively knew was important. However, after the computer classes had been tested for one year, they were made mandatory at the school. Regardless of the teachers' good intentions to bring everyone up to speed on technology, most students still lacked sufficient skills to work with a computer after graduation because there was no distinction between users and developers at that time, which made sense since a programming language was the only software for the computer—there was no software like the applications we know today. So logically teachers trained everyone to be a programmer.

I had no problem acquiring my programming skills fairly quickly in these classes; before the end of the first year, I had developed my first computer game for the Commodore 64 and sold it for $100 to a computer magazine. However, as a participant in the mandatory classes, it struck me that a language that was easier than the programming languages, such as BASIC or COMAL, might let more students learn to benefit from the computing power available. With that in mind, I set out to develop a new programming language with simpler and richer instructions; such a language would be easier to operate, as the user would not need to know as many commands to do complex things. For the technically interested readers, the programming language was programmed in BASIC on a Commodore 64; therefore, the user would have to pay severely in performance in order to get my proposed usability benefits....

I have retained the ambition to make computers easier to use ever since the days of the Commodore 64; however, the focus has shifted tremendously since the time when the challenge for the user was to program it. Today the challenge is to turn data into information and knowledge, and from there turn factual and experimental knowledge into wisdom. Turning data in computers into human wisdom has been a challenge for practically every organization I have been involved with while working in this field for the past decade. I have been privileged to take part in the challenges of organizations as a knowledge worker, a programmer, a software architect, an entrepreneur, as well as an executive. First and foremost, however, it was my involvement with hundreds of organizations around the globe, from small operations to Fortune 500 enterprises, as they attempted to meet the challenges of competing globally that gave me the inspiration as well as the confidence to write this book.

It seems obvious to me that there are three ways in which organizations fail to maximize their potential. First of all, we are not exploiting our talents and our minds to the fullest extent. We live in various degrees of fear that make us hesitate and restrict our lives. Second, if we assemble an organization from multiple individuals with these restraints we aggregate the loss in human potential while at the same time preventing ourselves from reaching a state of interpersonal synergy, synergy that is free from fear and mistrust. On top of these two issues, the third loss of potential is the problem I attempted to address in my first programming experience; namely, people's inability to interact with computers. This inability is what prevents us from using computing to the extent where it is capable of making an extraordinary impact.

In other words, a huge amount of potential is lost, potential that could have been converted into energy that would make organizations successful and people more contented, less stressed out, and most importantly, less burdened with fear.

Turning now to my own love for computing, I was compelled to research and describe some of my visions of how computing could change the scenario where potential is lost today and could continue to be lost in the future. My attempt to summarize my research and thoughts led to a concept for using computers to unleash their potential and apply it optimally in an individual and an organizational context. The concept is called CALM: Computer Aided Leadership and Management. Overall, CALM is a concept for unleashing the potential of both individuals and organizations through computers; in this case, potential is mental work only, meaning that I basically take the traditional workflow optimization through computer processing, as well as physical work through robotics, for granted. Few will dispute that people are gradually being displaced from these disciplines in favor of the raw physical strength of machines or basic computing power of computers. The CALM concept seeks to take the next step from there, as we traditionally see computing and human labor as very different. CALM is the exploration of short-term and long-term possibilities for using computing to unleash people's mental and emotional potential in either an individual or an organizational context.

In this book I will describe the environment that we live in and that organizations operate in. It is an environment that has been shaped significantly by computing in the past decade and will be even more so in the future. From this standpoint I will review some of the latest research in human psychology, neuroscience, and organization in order to identify ways for computing to address the restraint of fear. Next, I will share my theory and vision for computers to assist organizations in becoming more energized, meaning that they will have the necessary abilities to survive and to succeed. Energy in this sense is the unleashing of human and organizational potential, but it is also about using computing in revolutionary new ways for humans and computers to work autonomously and even in some cases "bend time." Finally, I will take the energized organization and add the strategic mind on top of it. The mind in this case is a combined human and computer effort; it is up to leaders and mangers to exploit computing to its very limits and to its full potential.

This book is intended as a flash of inspiration to the leaders and managers who seek to maximize the potential of individuals and organizations through computing. Bear in mind that computing is, so far, the only one of the three potentials that is evolving exponentially, and it appears to be doing so for both an immediate and a longer-term future. I do believe in the relevancy and potential of computers as the fundamental tool for leaders and managers today and in the future; computers will make organizations succeed or fail. Computers have already redefined our environment, and in the future they will redefine the tasks of people as they become displaced by computers more capable and intelligent than those now in use. The CALM leaders and managers will harness this power of change and be able to fuel their organizations in radical new ways by balancing evolving human and computer talent.

I have taken the concept of CALM for a spin in both contemporary times as well as the future. Additionally, I have sought to take it from practical implementation advice that you can start today to extreme potential applications of the future. Some might be surprised by the state of the art today, but would that be surprising? We humans often underestimate our own capabilities, so why wouldn't we do the same with computers?

1

How Computing Changed the World

The Evolution of Computers

Going through the evolutionary stages of computer history, we find there has certainly been a significant growth in the processing power, storage, and networking capabilities of computers. Today we take these factors for granted. Moore's Law states that computer processing-power and storage capacity double every 1.5 years and that its network capacity doubles every two years. These facts are almost considered laws of nature.

What is it about our approach to the interface that binds humans and computers together? The answer to this question is the critical element for allowing a person to tap into computing power and allow this person to unleash new thoughts and new ways of doing things as a consequence.

If we travel back down the line of computing history for about 170 years, to the early 1830s, we encounter the remarkable brainchild of Charles Babbage: the Analytical Engine. Despite being a lifelong pursuit, it was never to be a reality in more than theory and blueprints. During the most fruitful period of his pursuit, Ada Lovelace, a writer and amateur mathematician, collaborated with him on the quest. She is regarded by many to be the world's first software engineer. She wrote professional papers on programming techniques and accumulated over 7,000 pages of mathematical notes and diagrams that she used to interpret, explain, and present the new technology to the British government in book form. In this context it should be mentioned that some have disputed Lovelace's role as the world's first software engineer and see her role merely as Babbage's assistant, but in either case her role of synergic collaboration with Babbage as a promoter of his ideas and theories in public would at least turn her into the world's first software "evangelist." My point is not to discuss the roles of the partners in this col-

1

laboration, but simply to note that to work with computing technology at that time, one needed to be a mathematician, preferably a scientist.

Skipping more than 100 years forward in history, we find ourselves in the midst of World War II. The British mathematician Alan Turing was a key player in breaking the code of the German U-boat Enigma cipher for the British government. Turing and his team succeeded in breaking almost every significant German code, using a machine called Robinson. The world's first operational computer was built using electromagnetic telephone relays. When the Germans countered these code-breaking efforts by adding extra coding wheels, and thereby complexity, to their Enigma, Turing answered by developing an electronic version of Robinson called Colossus, which contained 2,400 vacuum tubes. Colossus, and nine other similar machines running in parallel, provided uninterrupted decoding of vital military intelligence to the Allied forces.[1] I think that it is safe to say that these highly classified machines were not user friendly, even though they were not tested by today's standards, because they still required a mathematician to operate them.

During the same period that Turing was breaking Nazi codes, John Mauchley and J. Presper Eckert, of the Moore School of Engineering in Philadelphia, designed and built the first all-electronic digital computer, the ENIAC: an acronym for Electronic Numerical Integrator and Computer. The computer was ready in 1946, just after the end of World War II, and its success was due largely to mathematician John von Neumann's logical program instructions, which enabled the technology to work. Later, von Neumann modified these instructions from the original design and thereby transformed the ENIAC into a programmable computer. After the war, von Neumann concentrated on the development of the computers, working from the Institute for Advanced Studies, IAS. He continued to develop the synergism between computer capabilities and the need for computational solutions to nuclear problems related to the hydrogen bomb. Von Neumann's logical design became the prototype for most of its successors; therefore those of us who program can thank him for the stored-program concept—the von Neumann Architecture. Nevertheless, though von Neumann took a good leap ahead in design, the computers of his time still required an elaborate understanding of programming in order to operate them.

However, from the 1970s onward we experienced a significant development in the leveraging of computer capacity, which was sparked by Alan Kay and his team at Palo Alto Research Center (PARC). The birth of the user interface, a combined graphical display and pointing device, was a radical improvement over the character displays and keyboard commands. The idea quickly caught the attention of both Apple and Microsoft, and both adopted the concept quickly. This type of user interface has become the standard *metaphor*, another word for user interface, for practically everyone developing computers and computer software today.

If we place the marker in the 1970s, we could say that during the past thirty years the potential of computers has been unleashed at an accelerating pace; this potential has led to a global information infrastructure that allows any digital entity to travel around the globe at the speed of thought. This digital force has had a tremendous impact on our world in the sense that it renders our environment fluent in terms of moving resources at a much more rapid pace. This is a consequence of computer development that has not only been focused on developing potential, but has also been focused on unleashing its potential for about half its evolution since it was conceived from thoughts to its physical form.

The word *technology* originally comes from a Greek word that means craft, or art; in ancient Greece the word was probably mostly used to describe ways that humans could use a technology, not how humanity was crafted *by* it. In this sense it is interesting to note how computer technology is not just an instrument used by humans, which we would tend to think when we sit in front of a computer. The collective force of people using computers means not only that this force is dependent on computers, but that it is perhaps even *crafting* the evolution of our society. This information-based society, where people relieve themselves of tasks by giving the work to computers, is becoming more and more productive, and is in turn being shaped by the computers from which it sought the productivity. We therefore need to master computers and have them aid in our quests for success as individuals and organizations; when our environment is already shaped by the power of computers, we need to harness this power in order to gain the momentum needed to succeed.

In the highly thought-provoking article "Why the Future Doesn't Need Us," Bill Joy explores the evolutionary challenges humans face as information technology (IT) becomes increasingly capable of undertaking human tasks through artificial intelligence and robotics. The IT disciplines, in combination with nanotechnology, could pose a threat to humans, either in the hands of madmen or as a simple evolutionary process of survival of the fittest. The theory of computers taking over the planet does not suggest that computers will initiate an exhausting battle against humans; rather it predicts that humans will gradually turn over power to computers as they become more and more capable.[2] The takeover of power will not happen in one day; it will instead be a natural evolutionary consequence of computers becoming more and more capable, and the world will demand these capabilities. These two factors in combination will displace human presence in the areas where computers gradually take over more and more tasks. Joy compares the application of computers in society to the application of nuclear science in weapons and power plants, and states that nuclear science requires highly specialized materials, whereas the application of computing in artificial intelligence and robotics does not. Therefore the threats against the stability to society, the environment in which we live, will increase, since a threat can be posed globally with few resources.

It should be noted that Bill Joy was head of research and development (R&D) at Sun Microsystems when he wrote the article, so not only did he have insight into the specifics of computing but he also had a track record of developing and watching technologies being absorbed by the market.

I do think that Bill Joy wrote a remarkable and provoking article; however I believe that the future does indeed need us. The potentials mentioned earlier in this chapter are far from the reach of computing today, so perhaps the best argument to keep our hopes up is that we humans do not even know ourselves well enough to define the computer that will perhaps be our equal, and even if we think of a computer that is so intelligent that it would know us better than we know ourselves, we would fail to recognize it because we have failed to know ourselves. If we do not recognize the relevance of a technology, we cannot apply it. We humans will be mastering the *art* of selecting which technologies should *craft* our world and thereby *craft* ourselves, at least for what in my mind is a foreseeable future.

However, Bill Joy's article tells a lot about the potential of computers; over time, computers will basically be able to run everything, from a purely operational standpoint. Although this time is yet to come, let us at least consider the fact that most companies today are virtually impossible to operate without computers. Some of our fighter planes, like the B-2 Stealth Bomber and the F-35 Joint Strike Fighter, are impossible to fly without computer stabilization, since they are designed to be unstable in the air to increase maneuverability.[3] Moreover, most of us rely on computers in the form of our cars' Anti-lock Brake System, ABS, to save our lives in traffic if we need to brake quickly in an emergency. We certainly need computers now, and will in the future, simply to live our lives.

In fact I think the most likely future is a synergic collaboration between humans and computers. This synergy will enable us to enjoy the benefits of computing, giving us more options to apply computers as capacity increases along the lines of their current capabilities. These laws, which can almost be described as laws of nature, at least computer nature, state the following:

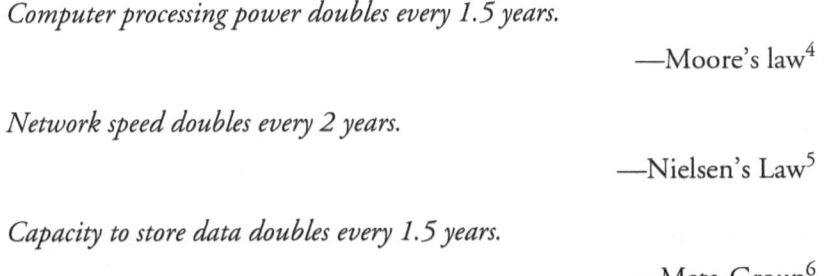

Computer processing power doubles every 1.5 years.

—Moore's law[4]

Network speed doubles every 2 years.

—Nielsen's Law[5]

Capacity to store data doubles every 1.5 years.

—Meta-Group[6]

Computers will undoubtedly be faster, smaller, and have more storage capacity, and development in Internet bandwidth will allow more digital content to be transferred even more swiftly. These factors all mean that the world we know today will become increasingly volatile, and we can most definitely count on computer technology to help us survive and succeed in that environment. As we will see in the following chapters, computers will enable organizations to become more flexible and aware in the global economic environment. Computers might even give us (and our organizations) a flexible backbone of infrastructure that allows us to evolve our knowledge and core competencies, pretty much like the software layer in the von Neumann Architecture.

However, the most remarkable thing about computers' potential is, in my mind, not raw processing power, but the fact that computers interconnect millions of people on the Internet. This means that we suddenly have a global pool of information, knowledge, and resources at our fingertips. We can almost think of it as telepathy, in the sense that we can communicate thoughts globally in milliseconds. I must of course admit that this channel of virtual communications has its limitations compared with face-to-face communication, but as Internet bandwidth increases, we will perhaps be able to unleash an even broader spectrum of emotional and mental energies across this channel.

It did not really strike me until I started to build my personal Web site that the Internet is just as much a human phenomenon as it is a computer phenomenon. This learning was ignited by a task for my PhD at Rushmore University. Before I knew it, I was corresponding with best-selling authors such as Peter Urs Bender. The Internet provided a channel for others to comment on and ask about my research, and I met people virtually whom I would probably never have met otherwise. These people inspired and challenged me, thereby helping me refine the substance and findings of my research. Ten years ago such a process would have been literally impossible, and yet here I was hosting a Web site with thousands of visitors who, by either their behavior or communication, were assisting me. Technology crafted my projects and my beliefs much more than I would ever have imagined, all because I probed the Internet by putting up a Web site. In another context, a couple of my friends and I have a rap band in which we share the fun and energy of composing music and writing lyrics; through the Internet a happy bunch of amateurs like us managed to get airtime on radios in thirteen different countries across the globe through a concept we called "The Virtual Earth Tour." We even got to be band of the week in Beirut! I should point out that we are not that good, but the goodwill of people around the globe, interconnected on the Internet, managed to carry us around the world anyway. To me, these incidents tell of an unprecedented potential that can be tapped and developed with very little effort—simply start using the Internet and see what happens. It should of course be noted that both these cases deal with content that can easily be distributed on the Internet, or rather content that is part of the Internet community; therefore no commercial lessons can be learned from these experiences. However, these experiences have unveiled to me the global hyper-volatility on the Internet.

Another interesting aspect of this new computing dimension of global interconnectivity is that we connect with it only when we see fit. This gives what I like to call the fifth dimension in the world: asynchrony. If we think about it, all people are different; for one thing they live in different places across the globe, but even if two people are in the same geographical place, they may have very different learning patterns that allow them to excel in their performance. Through things as simple as e-mail, it is possible to create asynchrony; this means people can deal with issues when they have the most energy. Perhaps some of the stress we experience when we strive to coordinate our efforts with the pace of the computerized world can be relieved if we do not have to interact synchronously; perhaps the potential to allow people to deal with issues in their own rhythm of life is a much better and more effective long-term approach to productivity. The technologies that could help harness personal energies in a less stressful way and thereby unleash unused computer potential are already available today in the form of Internet technologies.

Going forward, there are of course many things that can further accelerate the movement of resources and information in our world. Ray Kurzweil, author of *The Age of Spiritual Machines: When Computers Exceed Human Intelligence*, has a theory that combines the law of increasing chaos and the law of accelerating returns. Essentially, this theory states that in a process, the time interval between salient events expands or contracts along with the amount of chaos. Kurzweil combines this with the exponential growth in computing and makes the case that artificial intelligence will be able to pass the traditional Turing test in convincing new ways. In other words, the evolution of computing power will introduce order and thereby reduce chaos, thereby facilitating more salient events at an increasing pace; a new intelligence would emerge from these events. Kurzweil envisions that intelligent systems during the coming century will influence education, people with disabilities, communication, business and economics, politics and society, and, not unimportantly, art and philosophy. Obviously one would intuitively anticipate that systems we know today will become more efficient, but consider having intelligent systems participate in the discussion about whether they possess a soul or not, as suggested by Ray Kurzweil.[7]

One could of course completely disregard Kurzweil's suggestions and simply say that it is unscientific to expect these miracles or salient events in computing; however, reading Kurzweil's work is also what inspired Bill Joy, so at least Kurzweil's hypothesis of potential future intelligence is taken seriously by some. From my personal perspective, having worked with artificial intelligence for more than a decade, I must say that I find Kurzweil's suggestions rather interesting, and I would say that disregarding the possibility that any of them will come true is probably equivalent to people a little over 100 years ago saying that it would be impossible to get a plane that is heavier than air to fly.

My point is that there is incredible potential in computing, much of it already available today, and this potential is increasing exponentially by the hour. A wise application of this potential today is the best way for individuals and organizations to reach their goals in the already computerized environment. The reason for this is that computing creates the environment, which means changes in the environment strike at the speed of computing. Therefore, if we move at the pace of computing we will be able to counter the threats and exploit the opportunities of these changes at the pace demanded by the environment. Computing power is not everything that contributes to the potential of the computing aspect: through global interconnectivity we have the potential to move knowledge and ideas in digitalized forms at the speed of thought. The only way to discover the power of this resource is through probing the Internet and learning what happens; the Internet is the collective mind of people, and since we cannot fully grasp the concept of our own minds, we certainly cannot grasp a collective mind either. Therefore "living" the Internet, in the sense that we incorporate it appropriately into our lives, seems to be the most appropriate approach. After all, that is what we do with our individual minds. If we successfully harness the potential of the Internet, we will tap into a knowledge resource of unprecedented vastness, and perhaps we will also even be able to work differently with the time dimension to optimize individual potential and relieve stress, effectively changing Peter Drucker's definition of time as the one critical resource that is inelastic.[8]

Moving with the computing potential into the future, we will most likely find more and more intelligent and smart systems. Today it might not be possible to develop a computer that argues with us about whether or not it has a mind or soul, but no expert can say with certainty that this stage will not occur in this century. Whether we make it to that stage or not is perhaps not critical, but it is a peek into where computer sciences might be heading. We might not end up soon with a computer with an independent mind, but think how much impact a car that could drive independently would have. Even applications that would be equivalent to catching the moon when reaching for the stars will be revolutionary. So in order to harvest the potential of computing and be able to survive and succeed in the world of the future, we should understand this direction of computer evolution and apply it where it is reasonable to do so. The potential of artificial intelligence will redefine the computing potential during this century; in general, artificial intelligence will mean that computers will be able to do more and more things autonomously. In the beginning this autonomy will emerge as more pleasant user interfaces that appear more intelligent; the user will experience that more work is done with fewer instructions since the computer "knows" the user's preferences and intent. These interfaces will gradually build a bond of trust in which the user will rely on the computer to do more and more to the extent that it works autonomously on an increasing number of future tasks. Time will show exactly where and when the line between the user and the computer will be drawn in terms autonomy, but the trend toward autonomy is already here.

So in summary, the potential of computers will evolve around three main development streams: capacity (processing and storage), connectivity (bandwidth and Internet size), and autonomy (artificial intelligence). If we want to develop the computing potential under given circumstances, we should consider these three aspects and seek the optimum for all of them.

The Hyper-Volatile World

During the time I have been involved with computers, we have seen the world change dramatically. Politically, we have watched the Cold War end with the fall of first the Berlin Wall and then of the Soviet Union, and we have seen China rise from Tiananmen Square to become one of the biggest factors in the global economy. We have also seen our longing for peace put through the test of a new war against global terrorism, which has again sparked a dialogue on human rights and on cultural and religious integration. Technologically, we have seen the Internet phenomenon emerge as a factor with its own life. It has both disrupted the global economy during the dot-com rise and crash and has changed, once and for all, the way we do business and organize ourselves around our interests. Let us just say that a lot of things have happened in the past two decades.

Philosophically, I would say that the biggest thing, which has also had the most impact on the future of all the other things, is indeed the Internet. There is nothing new to shifts in political and economic power—wars and empires come and go. But the Internet seemingly came out of nowhere, and once it wired us together globally, there was no turning back. With the Internet, any thought, idea, financial transaction, or digital product could circle the globe in milliseconds. Global business and financial transactions became available to everyone with a computer and an Internet connection. This infrastructure was just what the global economy needed. From this moment on, the market economy seemed unstoppable for even the most protectionist economies. Customers and vendors could be recruited anywhere—markets and competition are effectively becoming global.

However, a much more interesting thing that happened with the birth of the Internet was that our economy potentially shifted toward a knowledge economy, meaning that intangible information assets in different forms became worth more than physical assets. We saw, for example, small companies with few physical assets but skyrocketing turnover from trading goods that they not only did not produce or see, but more interestingly, didn't even own. Think, for instance, of companies like eBay that emerged from this age: for such companies, the intangible assets are their only true value, and all intangible assets are digital.

Any digital asset can be moved across the globe in milliseconds, so not only has a company or organization global access to both customers and vendors, but it can also move itself around globally through digital teleportation. The world in which such potential exists for movement of big assets in the form of transactions, information, or entire companies is what I have chosen to label, a Hyper-Volatile World. In the Hyper-Volatile World we can move anywhere rapidly and with very little effort. It seems that global movement has become something as frictionless as a puck in an air hockey game. If we consider physical assets in this context, we will find that the Hyper-Volatile World is also having an impact; the more information we have about an asset, no matter how complex, the more it becomes a commodity. The more it becomes a commodity, the more we can use the global interconnectivity to acquire the physical asset anywhere. Therefore, even though physical assets do not move as electrons, they still appear more mobile in the hyper-volatile environment, and as such they are also subjected to the effects of the continually increasing pace of global movement.

Another remarkable event that disturbs the traditional market economy is the birth and rapid growth of the knowledge economy. The knowledge economy is about exchanging knowledge and ideas rather than money. Both can be expressed digitally, which means that one can choose to exchange knowledge and ideas as many times as desired without losing them. The traditional trading perspective has changed: If two people each exchange an idea with the other, they both end up with two ideas. This expands the richness of their economy to four ideas. This is remarkably different from the traditional market economy, especially considering that knowledge and ideas are worth more than physical assets in the Hyper-Volatile World. One can of course also choose to wrap the knowledge in a way that makes it usable by the recipient only in a certain way. One can then sell it over and over again without additional costs; this is perhaps where the software industry should be thanking von Neumann.

Examples of the huge impacts of the knowledge economy at play can be found in the identification and containment of SARS, in which a global sharing of information led to swift containment and brought us very close to eliminating the disease. It is especially remarkable that there was no overall management of the sharing process; there was simply the synergy of great minds in various organizations, with the overall mission of stopping the disease. The Internet made such an unprecedented process possible, just as it facilitated mapping the human genome.

The consequence of hyper-volatility is that change happens faster; extreme changes can be made with less effort, and change is global. From a purely statistical standpoint, the fact that we all experience the local impact of the changes made by others throughout the globe means that more people will have an impact on us than when we were influenced only by local actions. In addition, since change can be conducted with less effort, chances are that more people will conduct change—some perhaps without even realizing it. The aggregated effect of these two trends renders each of us a participant in the Hyper-Volatile World, exposed to changes at an ever-increasing pace.

"Give me matter and motion, and I will construct the World," wrote the seventeenth-century philosopher René Descartes, who saw the world as a logical and mechanical process.[9] He shared this logical approach to understanding the wonders of life with Nobel Prize–winning mathematician John Nash, who at age twenty-one managed to take conventional mathematical modeling of behavior at the time to the next level by adding complexity to the traditional zero-sum, "pure rivalry" games in game theory. By outlining his "Nash Equilibrium," he opened the eyes of the world to a type of behavior in which parties that normally competed could become mutual winners—in other words, a mathematical model for synergy through win-win situations.[10] I wonder what great minds like these would say about the Hyper-Volatile World. Perhaps they would arrive at the conclusion that chaos theory is probably the best way to describe the fact that we have to accept an incomplete description of the world. Chaos theory has emerged during recent decades, and for now it appears to be the most appropriate mathematical application to describe why life appears, at least within contemporary science and reasoning, impossible to describe in detail, let alone understand to the extent that it can be predicted. The perspective of incomplete detailed information is the essence of chaos theory, in which we deal with nonlinear systems with sensitive initial conditions, and in which timelines are the drivers of deterministic processes. This means that the current state of the system is affected by the previous state, which again has an effect on the next.

The idea that a disturbance at the molecular level of a butterfly can lead to a hurricane on the other side of the globe is probably the most well-known example of chaos theory[11], and if we lubricate this process with a global network of computers that serves to transfer the butterfly effect instantaneously around the globe, it is probably not hard to understand that the Hyper-Volatile World will feel more and more like chaos in its original meaning. Whether we think that life is chaos in a technical sense or see it as random incidents, life in the Hyper-Volatile World will become increasingly unpredictable.

The devastating consequences of a hurricane triggered by something as innocent and gracious as a butterfly are a good analogy of the potential consequences of seemingly minor and innocent deeds. Think about a teenager who just for the fun of it makes some minor modifications to an innocent program. That is how it looks on his local computer, but within seconds he has suddenly launched a devastating attack on the information society and the global economy. The line of teenage computer virus authors is growing by the hour, and many of these situations seem to be cases of a person doing what seems an innocent joke, but "butterflown" away it can lead to massive financial losses and destabilization of the information society.

The threat against us has been multiplied by the same factors mentioned on economics, and today our infrastructure and tools of production are as much our masters as they are our servants. They help us harness the power of change, but at the same time they make us extremely vulnerable; the infrastructure can be disrupted with a destructive effectiveness based on the same momentum from which humans are gaining productivity. Such disturbances in the infrastructure, whether they are competitive actions, chaotic "butterfly" effects, or plain and simple acts of terrorism, add to the feeling of chaos in a Hyper-Volatile World.

So what does this mean for us as individuals and as participants in various organizations? First of all, we are in a world of opportunity; never has the individual action been able to accomplish so much with so little effort. If we understand the opportunities we have at hand, there is virtually no stopping our ideas from global growth. However, we need to realize that we have to act or we will be acted upon, since the potential alternative actions that can impact us are also global. As organizations, we can enjoy the benefits of collaborating and sharing globally, but at the same time we have to understand that traditional organizational models cannot compete with models that, as opposed to being rigid systems, incorporate awareness and flexibility.

Basically, organizations in the information age need to act and react more quickly on different issues because they are faced, as a consequence of global competition, regional instability, and vulnerability, with a business environment of rapid and disruptive change, fleeting opportunities, incomplete information, and an overall sense of uncertainty and disorder.[12] Second, the individuals who collectively constitute an organization are seeking more empowerment and involvement. The number of managers, therefore, has increased as a percentage of the organization, and although these individuals might not be managers in a classical sense, they are becoming more and more dependent on information to support their decisions.[13]

2

Human Potential

The Potential of Human Individuals

If we turn our attention from the computerized globe of today and glance backward into our past, the greatest scientists from NASA would tell us that the creation of the universe began with a big bang somewhere between 10 and 20 billion years ago.[14] If we consult geologists researching materials found on earth, they would tell us that the Earth in the form we know today is about 4.5 billion years old.[15] Jumping a little less than 4.5 billion years forward, our science tells us that it has only been about 15 million years since the first humanoids emerged. These humanoids distinguished themselves from other animals by walking on their hind legs and having large brains, particularly in the area of the highly convoluted cortex, which is responsible for rational thought. Dating back 500,000 years from today, we find the first evidence of the species *Homo sapiens*. Jumping an additional 400,000 years forward to about 100,000 years before today, *Homo sapiens neanderthalensis*, or simply Neanderthals, can be found. Among Neanderthals, our closest relatives as a species, we find the first evidence of culture, such as funeral rituals that included ornaments and flowers. If we move 10,000 years further ahead to about 90,000 years ago, we find *Homo sapiens sapiens*, our immediate ancestors.

To obtain information like this, we have to search information by acting as forensic detectives; but what other choice do we have? Our modern-day written history dates back only about 3,000 years.

In other words, it seems that we humans have done a lot poorer job in our evolutionary chain, compared to computers, in rendering our mental work in a form that is easily interfaced so it can benefit successive generations. Computers may have had a head start because humans conceived them at a time when we are at our best performance ever in providing information about ourselves and other things, but the fact remains that our inner potential is much less accessible than it potentially could have been if we had started to document it earlier. I would even argue that our full potential is much less accessible to us than is the potential of a computer. Today we usually design new software that craves more processing power before such power is even available, while in the meantime our scientists estimate that we use only about ten percent of our human brain capacity. In this context it is perhaps equally interesting to note that we have learned ninety percent of what we know in the field of neuroscience in the past decade![16]

So with so much potential, what does it take to unleash it? First of all we need to accept its existence; secondly we need the wisdom to unleash it. While we know the exact metrics of computer potential, how much do we really know about our own potential?

If we take our knowledge about our existing mental potential, I would be inclined to say that our sciences are, by Western world definitions, just a little more than 100 years old in terms of psychology. Putting that into the time perspective of the evolution of our species, *Homo sapiens sapiens*, let alone the evolution of humanoids in general, we discover that our empirical findings are the equivalent of three seconds, or a little more than a thousandth of our total knowledge of ourselves in time. If we divide this figure by ten, we have the amount of knowledge we have of ourselves in terms of neuroscience, which may be even more important, since it is at this level that we will be able to bridge some of the gaps in our knowledge about our mind with other sciences, such as physics and biology.

When Freud did his pioneering work in psychology, he was not the first to invent the idea of the conscious versus the subconscious mind, but he was the first to suggest that the subconscious mind was a much bigger part of our mind that the conscious. According to Freud, the subconscious is the source of our motivations, whether they are simple desires for food or sex, neurotic compulsions, or the motives of an artist or scientist. Yet we are often driven to deny or resist becoming conscious of these motives, and they are often available to us only in disguised form.[17] Later, modern psychological research proved that these suggestions were right, and today it is a common belief that we only use about ten percent of our mental capacity.[18]

Glimpses of the unused capacity in our brains can be seen when we observe extreme abilities in people at the boundaries of what we would label normal people, namely the *idiot savants*. Idiot savants are people with autism who have extraordinary skills in certain domains in spite of cognitive deficiencies in most others.

Some autistic individuals with savant abilities are incredible artists, such as painters or musicians. For example, a child named Nadia drew beautiful pictures of horses, and her drawings have been compared to those of Rembrandt. Interestingly, she lost her drawing abilities when she started to learn to speak. Music is another common savant ability. Many performers with autism have perfect pitch and a great memory for music. In some cases, a person can hear a classical piece once and play it back in its entirety. The reason why some autistic individuals have savant abilities is not known. There are many theories but no solid scientific evidence, and among these theories, the one that appeals most to me speculates that these individuals have an incredible ability to concentrate and can focus their complete attention on a specific area of interest.[19] However, the fact that these phenomena exist and yet cannot be described by our science today is testimony to the gap between what we are and our scientific understanding of ourselves. Interestingly enough, many researchers in psychology feel that we will never truly understand memory and cognition until we understand the autistic savant.

Considering the fact that we appear to be lagging significantly behind in documenting ourselves and the potential of our minds from a scientific perspective, it seems odd to me that we cling to the brief period of documented science alone, especially since some ancient practices have been passed on through timelines and generations that exceed our relatively short period of documented scientific experiences. The age of the discipline of philosophy will of course vary depending on whom we select for the title of the world's first philosopher, but if we let known history speak for itself we will find that Pythagoras (about 569 to 475 BC) was the first to label himself a *philosopher by Western definitions*.[20] Did Freud wake us all up, a little more than 100 years ago, to a level of understanding that should allow us to disregard things that scientists documented through generations and more than 2,500 years? Admittedly, even if their findings don't constitute proof by modern standards, it merely leads us to describe a mental minute in the "hour of man" as one minute instead of three seconds. To me, it seems that our modern scientific principles would demand that we investigate these ancient claims before disregarding them. Who knows? There may yet be some relevance in some of these ancient philosophies and sciences.

So how deep into a subject should our science look to understand it? Although it seems from the theory about idiot savants that we should feel compelled to dissect a subject to understand it and benefit from scientific findings, the problem may very well be the depth to which we try to look. We might end up searching for the forest even though, or perhaps because, we are surrounded by trees.

In our science we have been willing to accept the distance between physics and spirituality, perhaps for the simple reason that we have not been able to fit our soul or mind into either a mathematical or a physical frame of reference. Being a philosopher with a preference for the purity of mathematics on the one hand, and with the acceptance of a soul on the other, René Descartes sought to bridge the gap between mind and matter with six meditations on "First Philosophy," published in 1641 and designed for the philosopher and for the theologian. The meditations addressed the following areas:

-Of the Things that we may Doubt;
-Of the Nature of the Human Mind;
-Of God: that He exists, of Truth and Error;
-Of the Essence of Material Things;
-Of the Existence of Material Things;
-Of the Real Distinction between the Mind and the Body of Man.[21]

Although many scientists of the time were opposed to Descartes' ideas, I still find it remarkable that his solution to the problem was meditation—a mind tool very much aligned with what we could find in ancient Eastern life philosophy.

So how much of the potential value from ancient inspirational sources have we succeeded in incorporating into our modern lives? From my point of view we are heading in that direction, but there is still room for improvement. As I grew up with a father who was a doctor, I often listened to his skepticism of ancient methods of treatment, such as acupuncture, reflexology, and zone therapy. However, in comparison, his trade was not widely accepted 400 years ago either, at a time when we accused people of witchcraft and subsequently burned them. I am by no means arguing that a linear quality comparison of four centuries versus thousands of years is fair, as we have undoubtedly evolved exponentially in scientific efficiency. However I do believe that a rejection of Eastern medicine that has evolved through refinement from generation to generation, without any objective assessment of it, is equally wrong. In this context it is encouraging to see that ancient Chinese healing methods, such as acupuncture and reflexology, are beginning to be recognized among new generations from medical faculties where some medical experiments have even included acupuncture[22] and meditation[23] in fMRI[24] brain scanners.

We seem to be getting closer and closer to the point where there is greater acceptance and willingness to experiment down the alleys of our mind, but there still appears to be a gap between the older and the younger generations of doctors in their openness to knowledge in this field.

There are various definitions and ways of describing energy, but in my writings I will go with the definition that there are three overall categories of energy, namely emotional, mental, and spiritual.Emotional energy is typically what we feel through our heart and stomach, and mental energy is what goes on in our head, rational thought and creativity in both visual and abstract forms. Around these two basic energies we have the spiritual energy embracing them both. Spiritual energy is the source that most of us would probably refer to when we are telling others about how energized we feel. Not feeling energized, or feeling fatigued, will also typically lead to more emotional fluctuation and less mental concentration. Hence if we bleed spiritual energy, we will most certainly feel a drain in our other two energies. On the other hand, if we feel completely energized we will feel much more resourceful when we are emotionally affected, and we will feel capable of doing mental work effortlessly. We experience flow when our spiritual energy is high.

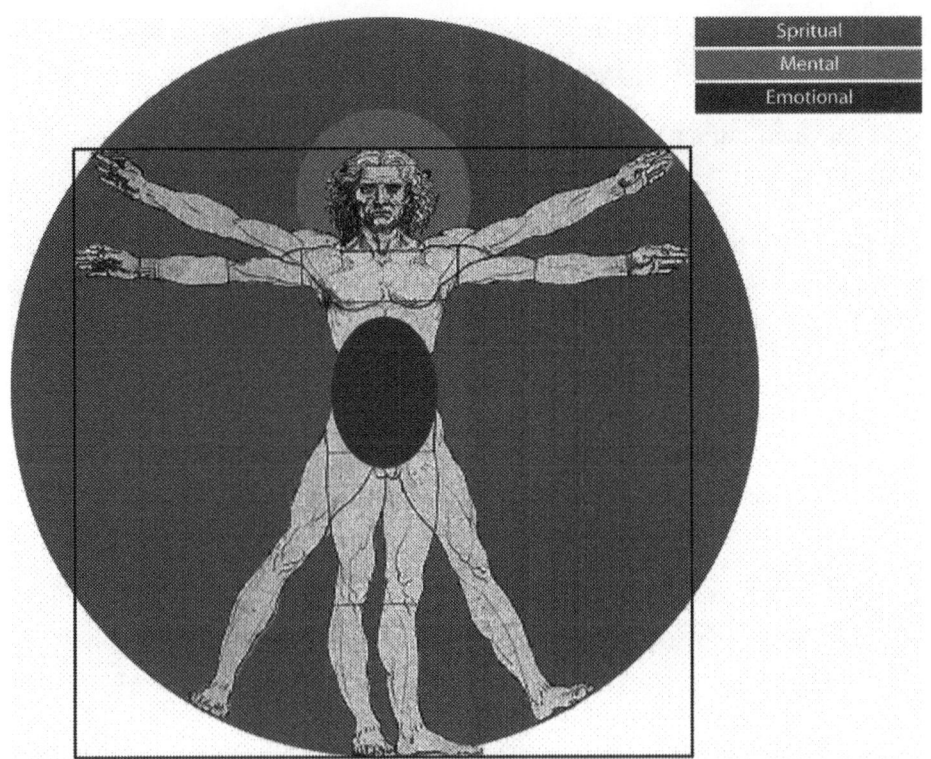

Figure 2.1 Three Human Energies

Figure 2.1 shows the locations of the energy systems. In the next chapter I will provide the findings of neuroscience that justify making the distinction between mental and emotional energy; and from this perspective we could simply regard spiritual energy as all the other energy that does not fit into the emotional or mental categories. These three human energies will serve as a frame of reference in my discussions of areas of human potential as well as synergy with computers.

Having assigned all human energy to these three categories, we find that that some of the energies are better accommodated by contemporary computing than others. The mental energy is highly stimulated, in particular in its abstract form as mathematics. This is not surprising, as the dawn of computers arose from the mental energy of mathematicians. However, it is interesting to note that the creative side of our mental energy seems to be the highest priority for software developers these days. The latest operating systems, such as Windows XP from Microsoft, have prioritized tools for multimedia presentation and editing, and there are also a number of other free or affordable applications available for music composition. This trend seems to be continuing, and suggestions for use of future computer capacity will undoubtedly bring us 3-D animation tools so we can make our own animations and dive into universes of learning such as edutainment.[25]

We don't seem to have progressed very far in developing systems to help us gain extra emotional or spiritual energy. There may be applications on the Internet that can help us live healthier lives, find the love of our lives, and the like, thereby adding to our spiritual and emotional energies respectively, but in reality these applications are by far inferior to the applications for stimulating our mental energy.

Mihaly Csikszentmihalyi's research into creativity illustrates another aspect of the mind. Some of his findings regarding the environment where ideas emerge are hard to ignore. In a study on the origin of ideas, he found that few people got their ideas while sitting at a desk in the office; people typically get their ideas when they are not focusing too hard on the problem they are trying to solve. This appears, at first glance, to be in direct contrast to the theory of idiot-savant abilities as a way to understand our potential, but on second thought, if we refer back to Freud's distinction between conscious and subconscious minds, Csikszentmihalyi's findings might very well complement Freud's. Perhaps the ability to focus is a way to optimize our conscious mind, whereas the distance from the problem is a way of employing the subconscious mind. So let us assume that both focusing and distancing ourselves are ways in which we can find mental resources that can benefit us in pursuing our goals more successfully while we are conscious; using this rationale, focus and unfocus are both access paths to mental energy beyond the average ten percent brain utilization, so to speak. But with reference to the idiot savant examples, it should be noted that the healthiest way appears to be to use the unfocused approach, since the conscious mind might have a more limited potential overall compared to the subconscious, and once we approach the boundary of our conscious capacity, our knowledge and abilities might compete for the available space. There is no evidence of that happening when we employ the capacity of the subconscious, unfocused approach—and according to Freud, this is a bigger capacity anyway.

I am personally a believer in meditation as a tool for unfocusing and thereby unleashing ideas from the subconscious, or perhaps even gaining inspiration from a higher order of truth, depending on one's belief system. Although there are many systems for meditation, they typically include relaxation and clearing the mind. Such an exercise is important in itself, and should it end up being the only experience one gets from meditation, it is still worthwhile. Actually, I am of the opinion that the simplest meditation is available to all of us from nature, in the form of sleep. It is remarkable how different a problem looks after sleeping; if any problem has significance, in most cases it is best solved after a night's sleep. Sleep seems to help us digest and bring the problem into perspective, a perspective that can usually turn a problem into an opportunity.

> *Sleep that knits up the raveled sleeve of care, balm of hurt minds, great Nature's second course, chief nourisher in life's feast*
>
> —William Shakespeare

At the dawn of philosophy, where this section started, we can find indications on a broad life perspective. Pythagoras and his followers developed the disciplines that enabled them to make discoveries ranging from pure mathematics and numbers, over matter and atoms, all the way to the occult and mysticism. In other words, these ancient scientists were pretty farsighted, yet they also accepted that conventional tools might be of little use in discovering the secrets of the mind. Bearing in mind this and the fact that there are many aspects of our inner life that contemporary science has not yet been able to describe, perhaps it is merely a question of time before we have enough empirical findings, and by then we may have established another science that cover even more of these areas.

Perhaps broadening the perspective to look at contemporary and ancient wisdom together could be a source of inspiration, and perhaps not broadening it leads us to a potential loss of potential. Computers, as we will find later on, can even assist us in looking empirically at the knowledge and discoveries we already have and bring them into a broader perspective by using computer capacity to elevate ourselves. The reason for suggesting that a scientific paradigm shift is necessary can perhaps be justified by quoting Albert Einstein:

> *The significant problems we face cannot be solved at the same level of thinking we were at when we created them.*
>
> —Albert Einstein

I found a great inspiration for this book when I read Ray Kurzweil's *The Age of Spiritual Machines*. In this book, Kurzweil states the law of time and chaos, which is a combination of the law of increasing chaos and the law of accelerating returns. The combination essentially states that "in a process, the time interval between salient events expands or contracts along with the amount of chaos." One outcome of this law is that our human species will become more and more productive, since the chaos in the evolution of our species has decreased in comparison to the time when we came out of the water. In an evolutionary process we moved from chaos toward higher order, which means that the salient events slow down over time. As a consequence, the returns on productivity increase as chaos decreases. Think of our lives: during our first nine months, a remarkable chaos of creation is turning into a baby, and in this magical process a mind develops and increases its efficiency throughout the person's life. A funny way of thinking about it is that we do not have to "worry" about growing extra limbs, so this energy can be converted into being efficient with the limbs we have.

Ironically, the higher productivity we gain from the higher degree of order again leads to the Hyper-Volatile World, which might also be order in a mathematical sense, but it appears very much like chaos from a human perspective. Perhaps this is the reason some people are so fixated on their own knowledge domain; if we keep what we have in our heads now, at least chaos will not increase in that part. We would like things to stay just the way they are for the most part, and I would argue that fear of and reluctance to change are inherent human traits. At the dawn of the era of *Homo sapiens*, this fear probably kept us alive. Any change in sound, or any movement in the leaves of bushes around us, could have meant that we were about to be the prey of a fierce prehistoric predator. Fear could mobilize the resources to think sharply and react most efficiently to ensure the survival of the species. But between then and now, there is one big difference; at this evolutionary stage we were very far from the global society to which our world has come.

To align Kurzweil's theory to the hyper-volatile environment we have today, we need to apply Kurzweil's thinking more broadly; we need to think of evolutionary processes as happening in waves. Whenever evolution reached a stage in which returns were increasing exponentially, this acceleration had the potential to create an event that would start an entirely new evolutionary process, moving from chaos toward a higher order. We see this all the time when new technologies are applied: first most people meet the technology with neglect and denial; it is kept alive by a few enthusiasts. Then the technology picks up, fueled by the enthusiasm of the masses, and, just as it appears that the technology has taken on a life of its own, it can suddenly create an incident that brings chaos to a new level. From this new level, one or more new evolutionary processes can begin. So in essence, we have multiple evolutionary processes derived from a single process. In technology in particular, such incidents can result in more chaos, which in turn brings more information and processes.

Think about how the Internet has left us with more means of communication. This effectively means that regimes suppressing their citizens through misinformation are crumbling. The Internet has also provided a theater in which warfare and vandalism seem much more attractive, which again has led to new technologies in computer security. Think about how the Internet has not only redefined the opportunities for doing business, but has also redefined the global economy and shaken its traditional means of accessing financial values.

I will restrain myself from getting into a discussion of whether our world is moving toward more chaos or toward higher order and simply conclude that changes in our environment, whatever their direction, will be happening at an accelerating pace. When change is the accelerating rule of our environment, where can we turn, and what is the key to addressing the fear that evolution has given us?

The Potential of Human Organizations

Since the dawn of mankind we have been organizing ourselves into groups to overcome the obstacles we face. From tribes of humans simply fighting for survival, the modern day organizations of people seeking fulfillment for themselves in terms of physical, emotional, mental, or even spiritual needs has developed gradually. The organization today can in many ways be compared to an ant colony: by participating in an organization we achieve greater things than we could as individuals. Through collaboration we are stronger than we would be on our own. But the organization is very different from the an ant colony in many other ways because we are humans with options to choose our behavior; we are people with emotional, mental, and spiritual energies that define us uniquely while, paradoxically, also binding us together.

If we are considering the most limiting resources—people, finance, and time—we can say that from a personal standpoint we usually trade in human capital and time to benefit financially on the personal level, and vice versa from an organizational standpoint. From the total outcome in such an organization would be deducted the cost of organizing the resources, and the remainder could then be distributed among its participants. In other words, from a market economy perspective, an organization is only relevant if it is able to undertake a task that could not be done by an individual or multiple individuals working independently, because organizing the work would only mean adding additional administrative loss to the equation.

If the world really worked along the lines of this simplistic model, many organizations would not make sense in the Hyper-Volatile World. It is easier to undertake a task with fewer people and less finance, so independent workers could in principle work alone; all it would take is perhaps more time to get the job done. This simplistic market economy is, however, far from the reality in the knowledge economy, especially if we consider organizations from an energy perspective.

In the knowledge economy, two people exchanging the same amount of knowledge and ideas end up having double the amount after the transaction. In the market economy $1 + 1 = 2$, but in the knowledge economy $1 + 1 = 4$, so to speak. This means that for an organization to make sense, we do not need to worry about what is possible or impossible from an individual standpoint. We should simply look at the total amount of knowledge generated in the organization; the total knowledge in an organization should surpass the accumulated knowledge of the individuals in it. If we assume that we have a number of people with the same amount of ideas and knowledge, and that there is no overlap between their knowledge domains, we find that the total knowledge in such an organization, before the cost of administration, would be: $(individual\ knowledge)^2$.

Granted, the knowledge should be relevant and applicable to the task that the organization seeks to undertake, but if we theorize that we are able distribute relevant knowledge among all participants, and that everyone complements each other, it is easy to grasp that we do not need very many people collaborating before the idea of an organization becomes highly attractive for the individual in terms of outcome, even after the deduction of organizing costs.

Most of us have probably felt that working with others on ideas and sharing them usually generates new ideas, and indeed I would suggest that the most realistic equation for total knowledge is based on synergy rather than collaboration. By synergy I mean the things that happen when we are sharing ideas and knowledge. At these times we usually either come up with new ideas or refine the knowledge we have. In other words synergy is the spice that leaves everything a little better than it was; synergy is ideas and knowledge in flow, the place where inspiration flows effortlessly.

Perhaps synergy is what happens when our individual energies merge with those of other people; we appear to be emotionally, mentally, and spiritually on the same page, or we have a deep appreciation, understanding, and respect for each other's energies. In such an environment, where we understand each other, there can be no fear. Fear is essentially the irrational blocking of initiatives based on our evolutionary worst-case negative thinking. In synergy we are compelled to think more positively about a potential outcome; perhaps we are driven on by the enthusiastic spiritual energy of others, or perhaps we feel supported by other people's energies and so do not mind taking the next step, making the first mistake, or sharing the next idea. I would hesitate to take such a mathematical approach to synergy as I did to knowledge, but I would say that synergy can only exist if we are in balance with our energies. I do believe, however, that synergy can compensate for individual imbalances so that the organization or group becomes balanced overall. Think about the energy levels you entered a meeting with and the ones you had after it. If you experienced a change, you were influenced by others' energies. If you experienced a positive change, then by my definition you experienced synergy. Likewise, it is probably not hard to recall a situation in which the synergy was less than one, meaning that we needed to use excessive energy simply to share knowledge. This could happen if there were too much hostility and arguing or mistrust and questioning of each other's knowledge.

Having quoted Einstein earlier, I cannot help thinking of the following way to express the potential knowledge energy that resides in an organization:

$$\text{Energy} = \text{Synergy} \times \text{Knowledge}^2$$

Theoretically, the potential of an organization is equal to the energy it can possibly unleash in terms of knowledge applied in action toward a chosen objective. Synergy is a way to express the organization's ability to move from pure collaboration = 1 to synergic collaboration, where the synergy is greater than 1. Now, the degree to which we feel synergy is perhaps hard to explain. Is it a doubling or is it an almost infinite number? For my arguments it is not necessary to quantify the specific synergy constant; it is simply a matter of distinguishing between collaboration and synergy. For further simplification, let us consider knowledge—the average unique individual knowledge per person in the organization—and let us also assume that each individual's knowledge is complementary to the knowledge of all the other individuals. The exchange of ideas is then effectively a 1+1=4 transaction.

Now, the energy mentioned here is the knowledge energy, so the impact of this expression has different impacts on organizations depending on whether they require more or less knowledge to produce their goods or services. However, the expression shows the importance of sharing and synergic collaboration and the impact it will have on knowledge. The expression is, to my mind, highly relevant. Bear in mind that, since most modern organizations are indeed based on, or at least highly dependent on, knowledge to succeed, this tendency, and therefore the relevance of the expression, seems to be growing as the Hyper-Volatile World promises to turn us all into knowledge workers in the future, unless we already are. Think about it this way: how much of your time is used on actual production compared to either generating or applying knowledge?

According to Bill Gates in *Business @ the Speed of Thought*, the knowledge age is characterized by the ever-increasing availability of information. A digital nervous system brings an organization to life in that it creates a constant awareness of the globally competitive environment in which the organization operates, and furthermore it transports the impulses to the right people, thus facilitating rapid situation assessment and reaction. We shall go more into detail about the actual application of computer technology to the organization in the next chapter, but my point in referring to Gates is the terminology he uses about bringing an organization to life. He describes the organization as an organism with a nervous system. Perhaps we should discuss which organism would be ideal for survival and success in a changing environment; is the organism that is most likely to succeed going to mimic a human, or perhaps an ant? As with other things, the narcissism typical of humans tends to explain why we create even divine things in our own image.

The CALM Hypothesis of Unleashing Potential

No one can predict the future now. No one can make long-range plans. The best we can hope for, to quote Robert Bridges, is "the masterful administration of the unforeseen." Ride the whirlwind. That's the most we can do.

—Arthur C. Clarke

To use the potential of the Hyper-Volatile environment, we need to understand and accept its chaotic nature. I like to think of it as an environment in which wisdom makes it possible to channel vast resources and energy with very little personal effort. This, though, is very much inspired by martial arts such as Tai Chi in which the martial artist flows with the energy; metaphorically he is being strong, like a straw that bends in the wind. The straw accepts the wind and does not compete with it, but the strength of the straw is evident when someone tries to tear it apart. In the Tai Chi mindset lies also the idea that if one fights an enemy with very little effort, the martial artist will preserve his energy, which can then be applied much more efficiently when it is needed, and at the same time the opponent will consume his energy and eventually tire out.

Since change is the only constant in the Hyper-Volatile environment, we need to make ourselves and our organizations understand our strengths and apply them wisely in accordance with our acceptance of the forces of nature at play. In Jim Collins' book *Good to Great*, he documents research on companies that have enjoyed fifteen years of regular growth but that suddenly found the key to success and subsequently enjoyed fifteen years of extraordinary growth. He tells the story of "The Hedgehog and the Fox," which in short goes like this.[26]

A fox tries to outwit his prey, a hedgehog. He tries many different strategies, trying to come up with a cunning attack, but whenever he attacks, the hedgehog rolls up into a spiky ball and the fox fails. The fox spends all his energy trying to come up with a winning strategy, but every time he fails and goes to bed hungry. The hedgehog, on the other hand, goes about collecting food except for those short times when he is under attack, so he never goes to bed hungry.

The key to survival and subsequent success in this short fable appears to be something as simple as core competence; if we know what we do best and apply it appropriately to a situation, chances are we will succeed. But if we spend all our time strategizing scenarios that require much coordination and energy, chances are we will fail in the long run for the simple reason that we are spending our energy attempting something that is impossible in a world of chaos, a Hyper-Volatile World.

Peter Drucker, author of *The Effective Executive*, describes the most limiting resources in all matters of achieving an organizational goal, whether in business or elsewhere, as time, people, and money.[27] In his writings he describes time as the only one of these three resources that is totally inelastic. Taking into consideration the dynamics of the Hyper-Volatile World, we find that both financial and human resources have certainly become much more flexible, since the global availability of them is continually improving. However, even more interestingly, the Hyper-Volatile World has an impact on time, or rather the pace of changes. Basically, if we perceive time as inelastic and combine this with a world that is changing at an increasing pace, the concept of applying resources needs to be rethought. Thinking of these three core resources as abstractions of a leader's options makes pretty good sense, but the time we, as individuals or organizations, have to consider our options using these abstractions has changed dramatically. Essentially, my point is that perhaps we should start thinking of time differently; perhaps we can bend time to a certain extent in the Hyper-Volatile World?!

For example, computer capacity can give us new options through the availability of traditional artificial intelligence. First we stretch time by allowing experts to train and educate a given system to react, and in this phase we have all the time we want. When we subsequently collapse time by letting the computer react in the real world at a pace that is millions of times faster than human reactions, we have effectively changed the time resource. Essentially, what we did was invest more training in our new digital employee than we would in a human, but provided we selected a task that the computer eventually learned, it would all come back to us, and more with it. Future leaders might gain dramatically if they have the wisdom to select the right distribution of tasks between humans and computers.

Another example of such tradeoffs in capacity between humans and computers can be found in the idea of "massive empirics"; the idea is that computers might not be intelligent by our own standards, but their processing capacity might be able to compensate for this by simple trial and error. By creating an environment in which the computer can simulate different choices and behavior, the computer can gradually learn the optimal solution to a problem through, for instance, evolutionary algorithms. All we need to do is to flick the switch of inspiration and show it where to look; computers will then do the rest effectively and perhaps suggest new paths to success that we might never have seen. Additionally, massive empirics has the advantage of being unbiased and extremely capable of building relations among multiple factors, and, because it is unbiased, no one has to have guesstimated the outcome or have had a hunch for an outcome to be found, as our previous scientific methods would have required.

Perhaps all it takes to make future leaps in the sciences is to apply our human ingenuity, in the form of creativity and inspiration, to find the areas we want to explore, and then apply the massive computing powers available to data mine the findings for relevance and significance. Such a symbiotic teamwork between human and computer might be the key to progress in sciences about ourselves and thereby further allow a hidden potential to emerge. Although we might feel intuitively that there is something out there, it is important that we not disregard either ancient or contemporary science on the way. To my mind, the worst mistake we could make at this point would be to attempt to simplify and narrow the boundaries of our quest. Given our current scientific stage, we should accept questions that we might not even think can be answered, since the massive empirical powers of computers might answer them in an entirely unexpected way.

There are many areas in which we could benefit from applying computing power that is unused today; granted we should distinguish between areas we would like optimized through computing and those we would like to remain dominated by humans. Such choices need to be based on an understanding of the alternatives, and in a hyper-volatile future, which is going to demand more flexibility, effectiveness, and efficiency, we should at least consider the computer our closest ally, even though it is also the culprit primarily responsible for our world's becoming hyper-volatile.

In general, computing will evolve along lines that in the short run appear to be pretty predictable. We will experience much more graphic and speech-aware applications from capacities that will emerge as processing power and storage increase. We will also see computing become much more pervasive in the form of different specialty computers that are task oriented and embedded everywhere from household goods to our clothes; these trends will emerge from the increasing Internet connectivity and speed combined with the decrease in physical size.

These trends in combination will lead to the point that, to my mind, will be the most interesting: the day computers become invisible. This will happen when computers become fully embedded in various parts of our everyday life. The computer will be a natural extension of physical objects, or it will be so small that we do not notice that we are carrying it. But first and foremost the computer-human interface should provide such usability that we do not consider something a device or a user interface, simply because all interaction with the computer will become natural, intuitive, and perhaps even mental or guided by the mind. However, for the time being, let us leave it at the point that we as humans are challenged by change while living in a Hyper-Volatile World, and computers might have unused potential that can be applied and in time help us discover and unleash even greater parts of ourselves as humans. The trends in computing will be further discussed in Chapter 4.

In today's hyper-volatile environment it is possible to accomplish things with few resources by understanding the environment and applying the appropriate energy and resources. The art of leadership in the Hyper-Volatile World is to take into consideration which tasks can be optimized by computers and which cannot; such wisdom will allow the optimal employment of resources and energy of both humans and computers, thereby unleashing the full potential of both.

This leads to the hypothesis of this book:

The evolution of man and computers has, in combination, rendered our world in a hyper-volatile state. This means, on one hand, that great achievements can be accomplished with little effort through the use of computers, while on the other hand it means that threats can "travel" effortlessly and rapidly toward us and strike at a pace that appears random. In essence, we perceive the Hyper-Volatile World as chaos.

For an organization to succeed in the Hyper-Volatile World, the traditional strategies and long-term planning cycles are inferior to tactics that seek to seize the moment. The reason for this is that time is more important than the other traditional limiting resources: people and finance. In addition, it will be virtually impossible to predict action and reaction, which is the key to strategy formulation. If an organization accepts its environment as unpredictable, it can start working constructively with all its strength and energy and continuously strive toward survival and success.

If we break the organization into its components in order to ensure the maximum effect in any given situation, we find that there is some inherent unused potential in the utilization of both individual human capacity and computer capacity. In addition, this unused potential can be accumulated and used by an organization. It is the challenge for leaders and managers today and in the future to understand their environment and apply the unused potential of their organizations to get the energy needed for survival and success.

From this hypothesis, "Computer Aided Leadership and Management," CALM, emerges as a discipline that seeks to unleash the potential of the three entities: individuals, organizations, and computers. This book identifies the practices of the CALM discipline and gives guidance on how to unleash the potentials and apply them for organizational survival and success in the Hyper-Volatile World.

It should be noted that the scope of this book is limited to the disciplines of leadership and management in maximizing human and organizational success. This makes the content relevant for practically any organization, but it excludes disciplines such as operational optimization through robotics and the like. In other words the aim of this work is to maximize the combination of humans and computers in any organization, from a "collective mind" perspective. The gain from the automation of physical labor that in many cases complements this perspective will not be investigated.

In addition, the terms *organization* and *competition* will be used in this book to cover both profit and nonprofit organizations. This could perhaps lead some readers to believe that the findings described here concern only for-profit organizations in the market economy. However, the Hyper-Volatile World has an effect on any organization, whether it competes for market share or for a cause. This can be justified by the fact that whether we set out to capture a share of other organizations' or individuals' income, or a share of their mind and time, we are still within the constraints of the three most limiting resources: people, finance, and time. As these resources are all affected by the hyper-volatile environment, the organization that is dependent on them will also be indirectly affected. Therefore the investigation into environment, potential, survival, and success applies to both profit and nonprofit organizations, although it should be mentioned that their individual criteria for measuring survival and success are, of course, different.

From this point on, let us follow this train of thought and investigate the extent to which unused human and computer potential exists in organizations and, ideally, investigate how we can unleash this potential for the organization's success in its global environment.

3

Eliminating Fear

Acting Despite Our Inherent Human Fear

I have always been fascinated with the acceptance of the "now" in decision making, best exemplified in what I would label "ant decision making." It seems that the collective minds of ants are able to react and overcome basically any circumstances, whether it be the coordination of a huge challenge such as carrying a leaf many times their own weight, or an even more destructive scenario of somebody putting a stick into their nest. Whatever the circumstances, an observer sees swift adaptation and reaction to the given situation. Obviously this kind of behavior is a very basic pattern of reaction to stimuli, but it is the complexity of the aggregated behavior of all the ants that is my point. The fact that every ant knows exactly what to do in this situation is what makes it interesting; it seems that the individual ant continually reacts in the right way, and this aggregates into a complex collective achievement in which the job is done in what appears to be the most efficient manner.

It seems that no one is leading or organizing the individual ants, and yet it is hard for a spectator to imagine what could and should be done to improve the process. Additionally, one does not see very much hesitation among the ants, which to my mind suggests that every ant at any point in time accepts the situation; no time is spent feeling sorry for itself, no time wondering, "what's in it for me?" just a clean flow of reaction to stimuli.

We humans are of course very different from the ants in the sense that a key ingredient in our consciousness is the ability to decide our reaction to a stimulus. According to Stephen Covey, author of *The Seven Habits of Highly Effective People*, between stimulus and reaction, man has the freedom to choose. This freedom is significant, as it is both what distinguishes us from any other animal, among others Pavlov's dogs.[28] However, this great power of our minds to make a choice after the stimulus and before responding is also a potential pitfall: since we have the ability to choose our reaction whenever something happens, we also have to employ the entire thought process from gut to heart and on to brain whenever we encounter a stimulus. The flip side of this capacity is the potential to become passive due to mental overload and perhaps even collapse from stress. Psychologists have investigated the characteristics of people who are capable of achieving remarkable results, and it seems that the key to resolving any situation with success is rapid acceptance of the situation, good or bad.

Whether we look into the high performance of NASA astronauts, elite sports men, elite soldiers, or high-performing teams in their workspace, findings tend to suggest that a combination of accepting facts and remaining positive enables us to overcome the biggest challenges and excel in our performance. I cannot help being impressed when reading stories about top performers who, under the most extreme conditions, can remain calm, make structured choices, and execute those choices to perfection. To me, such stories serve as inspiration and put into perspective the level of pressure that most of us are under in our day-to-day jobs. Take for instance the astronauts of Apollo 13, who were under constant pressure for six days as Murphy's Law ruled and everything collapsed around them. They walked themselves methodically through each and every problem in collaboration with the crew in the control room. Although fear would have been a very natural reaction in the situation, it was controlled by calm analysis and assembling facts that, at the end of the day, brought them back to Earth.

Imagine being Commander James A. Lovell around 10 p.m. (EST) on April 13, 1970, while orbiting Earth on what seemed to be the best NASA mission to date, then suddenly finding that a routine stir of an oxygen tank has caused it to explode. With limited visibility of what has actually happened, you find that power is dropping to the extent that the lunar landing will have to be canceled. The disappointment of missing a lunar landing is quickly and dramatically changed to a fight for mere survival as you find that so much oxygen is leaking rapidly from the command module that it can be seen by amateur astronomers on Earth. Would you focus your assets and methodically work yourself through every single crisis on your way back to earth?

As it turned out, Commander James A. Lovell had tremendous assets in terms of his flight crew, along with the ingenuity and skills of mission control. Without losing focus, he and his crew used the lunar landing module Aquarius as a lifeboat by stretching the intended capacity from supporting two men for two days to taking care of three men for nearly four days under conditions that would have broken many men. He describes the physical conditions while orbiting Earth in uncertainty of their return:

> *The trip was marked by discomfort beyond the lack of food and water. Sleep was almost impossible because of the cold. When we turned off the electrical systems, we lost our source of heat, and the Sun streaming in the windows didn't much help. We were as cold as frogs in a frozen pool, especially Jack Swigert, who got his feet wet and didn't have lunar overshoes. It wasn't simply that the temperature dropped to 38 F: the sight of perspiring walls and wet windows made it seem even colder. We considered putting on our spacesuits, but they would have been bulky and too sweaty. Our teflon-coated inflight coveralls were cold to the touch, and how we longed for some good old thermal underwear.*

> —James A. Lovell in *Apollo Expeditions to the Moon*

Having survived under the extreme conditions for days, the time came for what he describes as the most critical crisis. At that point they needed to burn the thrusters of the lunar module to commence their return through the earth's atmosphere. They needed to rely on manual navigation, using a star as a fix point. But the problem was that they could not spot any stars due to the large amount of debris floating around the spacecraft. In the midst of their despair, a bright mind at NASA thought that they should simply use the sun to navigate—even though it was imprecise it was better than nothing. Again, an idea that had never been tested was entered into the chain of improvisation that led to their safe return to Earth on April 17, 1970.[29]

Another example of such bravery combined with calm under pressure serves as yet further proof of the concept. It took place when members of the Danish Frogman Corps were on an exercise in Hamburg Harbor. To those unfamiliar with this unit, it is an elite military unit equivalent to the Navy Seals in the United States. During an exercise, members of the corps have to move around on the seabed, following the pier wall. However, they were unaware that their detailed planning was based on a map that didn't take into consideration some rebuilding of the harbor, which had resulted in a big cave. While seeking the surface for orientation, the knowledge that they were in fact in a cave became frighteningly clear. This fact, in combination with the limited visibility in the water and the limited supply of air, made it a life-threatening situation. Again, panic would be the most likely spontaneous reaction. However, quick assembly of facts and options made a difference. As one frogman recalls, there were actually a few facts to be positive about: they were not cold, they had no urgent need for an air supply although this resource was limited, and they knew roughly which way they had gone in. Working methodically from this platform of resources in their favor for what is referred to as "a very long half hour," they made it out alive from the claustrophobic darkness.[30]

Being able to face facts and analyze the situation while remaining positive is only the beginning; it is this platform from which we should launch a lot of energy toward the desired results. Later in this chapter we will look into ways an individual can build up this energy and even enhance it through synergic collaboration between individuals, but let us for a moment stay with the individual seeking a platform from which he can launch the most effective actions. When we face facts, fear is replaced by a calm overview and a feeling of readiness.

In *The Other 90%*, Robert Cooper spends some pages explaining the latest neuroscience findings regarding how our brain, or rather *brains*, work. According to these findings, we have not one, but three brains: one in the gut, one in the heart, and one in the head. Essentially, the latest findings conclude that an input does not go through our five senses directly to the brain in the head to be thought through and thereby turned into some kind of action. In reality, the input travels through the intestinal tract, the gut; then to the heart; and from there to the brain in the head, with which we are all familiar.[31]

The brain in the gut is an elaborate system of nerve cells and neurochemicals in the intestinal tract, where there are more neurons than in the entire spinal column—about 100 million of them. This system is capable of acting, learning, remembering, and influencing our perceptions and behaviors independently. In nonscientific terms, haven't we all felt butterflies in our gut, or felt it tighten up in different situations?

The brain in the heart comprises more than 40,000 nerve cells called baroreceptors. Along with a complex network of neurotransmitters, proteins, and support cells, this heart brain is as large as many of the key areas in the brain. With each heartbeat, a pressure wave travels through the whole body, much faster than the actual flood of blood. Each of our trillions of cells feels this pressure wave and is dependent on it in a number of ways. Another route the heart uses to communicate is by transmitting messages through chemicals in the hormonal system; one of these chemicals is atrial peptide, which is a primary driver for motivated behavior. We have to *feel* our values or goals; otherwise we can't *live* them—such feelings are the input from the heart brain.

The brain in the head is the one that has been known to us for ages. Interestingly enough, it is also the one with the most potential for making us conservative. The information from the gut and the heart travels to the base of the brain, known as the medulla oblongata, and from there it reaches the reticular activating system, RAS, which is its third stop. The RAS is a part of our brain that connects with major nerves in the spinal column and the brain in the head; this part of our brain is a result of millennia of evolution, and it holds an inherent tendency to magnify the negative and minimize the positive impressions. So as Robert Cooper puts it, "Although human beings today live in a technology-driven world of galactic voyages and virtual realities, we still face everyday life with deeply embedded traits of Stone Age hunter-gatherers."

The RAS was most likely the key to survival in the jungle, where any unfamiliar sound in the bushes could be the prelude to an attack by an animal, but today it continuously signals, "Danger! Danger!" at the same strength as it has for eons, before we faced the changes that shaped our modern environment.

The brain in the head certainly has an important role in terms of our thinking, but the potential of the other ninety percent appears to lie in bypassing the immediate signals from the RAS. So in summary, we need to be aware of the functionality of the RAS as well as of our two other brains. If we pause a moment whenever we encounter a situation in which our immediate systems say, "Danger! Danger!," and compare this information with inputs from our heart and gut feeling, we will be able to make sounder decisions by tapping into the vast resources of our intuition and feelings combined with our logical thinking.

In other words, our natural reaction to a change in the environment is to see it as a threat; so even though we are the masters of our entire mind and can choose our reaction to a stimulus, we still need to master positive thinking to make this choice wisely, because this kind of thinking in these circumstances is not our natural response.

So how do we achieve positive thinking in a changing environment? If we acknowledge the description of the three brains offered by Robert Cooper, we can as individuals start a process of becoming more aware of how to use these brains in combination to make more balanced choices in our lives. Positive thinking might not be our automatic response, but from personal experience we will be able to recollect and compare situations in which we encountered change for the better. The mental map of these incidents, in combination with the feeling in the gut and the heart, can serve as a tool to remaining positive even under difficult circumstances. Building a mental map requires us to take the time to reflect on our performance in different situations. If we do not invest this time to learn from our experience, the impressions will slowly fade, and our evolutionary habit of seeing change as a threat will remain.

If we refer to the energies shown in figure 2.1 in the previous chapter, we will see that the road along which an input or stimulus travels influences the emotional and mental energy, by definition. Using this model, one could say that emotional energy should be monitored continuously with a little mental energy; such an investment of mental energy will enable us to optimize both energies, and make us better able to cope with changes in our environment. Over time, such monitoring of our energies in our natural environment will make us more secure and self-aware, even in a changing world. There are, however, situations so radically different from our natural environment that we have great difficulties relating to them.

I recall parachuting for the first time, which was an amazing experience. I wouldn't describe it as frightening as much as it was a feeling of extreme sensory overload, in the sense that everything felt unreal. I guess this feeling comes when you are receiving so much more input than you have ever felt before. In my first jump I had to concentrate very much while climbing out of the plane. As I let go on the jumpmaster's command, it was as if I blacked out until the parachute opened by static line. The period between letting go of the plane and the parachute's opening was probably no more than two or three seconds, but it was very strange to feel how my mind reacted to being in midair, 3,000 feet above the ground. Having experienced this emptiness of the mind once, it was remarkable how quickly I adjusted to receiving this input; on my second jump I could feel the entire fall and was much more aware of everything that was going on. It seemed that my senses had adjusted and were able to capture what was going on, even though I had had just one previous experience of this kind. More than a decade later, I treated myself to a skydiving education that took me freefalling 12,000 feet for fifty seconds until I pulled the parachute ripcord. The interesting part from a sensory standpoint was that even from the first jump I was able to enjoy and feel the experience to the fullest, although it had been quite some time since I had parachuted. Another thing I found in "my personal lab" was how I dealt with fear. Logically, there is a certain amount of fear involved in jumping out of an airplane, but I found that after proper instruction and training, at the critical moment when we were lifting off and jumping seemed inevitable, all fear suddenly fled. It was as if the acceptance of jumping turned the nervousness in the gut, which I felt on the ground, into a decisive knowledge in my head that I knew what to do and was capable of doing it, no matter the circumstances. It was remarkable how much spiritual energy was available to me once I had conquered fear and felt fully in control of the situation. Following this path even further to jumping a number of times, I felt how the experience of jumping becomes more and more natural; suddenly the feeling of fear vaporized entirely, and the joy of the ride emerged to the fullest. I guess the best way to describe these calm jumps is that the parachute becomes a natural extension of my body when I step out of the plane and start exploring an exciting new environment while balancing on a pillow of gravity and air.

I would not guesstimate what it takes to allow our senses to adapt to a radically new situation; however I do think that if we stimulate our senses to adapt to different kinds of situations, we can reduce this time, and perhaps even prevent ourselves from having a "blackout," whether literal or metaphorical. Testing and expanding our boundaries will, to my mind, improve our ability to adapt. We can use these types of experiences to expand the scope of our sensibility, and this, in combination with experiencing the mix of fun and anxiety followed by the joy of overcoming the situation, can help us program our minds to feel positive in such situations, thereby allowing us to enjoy the benefit of improved levels of all three energies, namely emotional, mental, and spiritual. Conversely, if we do not update this mental map of our energies with each new experience, there is a chance that a changing environment will consume our energies—and where's the fun in that?

Stephen Covey defines habits as the intersection between knowledge, skills, and desire. For something to become a habit, all three areas must be covered; we must have the knowledge of what to do, we must have the skills to do it, and finally we must have the desire to do it.[32] It is interesting to combine this with the areas of energy, since we find that each of the habit components is influenced by all three energies. We probably think that knowledge and skills are all in our head, but going back to the description of how impressions travel through the gut, heart, and head, we find that we should be wising up. We need to combine our thoughts with our feelings in the gut and heart if we are to use our entire source of knowledge. The same rationale can be applied to skills, as they are merely a deeper subset of our general knowledge. It is different with desire: one would be compelled to say that desire arises from the gut and heart and then is sometimes suppressed by our head. How many of our desires are not actually suppressed by rationalizing about our resources? Regardless how we look at it, we need to involve all three energies to have a habit, whether we do it consciously or subconsciously. If we are low on any one of the three energies, chances are we will have greater difficulty and energy consumption in our habitual reactions and vice versa.

When the Danish author Sjak Svendstorp was writing a book about experiences in the Frogman Corps, he noted that it appeared that each elite soldier had a certain look in his eyes, a certain look that seemed to hold no fear of anything, combined with an attitude that suggested inner peace. Could it be possible to eliminate all fear by accumulating enough experience of extreme incidents to wire change into a habit? Most of us will probably never know, but we can all start rewiring our evolutionary propensity to see change as a negative thing in our daily environment. It simply requires a little bit of reflection from time to time.

A tool I have found useful when reflecting on a given incident or impression is to consider that everything holds both a positive and a negative potential. This means that even though a change initially strikes us as negative, it might have a positive flip side. If we combine this with the fact that we are in a Hyper-Volatile World, we are actually able to move toward the positive aspect of an incident. This can be done with little effort; the cost in terms of energy is low. In fact if you look back on your own individual history, how many incidents can you find, regardless of how tough they were during the process, that have not had some influence in shaping the person you are today? How many times have you failed because of a weakness and not gained strength once you understood the weakness? Of course there are incidents in which we encounter things so traumatic that turning the experience into a strength seems virtually impossible, but these types of trauma do often strengthen the person, if they are handled properly. However, my point is not to address the types of deep-lying trauma that need professional guidance; it is rather to address all the everyday minor events in our immediate external environment that can be turned from negative to positive experiences with little effort. Whenever we deal with the external environment it is not hard to see ourselves as righteous and positive individuals, and at least from this platform it should be possible to gain strength through a thorough understanding of the hyper-volatile environment around us and our inherent negativity toward change. Working toward positive scenarios with little energy consumption will gradually increase our inner energy, and this positive energy will in turn influence our inner selves on emotional, mental, and spiritual levels.

Perhaps this attitude was what Jack Welch meant when he talked about harnessing the power of change; if we embrace change as an opportunity, it has limitless potential. We know that change will always be there, so if we find a way of harnessing it and turning it into positive scenarios, we are virtually able to turn all negative into positive potential. As Napoleon Hill, author of *Think and Grow Rich*, put it, "every adversity, every failure, and every heartache carries with it the seed of equivalent or greater benefit."

If we reach a point where we have a positive attitude toward change, and the inherent fear of change has gone, we can start to address reality from a neutral or perhaps even a positive standpoint. One of the first pieces of advice Jack Welch gives in his leadership secrets is that a manager needs to "face reality!" I take it that since the term "brutal facts" is not used, he means that facing reality should be a habit, along with being positive toward change. In his own words, Jack Welch puts it this way: "Stick your head in the sand and you will fail. Face reality and you may turn a bad situation into a great one."

Management consultant Jan Holmsgaard, who has been a great inspiration to me and many others in the business environment in northern Denmark, teaches that it is not until we accept reality that we can do something about it. To a spectator of life, this would seem almost too trivial, but to a participant in life faced with change, it makes a lot of sense.

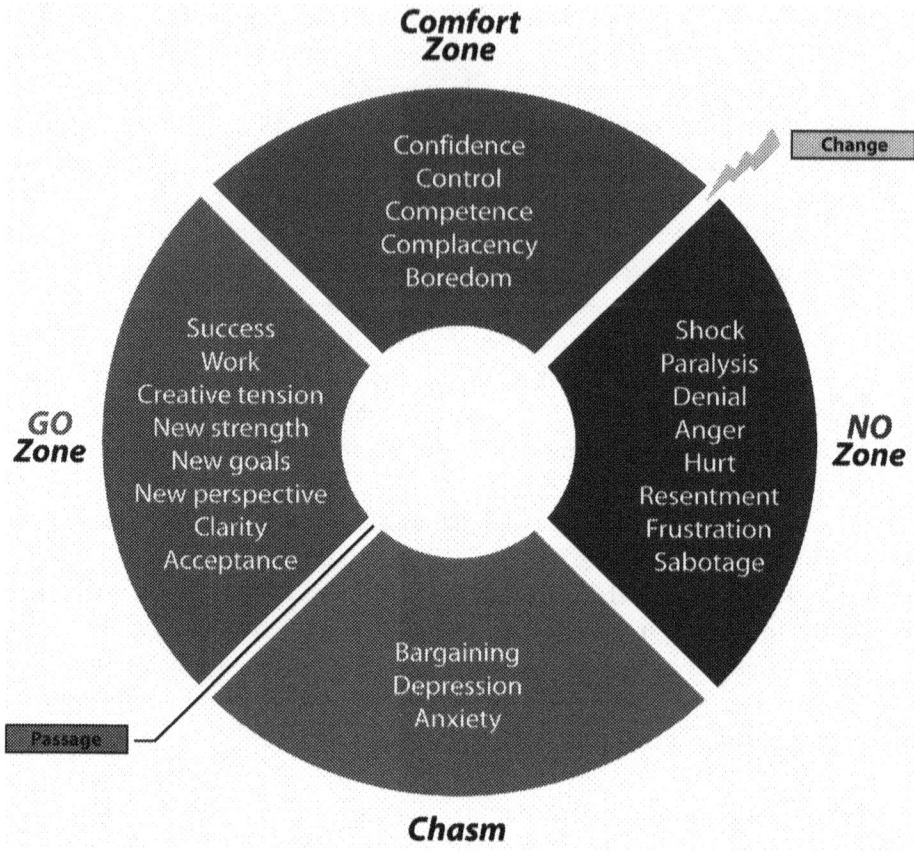

Figure 3.1 The Cycle of Change

Jan Holmsgaard introduced me to a version of Kevin Craine's "cycle of change," as shown in figure 3.1.[33] He described how the mechanisms in people subjected to change function. Our first reaction is denial, meaning we fail to accept the "danger" at all; we say to ourselves, "this isn't happening." At some point, though, reality strikes, and we can no longer deny the fact; we then find ourselves in a limbo that can leave us feeling depressed and anxious. This chasm is the second unproductive phase. Both the "no zone" and the "chasm" could easily be explained by the RAS, mentioned earlier. However, moving on from these first two unproductive phases, we come to terms with the facts. We have the opportunity to accept our situation and assess the knowledge we have at hand, and from this stage we can start to act. Once we start getting into action, we are in the "go zone," and here we have the opportunity to work toward the most positive scenarios given the circumstances. We can direct the full power of our available resources to optimizing our situation, and the more we operate in the "go zone," the more comfortable we become, until change occurs and we journey through the cycle again. At any point in our individual lives, we will be at one of these stages, and we will travel this cycle multiple times during our lives.

I have personally tried changing my habit of running. Over the years I have done a lot of running, but I never really seemed to get to the point where I was confident that I could go on and on for as long as I wanted, the point that some people refer to as being in "the zone." This meant that whenever I ran I was actually doing it very reluctantly. This made me feel that I was not on top of the situation and left me longing to reach the finish line. In other words, running was definitely not a habit that came easily to me, and I was using a lot of energy while doing it because I was not enjoying it. To change this habit, I basically shifted my focus from the finish line to the "now" and to the state of my body. I started noticing the different phases my body went through while running. I noticed that after X minutes I would start to perspire and feel a weakness in my left knee; but most importantly I learned that after about Y minutes I would feel that I could go on forever—I made it to "the zone." By continuously monitoring the signals from my body, I noticed X and Y decrease. Additionally, I became very familiar with the different areas in which I would experience moderate pain, and while running I focused on these areas and noted how the pain faded again. To gain positive energy, I constantly tried to focus on the areas that were doing well. For instance, if I was feeling pain in my knee I was glad that I was not short of breath and felt energetic overall. So in essence, simply by using a very simple methodology of monitoring my body, I managed to reprogram myself to actually enjoy running to the extent that I miss it if for some reason when I do not have time for it.

It should be noted that even though we feel confident we can easily deviate from a habit, we might be surprised and experience setbacks while trying to do so. Robert Cooper tells about a paratrooper from his time in the marines who agreed to use a left-handed parachute rather than a right-handed one, and although he was an experienced jumper, he failed to reach and pull his parachute ripcord. When they pulled his dead body from the ground, they found his uniform was torn to pieces where the right-handed release would have been. He died trying to fight a well-known habit. So we may realize that changing habits, no matter how simple, might require a lot of work—and most importantly we would be wise to select the right place and time to reprogram the habit.

I have always enjoyed the song "Wish You were Here" from Pink Floyd; other than recalling my youth, Pink Floyd touches on what I believe is the biggest obstacle to unleashing our individual potential: fear.

> *How I wish, how I wish you were here*
> *We're just two lost souls*
> *Swimming in a fish bowl*
> *Year after year*
> *Running over the same old ground*
> *What have we found?*
> *The same old fears*
> *Wish you were here*

—Pink Floyd, "Wish You Were Here"

Shredding the Collective Fear

Much like the individual, our organizations are inherently subjected to the ineffectiveness of fear. Fear in this case resides in the individuals, and it results in individuals' not sharing information and knowledge. The fear in this sense is about other people's intent, their agenda. Covey has described a state of synergistic cooperation in which an optimum of synergy is released between people; he describes this optimum in two dimensions, namely the level of trust and the level of cooperation between the people. If we are able to reach a high degree of trust, in combination with a degree of cooperation where we aim for win-win situations for everyone, we are at this optimum. The idea of reaching this optimum is to release all the energy that would normally be spent distrusting and wondering whether other people are trying to trick us in a win-lose scenario; this released energy can be converted into positive and productive energy. It can effectively be converted into action.[34]

It may seem very logical that it is highly advantageous to reach this point, but in reality such an environment cannot be reached until we have aligned all three of our brains, our energies of emotion, mental activity, and spiritual drive.

In our head brain, based on pure mental calculation, we can consult the field of game theory, which is a mathematical model used by John von Neumann and Oskar Morgenstern among others since the 1940s to study problems in economics. Since then, its use has been emerging in political science and psychology as well. In short, these mathematical modeling methods are used to study human interaction in formalized incentive structures: games. Games, as abstractions of the real world, can be used to predict and study the actual behavior of individuals, as well as to determine optimal strategies for the games. Around 1950, John Nash developed a definition of an "optimum" strategy, known as the Nash Equilibrium, for multiplayer games where no such optimum had previously been defined.[35] A basic definition of the Nash Equilibrium follows: If there is a set of strategies for a game where no player can benefit by changing his strategy while the other players keep their strategies unchanged, then that set of strategies and the corresponding payoffs have a "Nash Equilibrium."

I remember an old cartoon where two donkeys are connected by a length of rope and are both trying to eat from a pile of hay in front of them, but the piles are just about out of reach for both of them. They struggle and consume energy trying to get to the pile in front of their eyes at the expense of the other donkey's not reaching the opposite pile. The struggle to win at the other's expense ends up as a lose-lose situation at first, but as they relax, a new strategy emerges: they each go to one pile and share it, and then go to the other pile and share it. Suddenly the situation is changed to win-win.

The moral of this story is that we cannot rely on others to fail for us to win, and even if we could, a lot of unproductive energy would be consumed in the process. Additionally, it might also be fairly easy to gain hands-on experience that in the real world win-win situations pay off better in the long term than do win-lose situations. It does not require more than a few tests or mere reflection for most people to see this. Win-lose tends to work only for the short term in the real world. Indeed, perhaps there is a reason we are not alone in the world.

Pure logic in the head brain only gets us so far in the story of the donkeys; the donkeys needed a bond of trust that they would both win by sharing. What would prevent one donkey from eating more than the other from both piles? The key here is trust. Trusting others involves using our brain in the gut, but more importantly trust has to do with the brain in the heart when we deal with others trusting us. My point is that if our intent in the heart is not pure, we are not worthy of being trusted. And if we are not worthy, then why should others be? Such thoughts are exactly the fabric from which distrust is made; we need to truly want a situation to be a win-win to have others trust our intent.

It gets even more complicated if we consider situations in which we are unsure of our intent, perhaps in situations where we are balancing on the edge of our own competency. In such situations we might even be protecting ourselves from being exposed as incompetent. It is interesting to note that in these circumstances, since we are unaware of what we ought to know anyway, energy is consumed totally unproductively defending something, but we do not know what. We therefore have no way of knowing what our intent really should be. Such a loop of incompetence is probably the worst-case scenario, since we are perceived as untrustworthy in a situation where trusting others would probably be the most productive reaction for us. Therefore we need to trust ourselves before we can earn the trust of others, and we need to trust our values and competencies to the extent that we feel confident enough to also admit our weaknesses. So the worst and most destructive fear that prevents a state of full trust is really not the fear of other people's intentions; ironically, it is the fear of the unknown within ourselves. As Plato put it, "Wisest is he who knows what he does not know."

From this point of view, in order to align our three brains we should be aware of our inner values and competencies, our principles and skills as Stephen Covey might label them. From this point we can clear our heart and materialize our intent based on the logic of the brain in the head. Secondly, we should not be naive and should apply the gut feeling as a measure of the level at which we seek to trust others. In my opinion, only if we succeed with this alignment do we have the ability to reach the optimum, which Covey suggests is full trust in a win-win environment.

So trust can really be a question of whether we trust ourselves enough to admit our strengths and weaknesses, not only to ourselves but to others. In addition, the potential synergic high performance is jeopardized if we enforce management systems such as control-and-reward systems that do not support a culture in which it is acceptable to make mistakes, admit weakness, and encourage knowledge sharing. In research conducted by Gallup, involving 198,000 employees, only twenty percent responded positively when asked if they felt that their strengths were at play every day, meaning that eighty percent did not feel that their strengths were put to work daily![36] Such findings are testimony that there are gaps in the organizational fabric where potential is lost, but why do these gaps occur in the first place? Is it because organizations do not build on the skills of the individuals, or is it because the individuals don't feel comfortable admitting who they really are, in terms of wants, strengths, and weaknesses? Another pitfall that could explain some of this discouraging finding could be Laurence Peter's 1969 description of "the Peter principle," in which an excellent employee is blindly promoted to the next level in an organization regardless of whether the competence of the employee, or his happiness for that matter, applies to the new level.[37]

This promotion to incompetence is still very much a reality today according to another Gallup study that covered more than 80,000 managers in over 400 companies.[38] If we continue to promote people methodically in this manner, competence gaps will eventually appear as the person promoted to incompetence flounders. Even worse, the synergic potential of the area under the particular incompetent manager will not be optimal. This will cause much more widespread organizational loss of potential because such a situation means that both the manager and the employees feel they could be better off elsewhere.

On the other hand, being too competent, especially as a leader or manager, has an inherent pitfall: underutilizing delegation. Underutilizing individuals' capacity also loses the potential synergy among them. In this case the leader ought to ask whether he is really the right person for the job; he might be better off leading a team with a higher level of skills so that delegation makes sense. Failing to delegate is, almost by definition, underutilization of potential.

Basically, failing to understand our own strengths and weaknesses can lead to an unproductive stage, as we are not tapping into the potential synergy. Failing to understand our own strengths and weaknesses puts us at risk of becoming victims of fear: fear of being unwanted in the organization, fear of not getting the job or project, and so forth. However, as we find it is exactly this type of fear that prevents us from creating synergy, we need to define ourselves and trust ourselves holistically in order to bridge this gap in the use of our potential.

This makes sense from a psychological standpoint as well. Jung describes four functional types that correspond to the obvious means by which consciousness obtains its orientation to experience. Sensation (i.e., sense perception) tells us that something exists; thinking tells us what it is; feeling tells us whether it is agreeable or not; and Intuition tells us from whence it comes and where it is going.[39] The way each function manifests in the psychology of the individual depends on his characteristic attitude. Whereas the extrovert is oriented primarily to events in the outer world, the introvert is primarily concerned with the inner world.[40] In other words, in Jung's typology we find four functions in two dimensions, namely feeling/thinking and sensation/intuition. Additionally, we find two attitudes in one dimension, namely introvert/extrovert. Combining these three dimensions gives eight different combinations in Jung's typology.[41] In different schools that are all derivatives of Jung's basic definition of human minds, we find different names for these typologies, such as Peter Urs Bender's four types of personalities—Analytical, Amiable, Driver, and Expressive—and their associated strengths and weaknesses.[42]

There are of course many more detailed models for categorizing the human mind from a psychological standpoint, but my point is that even on the roughest level we are dealing with at least eight distinct people profiles that all have an inherent set of strengths and weaknesses. So there is really no point in attempting to be what we are not; we should come to terms with who we are and build on our strengths. Psychological evidence suggests that we base our teaming up with others on finding people who complement our strengths by strengthening us where we are weak. Obviously there are many ways to identify people with whom we will be able to achieve synergic cooperation, but with psychological profiling we will at least be able to identify large gaps in the organization or team. Simply look for an area in which there are no individuals with the concomitant skills.

If we are in a situation where we do not feel comfortable and internally feel we should be somewhere else, we are bleeding energy. We will feel stressed out and frustrated that we are not where we feel we should be. There is hardly any evidence suggesting higher productivity based on stress, so it can complement fear in accounting for significant potential loss. Ironically, stress could probably be relieved considerably by admitting our weaknesses and letting others assist with the tasks we feel stressed about, but stress tends to intensify our mistrust even more. So adding stress to the equation means an even more powerful negative spiral that will constantly drain our energy to the extent that even simple things seem to require too much effort and energy. It is, however, interesting to note an article by Roderick M. Kramer in the July 2002 issue of the *Harvard Business Review*: "When Paranoia Makes Sense." The article exemplifies people who have gained the upper hand in situations by being paranoid, by completely distrusting others. The article introduces "prudent paranoia" as a healthy skeptical exercise to apply in situations where we are presented with information or observe others. Compared to Cooper's book, this is somewhat different from the "trust" cornerstone. As Roderick Kramer put it, "Two decades of research on trust and cooperation in organizations have convinced me that—despite its costs—distrust can be beneficial in the workplace."[43]

I personally believe that Kramer's article has some good points; we should not trust to the point of being naive—some people truly want bad things to happen to us. However, as leaders and organizational architects we should not even have such people in our teams and organizations. The organizational culture should in practice mean that such an approach does not pay off, first of all because it does not encourage sharing and openness, which are paramount components of synergic cooperation, and second because if we build organizations by such principles as trust, the paranoia would have no effect except inefficiency for the individual who practices it.

So in conclusion, the purest fear is really about not trusting ourselves; fear is equal to not knowing our strengths and weaknesses. If we do not come to terms with ourselves and thereby our fears, fear will prevent us from sharing information and learning in parallel, and worst of all it will distance us from the source of energy present when synergic cooperation takes place.

CALM @ Work: An Example of Facts Eliminating Fear

When we know about the inner workings of our three human brains, it is a classic management mistake to make a phone call to an employee simply asking him to come to a meeting: "Do you have five minutes....?" The reason for this being a mistake is the fact that the human brain will most likely start thinking negative about this neutral request; between the call and the actual meeting, the employee will ponder on what he/she did wrong.

Obviously the matter of the negative effect of being oblivious to the actual purpose of the meeting depends on his experience in this particular type of meeting in general. Both these types of information are in reality facts, and therefore facts can indeed eliminate the unproductive fear that the employee in this situation has.

All that is required to stop the employee's unproductive fear and boost his confidence is for him to know how he is performing against the actual goals of the organization. Alternatively, he should at least be told what he actually did do wrong. Even though the employee knows that he did in fact do something wrong, the factual knowledge could indeed help him being productive about his mistakes, thinking about what to do different and better.

The ability for an employee to have the knowledge to be confident and constructive under neutral conditions can easily be provided through a computer system that makes the actual performance data and goals available. However, the point of this example is not the system; it is the notion that facts eliminate fear, and the absence of facts breeds fear. Consider this: If the situation above was ignited by a rumor or a compet-itive action provided by an internal source, this would mean a period of fear accelerating with no actual meeting to defuse it. In such a case facts would yet again have been the cure, but there would be no alternative to facts for eliminating the fear, and worst of all: the damage to the organi-zations in terms of a loss in timely action and productivity would have been higher.

—CALM leaders and managers understand the nature of human fear and how computers can assist in eliminating fear through facts.

4

Computing for Wisdom

Knowledge to Accept and Act

Having identified the fears that can drain us as individuals and organizations, let us now look at how computers can assist us in minimizing fear or perhaps even eliminating it.

The most effective tool against fear is facts; the advice from Jack Welch to face facts makes sense in more than a logical way. The less we know, the more influence the inherited negative thinking of our head brain has. The more we know, the more brain food we have to process, and therefore the less processing capacity and perhaps less time we have to ponder the negative opportunities. Computers are brilliant at storing and calculating factual information; in fact they are brutally honest and impartial. Granted, facts stored in computers are no better than the facts we feed it, so we must of course ensure high quality of the basic data, but once this is taken care of, we have a pool of facts that can be applied to individuals and organizations to relieve fear.

If we use as many computerized facts as possible to cover an area of operation in which we need to be in present either as individuals or organizations, we effectively minimize the potential for fear, but we need to proceed further than that. The areas that are left uncovered, either because we lack the ability to access the relevant facts, or because we do not even have a clue what the facts might be, are still areas for the growth of fear. For these areas we need to accept a degree of uncertainty—the unknown. We are not powerless; we can appoint sentinels to warn us if these areas are changing, and perhaps facts will then start to emerge. Sentinels are actually key performance indicators, KPIs, for the environment around the organization, but they are applied to the organization's data most indicative of the external environment. Sentinels can initially be intuitively defined, but they must prove their worth over time. Most effective sentinels will be found in organizations in which there is already a record of which actual historical occurrences in the external environment can be compared with respective outcomes. Once the sentinels are in place, we use computers to monitor the data we control and thereby get a fair warning if something happens that can result in changes in the organization's immediate external environment.

If we apply these two computerization strategies in combination, we achieve the highest level of computing support in limiting and even eliminating our fear. If we accept that this is the most we can do and that this is in fact the foundation of survival in the hyper-volatile environment, perhaps we also prevent ourselves from trying to solve impossible or hypothetical problems. An appropriate strategy must ensure that we channel our efforts into problems that can actually be solved. For problems we cannot solve or that we are not certain exist, we need to rely on our sentinels to give us a fair warning, and trust that the warning we get is sufficient. This way we do not bleed energy by fearfully worrying about problems that are either out of reach or mere phantoms.

Referring back to the cycle of change, let us now review how facts affect the pace at which we travel the cycle. In the "no zone," facts allow us to move into acceptance and understanding the situation more quickly. We might not be able to use facts for very much at the relational stage, as the use of facts is not going to do anything to our human nature. However, at least we would spend less time in denial. At the stage of acceptance, facts can make all the difference, not only between making the right or the wrong decision, but also in our ability to choose the right course of action to execute the decision. This means that facts enable us to cross the chasm swiftly, perhaps even go directly from the "no zone" to the "go zone." The proper mixture of internal facts will enable us to understand our current situation in terms of strengths and weaknesses, and an updated environmental status report from our outer sentinels in the hyper-volatile environment will give us clues about opportunities and threats in the outside world. So the combination of facts and indicators from our sentinels will allow the cycle of change to move at a faster pace, from the unproductive "no zone" to the productive "go zone." Additionally, we can also ensure that we channel energy only toward problems we can actually solve. Worrying has no effect in the hyper-volatile environment; change is inevitable.

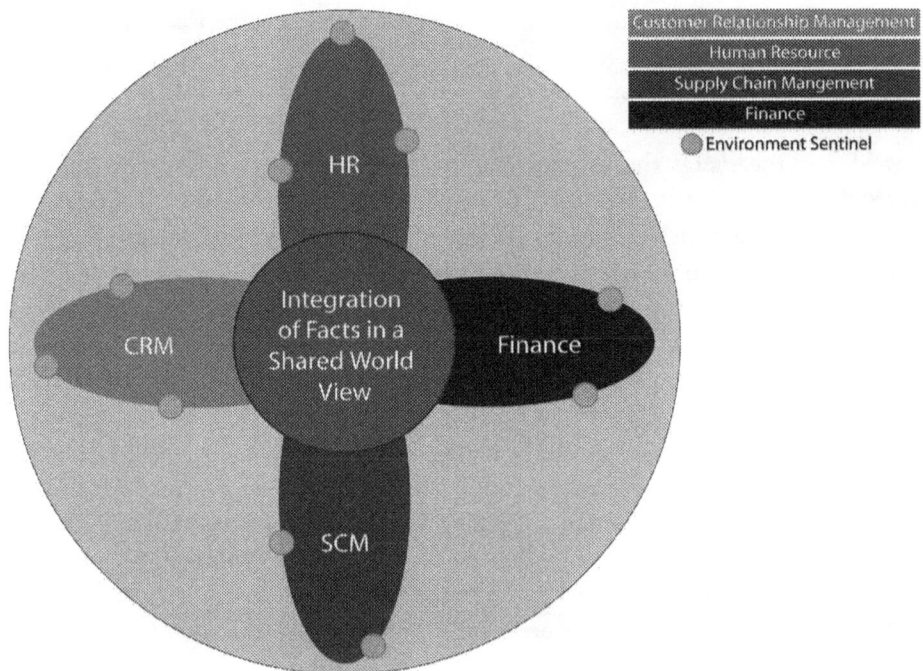

Figure 4.1 Example of Facts and Sentinels

In figure 4.1 we see an abstract example of an infrastructure and the distinction between facts and the indicators from the sentinels. Facts are the inner core of information across the entire organizational infrastructure, and sentinels are monitors for selected facts that have been empirically identified as indicators for the external environment. A way of putting it is that they mark the interface between the organization and its environment. As an example, one could look into the information arising from the customer relations management, CRM, system which, in combination with the finance system, would have facts about the number of orders, revenue, number of customers, and so on. The three sentinels around the CRM system provide the indicators of the environment such as number of offers, number of negotiations, number of meetings, and the like. In other words, the interpretation of information from sentinels should not be considered as reliable as facts, but by combining the historical relationships between the facts, some of which are sentinels and some of which are harder facts on which me measure our success, we can get both a feeling for what to expect and an early warning that something unexpected is about to happen in the environment. The example in figure 4.1 is an abstraction, so the concept should by no means be limited to covering only the four types of systems mentioned; in reality, the number of systems, the number of facts, and the number of sentinels will vary from organization to organization.

If we dissect the energy that is consumed by worrying in this context, we find that worrying is really a feeling of being threatened by factors to which we cannot pin an exact fact or sentinel. To minimize this unproductive energy consumption we must first be aware of the reality of a threat and accept it in as a fact. We then move to the "go zone" and start turning energy into action to counter the threat. Computers aid us in this process, first by making the facts visible and available so we can accept them, and then in the analytical process of identifying the appropriate countermeasure. Alternatively, if we do not have facts but we trust the position and quality of our sentinels, we can conserve the energy that would otherwise be consumed worrying, because if a threat is real and evolves into a situation, we will know soon enough to be able to counter it. In both these scenarios, computers play a vital part in enabling us to conserve energy rather then bleeding it while worrying; and all that is needed for the release of worry in the Hyper-Volatile World is a *trustworthy shared world view* based on the right facts and sentinels.

It should be noted that the term *facts* in this case is not used to distinguish the origin of data. Some data, such as financial data, are typically referred to as hard facts as opposed to soft facts like human resource and learning data, but the term *facts* in this context refers to all the data we control within our boundaries as individuals or organizations. This includes all the data in systems we control or have access to; systems that are not in these categories are simply part of the external hyper-volatile environment. The idea is that if we are fully aware of what we actually "know," in the sense of what data we have, and if we set up indicators in the boundaries of these data to warn us of probable impending changes to the data, then we can make the most of the data we have at hand at any given time. If we use computers to assist us in monitoring and analyzing these data, we will at any given time have the optimal computer support in the Hyper-Volatile World. Granted, we should continue to look for ways to expand the scope of the data we have, but making the most of what we have and deploying sentinels at the data boundaries will allow us to worry less about the data we do not have, and thereby free us of an unproductive fear that only consumes resources. The primary key to letting go of the fear is the knowledge that we do our best at any given time. What is actually the point of worrying whether our best is good enough?

I deliberately use the word *data* at this stage, since that is the raw material that we can refine into information by adding appropriate definitions and references to it. Information itself might not be worth anything until we apply it. We then benefit from it, and at this stage the information becomes knowledge. In its ultimate form, knowledge becomes wisdom. When it reaches that stage it flows smoothly to its proper application.

The wisdom triangle shown in figure 4.2 describes the layers in the process; the layers have been inspired by Pat Robinson's research update on "Sequential Data Distillation, Refinement and Learning Processes."[44] This illustrates the refinement process from data to wisdom. It is much like mountain climbing; none of the stages can be skipped, and some of them may be challenging to reach, but the clear panoramic view from the top makes the journey worthwhile.

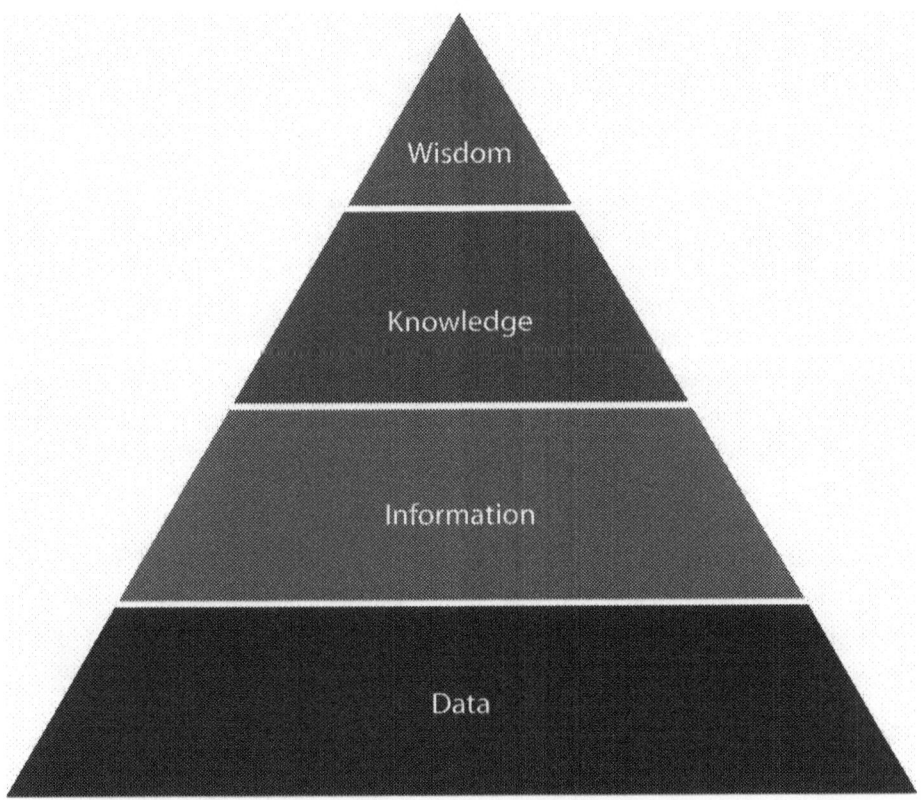

Figure 4.2 The Wisdom Triangle

The characteristics of the application of wisdom compared to knowledge is that the actions we perform with wisdom seem to happen much more easily, and we become intuitively attached to the action as we involve our combined mental, emotional, and spiritual energies. When we are acting wisely we do not feel fatigue to the extent we would under the same circumstances while operating only knowledgeably. With wisdom, we flow through the experience, spending less energy and achieving more. Later in this chapter we will look into details of the process by which data is refined into information, knowledge, and wisdom through the use of computing.

Technologically, most organizations find that there are already a number of systems in place that create the computerized foundation for systems that can be used to reduce fear and enable us to travel through the cycle of change. If we think about it, practically no large organization today could continue to operate without computers, so if we look into what systems they need we will also know a lot about what information is critical to their existence. Organizations have already been shaped by the hyper-volatile environment, so what has evolved is what was necessary for their survival. This is especially true if we consider the availability of facts. By definition they are present, and their relevance is axiomatic as the organization has survived in this Hyper-Volatile World so far. However, in my experience two critical challenges remain. We need to deploy sentinels appropriately and combine the facts with the interpretation of the sentinels to turn the data into information and knowledge, not just for a few individuals, but for an entire organization.

By information I mean data of unquestionable quality. I know that it is not necessarily easy to reach this stage, but it is worth the effort at an early stage to ensure from a centralized point that, should there be any problem with the quality of the data, the data will not be replicated. This prevents spreading inaccurate data and creating uncertainty whether the data can be relied on in a multitude of people. Chaos theory suggests that the lack of a good information foundation will potentially allow problems to evolve. Initially we will not know what is missing from the original data, and the consequences, little or big, will be deterministically replicated and multiplied throughout an organization, much like rings in water, or rather like the butterfly effect. Therefore, if we do not ensure data quality, we will effectively have data chaos in our foundation, and to avoid this, a centralized effort must be committed to ensuring proper quality.

The next stage is to turn information into knowledge. The key to reaching the knowledge stage is thinking about *actionable information*, or simply information that allows us to do the right things, information that allows us to take action, and information that allows us to eliminate fear and worry.

CALM @ Work: An Example of a Simple Individual Energy Journal

In the TARGIT organization, an employee satisfaction rating is integrated with the project management systems used. This means that every employee makes a daily rating based on a subjective impression; the rating can be "Dissatisfied", "Satisfied" or "Very Satisfied". The rating system has been in place for four years, and the developments of the individual as well as accumulated ratings are available to everyone throughout the organization.

Even though the ratings are fairly rough, the mere fact that the ratings are easy to enter and cover a long period of time will allow the TARGIT employee to gain new insight in his energy levels at certain times. The journal will allow him to cover a much longer period of time as the computer will supplement his human brain, which has a lot more limited and biased capacity. The computer will improve decision making by avoiding the human tendency to only remember situations that are fairly current as well as the inherent negative thinking of the head brain. The only thing an employee needs to do in order to gain these benefits is to use reporting and analysis on his performance to see his development in employee satisfaction and combine his ratings with his current perception, by doing this by doing this he will be able to get a more balanced view in time of which times he is bleeding energy and which times he is full of energy. Such wisdom will allow him to be more aware of the types of projects that may be more demanding than he anticipates and thus require more effort, focus or time. Planning with this wisdom in mind will allow the employee to make the most of his energies by perhaps combining multiple projects or tasks, and will prevent him from exhausting himself. Additionally, the historic record of satisfaction at a given time can allow him to understand the energy levels he had at a given time of change in organization, projects or life itself. The ability to understand how the long-term impacts of change can be positive will be a key ingredient for rendering him positive towards inevitable changes in future to come.

From an organizational perspective the overall planning and resource assignment can also benefit from the record of employee satisfaction. In many cases we have used the records to improve the satisfaction of the employee by correlating the work on projects and assignments with the satisfaction in order to find out which projects the employee is most satisfied working with; and thereby either fully or partially assign the employee to projects in which the employee is satisfied. The thoughts behind this priority from an organizational standpoint is that the tasks that the employee enjoys doing the most are also the tasks that he is best at doing, thus, the accumulated data of the employee's satisfaction makes a tool for revealing and continuously improving the competency of the organization.

—all it takes to gain these benefits for the employee and organization is less than five seconds a day to capture the moment...

Computing for the Full Organizational Potential

Obviously everyone is unique, so we should recognize the personal diversity involved at the knowledge stage. Referring back to Jung's profiling, there are at least eight profiles combined from the generic personality traits. Each of these personality types experiences and senses the world differently, so while refined information may be hard to dispute, we do not have refined information to tell us what the right thing to do is in a given situation, and therefore the right course of action can certainly be disputed. We should therefore understand that once we turn information into knowledge, the transformation process becomes sensitive to the diversified nature of humans, especially if we are looking to harvest the full potential of individuals and organizations, which will always involve personal views. We can only do this by empowering through interpersonal trust, since people's full potential cannot be reached simply by telling them what to do and what to think. In other words, true knowledge is a critical transition of information into meaning in the human mind in which it is interpreted by individual skills and principles as well as organizational values.

Even though doing this with information sounds to the manager of a computer system to be both fuzzy and uncontrollable, we want this transition to happen because the full potential and synergy between humans and computers lies in the multiplicity of human nature. We need to think up computer systems that accommodate this multiplicity, systems that have different behavior for different people, just as the talented leader uses different leadership styles with different employees.[45]

One example of a computer system that has the potential to cross the chasm between information and knowledge is the business intelligence application from TARGIT. My reason for mentioning the organization for which I work is that I have had the fun of being highly involved in the development of the concept of MetaMorphing, which is the process used to bridge the gap from a centralized refined set of data, referred to as "the shared world view," to a multitude of user-specific analytical and reporting applications that are used to shorten the observation, orientation, decision and action (OODA) cycle. This process, which can be used for any individual at any level in an organization, will be more fully explained in the next chapter.

In short, the concept of the MetaMorphing hypothesis is as follows:

There are a number of individuals running a variety of tasks through these OODA cycles throughout an organization. The ability to provide these users with a business intelligence system that will meet their needs became a challenge, especially since the information should be actionable in an organizational context, meaning that all the smaller units of information should have quality and integrity so that everyone has the same world view.

This can be achieved by allowing all the users to build their own applications according to their needs, through an interface that is easily understood. We will call this process MetaMorphing, which is the process whereby a user can both take predefined and analytical views or reports (morphs) and modify them to the user's needs. Furthermore, the user can decide to create something from scratch. MetaMorphing is an abstraction from data since these are represented by terms, called metadata. However, another important issue of the MetaMorphing process is the visual process, whereby the user creates the presentation and analytical interface using the metadata. This process should not bother the user with any aspects of data shape, integrity, or quality, as the business analytical system ensures that these issues have been taken care of by skilled individuals from a centralized standpoint. Furthermore, a user does not work with the actual data while MetaMorphing. Ideally the user should only be concerned with the business issues, and the business intelligence system should support the individual by allowing the user to pose questions and make analytical observations by using familiar business language and terms, with visual presentation aids that ensure that an answer to the question will get the user further in the decision and action process.

Traditionally, this kind of empowerment has been available to only a "chosen few," and most often the system has been manual; but empowerment of individuals through the successful introduction of business intelligence will shorten the cycles of observation, orientation, decision making, and action, and the staff at various levels in the organization will be able to react more quickly and autonomously, yet in total accordance with the overall plan, the shared world view."

MetaMorphing consists of two components:

1. A trustworthy shared world view

2. An application that allows development of user-or task-specific systems that improve observation, orientation, decision, and action (OODA) cycles with speed and quality

In other words, MetaMorphing appears to be the vehicle that would enable an organization to improve decision quality and speed throughout an organization. If successful, this would mean that an organization would be more aware and flexible since action would be taken more often and more quickly. Such actions could span everything from corrective action to opportunity maximization, and the key is that every action would tie into the overall mission of the organization, the shared world view.[46]

In general, MetaMorphing is one approach to unleashing individual and organizational potential by enabling *autonomous information and knowledge refinement;* that is, the user can tailor the information and refine the knowledge through analysis on his own terms. The idea is to ease the development of knowledge applications. In reality, it is a way of balancing the organizational resources so that the centralized IT department in an organization can focus on the task of turning data into information, and the users can cater to their own preferences in the process of turning the information into relevant personalized knowledge. This approach to the application of knowledge in any organization will make it much more scalable and resource efficient.

Another perspective that is equally important is the level of transparency of the computer system that gives individuals access to information. Therefore as much transparency as possible is the criterion for a system that will maximize the throughput and insight for the individual. In the MetaMorphing scenario, TARGIT's goal was to allow the users to do as much as possible with as few mouse clicks as possible. The rationale of such systems was that the fewer the clicks, the easier the operation and the less room for error. The goal of minimal clicks was achieved through application of common sense and graphic design in combination with artificial intelligence that intuitively adapted to the individual user's behavior.

Specifically, the idea that systems should be more intuitive in order to be more transparent has led me to even more radical experiments. In a joint venture with three other companies in Denmark—a musician, an idea lab, and a production company—TARGIT developed a prototype system that allowed a team at a production line to listen to music that changed characteristics depending on the challenges the team faced; for instance, the music played over speakers in a computer system would change tones and pace to let the team know if there was a shortage in supplies, problems in quality, and whether the pace of the production line was right, and the music even had different stages of intensity depending on the tasks (assembly, quality check, and hand over) in the individual's production cycle. All in all, it was a very interesting experiment to conduct in which the information was delivered not as numbers on a computer screen through the eyes, but through the ears, and perhaps even to the gut and heart as opposed to a more direct channel to the left side of the brain in the head.

More examples of such interfaces are emerging. In 2003, Ambient Devices, based in Cambridge, Massachusetts, launched its first products aimed at radically changing the way people receive information in their daily lives. In practice, the company builds products that use simple changes in lighting, sound, motion, vibration, and other sensory stimuli to convey information. One of the products is the "Ambient Orb." As shown in figure 4.3, it is an orb that can be configured to glow in response to information such as stock quotes, weather, pollen count, political polls, and the like. Another variation of the orb is a cube that uses weather forecasts to predict traffic flow, sailing or surfing conditions, and so on.[47] Such pioneering of different and intuitive channels of communication is likely to pave the way for even more radical information and knowledge applications.

Figure 4.3 The Ambient Orb

I have a strong belief that in the future more and more computer systems will allow much more transparent interfaces for interaction. These interfaces are most likely to address the parts of us that need information more directly, so rather than always sending information through our brain in the head for refinement into knowledge, perhaps these systems will selectively send the information directly to the relevant brains in the gut, heart, or head.

A final perspective is time, the limiting resource deemed rigid by Peter Drucker. Through the use of *computerized communication and collaboration* we can stretch processes that would otherwise have to be rigidly synchronized. In particular, I like the idea of allowing communication on things that would normally require a meeting. This would increase the slack time so people would cooperate more effectively and would feel less stressed. Later on we will look into how computers can also collapse time, but for now let us dwell on the stretching of time. The systems needed for us to benefit from the ability to couple ourselves more loosely together in time can be as simple as e-mail, or as complex as document workflow processes. If we used e-mail loyally as an alternative to meetings or phone calls, they would be quite effective in freeing us of some of the frustration and stress of people having to be available at the same time; this makes sense, as individuals have different performance curves during a day, and we can utilize their potential better. It makes even more sense if we consider the globalization; through methodologies like e-mail and document workflows we can operate globally with less stress.

In all fairness it should be mentioned that time stretching should be used selectively, as opposed to the pervious, more universal guidelines. The reason is simply that some processes need to be face-to–face, such as some customer-service functions or different types of synergic cooperation between people in which we seek to exploit the human energies that aggregate when people are together. However, this being said, we ought to give careful consideration to which channels of command and communications can be more loosely coupled through Internet technology than they currently are. The more we change to this way of thinking, the more effective and the less stressed out our organization will be in these areas; this also means that more energy will be available to focus on those channels that, for one reason or another, cannot be loosely coupled.

So far, so good. We have now identified examples of how computers can assist us in the transition of data into knowledge, and knowledge will enable us to travel faster through the cycle of change, as well as limit our fears and uncertainty. Additionally, computers can help us limit stress and consequently individual and organizational strain if applied wisely.

However, if we relate this back to the experiences of high-performance teams that are in the habit of facing facts and remaining positive, we realize that we have only dealt with the use of computers to help us to face and accept facts. The ability to remain positive comes from the feeling that we will eventually succeed, and the ability to mobilize this feeling can be stimulated by experiencing success in situations that we felt were hopeless. These types of situations are not hard to create if one is an astronaut or a Navy Seal, but they might be slightly harder to orchestrate in a traditional organization. Come to think about it, remaining positive in an extreme situation is perhaps the exact opposite of worrying in a normal situation. Consequently, the impact on our bodies and the effects on our energies are also very different. Computing can help us become more comfortable with unfamiliar or perhaps even extreme situations through simulations. We will explore this computer application in the next section. However, something as simple as keeping a track record of our ability to overcome situations could help us become more confident and have a positive attitude under unfamiliar circumstances. The key to positivity is to know not only our situation, but also that we can influence it for the better. As we approach this next level of knowledge, we approach wisdom.

From Knowledge to Wisdom

Assuming we are now able to eliminate or at least limit our fear using knowledge and facts, let us turn to the next level of support that computing can offer, namely wisdom. Wisdom is knowledge elevated to the level where it flows without friction to its proper application. A good example of the distinction between knowledge and wisdom comes from my good friend, computer and marketing pioneer Pat Robinson, in a discussion on the matter.

Consider the bush pilots who in the early 1920s flew over the northern American wilderness under extreme flight conditions, with little more instrumentation than a fuel gauge and a compass.[48] These pilots were still able to succeed although they lacked everything a modern-day pilot takes for granted. One could say they developed a certain intuitive feeling to go along with their limited instrumentation. In many ways these pilots made the most of what they had in a physical sense, but the key differentiator that made these pilots do what seems virtually impossible for a pilot today was the wisdom they had developed. Wisdom is a mixture: knowledge of the tools at hand is blended with experience of their correct application so that the performance comes naturally. The plane becomes an extension of the pilot, and the pilot senses every move and every sound of the plane. The pilot is not just flying by his mentally and physically guided head brain; he is involving intuition from his two other brains. The collaboration of these brains and their combined experience is, in summary, what enables him to fly and land in places where logically it would be highly risky or even impossible to do so. This is at least the explanation if we accept the previous definitions of the cooperation of the brains in the gut, heart, and head and account for intuition as their collaboration with logical thinking. However, no matter how we describe it, history bears witness to multiple situations in which these brave pilots defied logic and succeeded in delivering mail and life necessities under circumstances that would be impossible for a pilot using contemporary knowledge alone. If we project the bush pilot's application of knowledge and his ability to make the most of it to our personal lives, how can we then achieve the same extraordinary use of what we already know? Better yet, how can computing assist us in getting to this point?

By this definition of wisdom, we need to understand the interrelation of the three brains as mentioned in a previous chapter. According to Covey, we have the ability to choose our reaction to a stimulus; effectively, we can develop our own habits. This means we hold the key to reprogramming our desired reactions to any situation we encounter, and the stepping stone to this is understanding the feelings associated with our three brains' being either synchronized or out of sync. Traditionally, what we would need to do is get experience simply by trying to do different things and memorizing the different impressions in our head, gut, and heart brains. However, learning is a lifelong process. Therefore a certain level of wisdom will take a lifetime to achieve. The fact that learning is a lifelong experience is not up for change, in my opinion, but through the use of computing we can collapse the time it takes to achieve a certain level of learning by simulating the situations we need to learn. Furthermore, it might not even be possible to experience some situations that could be used in our learning without the risk of severe injury or death.

An example of how computing can be used is the air-combat training of modern fighter pilots in simulators, or the simulation of emergency situations for commercial airline pilots. Many pilots might not have a chance if the first time they encounter the situation is in reality, but through continuous training in computerized simulators, they gain the ability to meet the reality of these situations with experience. In fact, many of these simulations get an additional boost simply from the fact that more and more operations are computer assisted, so one could say that the computer does not even have to move toward the reality of the pilot, but in fact the reality of the pilot moves closer to the computer.

The idea of simulation through computers has been around for decades, but in the Hyper-Volatile World, simulation of our experience will be applicable for two reasons: first, the working reality for many people in this world is already based on computers, so the feeling of a simulation will be very realistic; second, the cost of computing power has dropped significantly to the level where, for instance, million-dollar flight simulators of the past are sold over the counter as entertainment. The closeness to reality and the cost are the parameters that make learning through both *individual simulations* and *organizational simulations* possible, and the idea that we can collapse time in order to get experienced people much more quickly is what makes it highly attractive from both an individual and an organizational perspective.

There are basically two degrees of complexity with which we can use computers for reprogramming our habits. The first level is simply keeping an electronic journal of the experiences we have had and the feelings we felt, a journal we will refer to as the *individual energy journal.* In this case we build on existing computing capabilities to store and later analyze data. This approach, although simple, will most likely be fairly effective in the sense that computers are becoming more and more online; this means that we will be able to keep these systems updated more easily wherever we are when we experience something. Additionally, this approach means that we have the individual energy journal available in a more structured form that we can analyze easily, and, as we accept things more quickly when they are presented as facts, we can move more quickly from a "no zone" to a "go zone." During my parachute training I found I could use a video journal of the jumps as a learning resource during debriefings, but more importantly I could use it as a way of getting in the mood to jump more often. Using something as simple as a video journal of ourselves can enable us to bridge the gap between our normal environment and an extreme environment, not once but many times. This is an effective way to adjust our habits and become comfortable with the new environment.

However, this approach is probably weak in the sense that we do not collapse time, except for a faster cycle of change in our habits. For this purpose we need to go with individual simulation.

In a more advanced application of individual simulation we can start applying game theory to a problem. By modeling the situation we want to learn in, we can start to simply play around and see what happens—much like a child at play. We can use our conventional wisdom to start finding out what works and what does not work, and thereby craft our reactions to a given situation. In effect, by repetition we are crafting our habits.

Simulations can also involve more than one individual. In a game, we can simulate multiple decisions and create a room where we can test aggregated organizational behavior, an organizational simulation. This of course has the potential for generating the wisdom for most effectively carrying out our strategies, but it also allows us to understand the reactions and intent of other people in the organization. By gaining such insight, we suddenly begin learning the mindset of our peers, thereby creating an opportunity for what Covey calls an "outside-in" perspective. However, no matter what we call this, in reality we will be able to understand much more about not only our own individual challenges, but also the ones faced by our colleagues and the organization as a whole. Through organizational simulation we will be able to gain insight into our own roles in the whole picture, and we will be able to understand the intent and motivation of others in the organization. If we apply this technology properly, we will actually have a vehicle for creating better understanding in an organization. This understanding can nurture greater trust between us, and if we play a sufficiently realistic game to identify the best win-win scenario, we will suddenly find ourselves computing for synergic cooperation. By playing the game, we are in effect creating a synergistic corporation through computing, which is the optimum gain for the application of game theory and simulation.

I have tried multiple simulators over time, and I usually find them to be fun and to contribute effectively to insight. There seems to be a trend toward progressively cheaper and more realistic simulations, even in scenarios where we are not just mimicking a situation from an abstract perspective. One of the most impressive simulations I have seen in terms of gaining historical insight is a game called *Battlefield Vietnam*. This game is an over-the-counter product, a first-person shooter game, and as such its primary market is perhaps people who are just looking for a bit of action. However, having always had a big interest in modern warfare, particularly Vietnam, I found myself learning a lot from the game. Not only did the game have a lot of factual information, but it created a mood with contemporary music, and, first and foremost, it allowed me to get a grasp of how it felt to move through the low-visibility jungle. Obviously a game like this is luckily far from the real devastation and trauma that could be experienced in this war, but to me it meant that I gained more insight into the subject than I had from watching many documentaries and reading about it.

We can simulate virtually limitless numbers of events in games, but, irrespective of the complexity of an application to a problem, a game that can simulate an environment and our actions is somewhat simpler than a game that can compute a solution. It therefore follows that applying one's efforts to developing a game rather than computing a solution to a problem is cost effective. It is arguably also more applicable to individuals and organizations today simply because we like to have a feeling that we are involved in making decisions. If the computer came up with the answer without involving us, we might not trust the answer: it would not be part of our own wisdom since we had not been in the process loop. However, as we shall see later when discussing massive empirics, we might in the future find we involve the computer in the actual empirical stage of more and more situations and thereby generate computer wisdom rather than human wisdom.

In conclusion, we have now seen how the computer systems outlined in table 4.1 can assist us in limiting the inherent fear on an individual level by leveraging facts transparently. The same process also allows us to travel more swiftly through the never-ending cycle of change; we can simply spend less time in the "no zone" if we apply computing. From this knowledge-enlightened place, with limited fear, we can use computing to move even further to a level of wisdom if we keep records or, even more effectively, play games that allow us to understand and perhaps change our behavioral patterns—our habits. If we apply computing in this form on an organizational level, we can gain the insight and understanding to dare to trust others and seek out win-win scenarios. If we apply computing at this level, we are effectively computing for the highest form of human cooperation: synergic cooperation.

CALM Components	Fear	Synergic Cooperation
Trustworthy Shared World View: Facts and Sentinels	√	√
Autonomous Information and Knowledge Refinement; e.g. MetaMorphing Analysis and Reporting	√	√
Computerized Communication and Collaboration; Time-Stretch		√
Individual Energy Journal	√	
Individual Simulation	√	
Organizational Simulation		√

Table 4.1 Systems for Computing Against Fear

Assuming now that we decide to make the effort and implement the CALM components suggested in this chapter, we can now proceed to the next chapter an investigate how we can use the energy we freed up from fear in ways that render an organization adaptable while at the same time aware and able to seize opportunities.

5

Optimizing Individual and Organizational Energy

Harnessing Energy and Change

Once we make a habit of meeting changes with a positive attitude, we arrive at a place where we can employ our actions in the way we choose. Robert Cooper describes this platform as a calm and alert state in which we are aware of our surroundings and still have the energy to make decisions with all our three brains. One should note that the state of being alert should not be mistaken for the state of being stressed; these are very different states. In the calm and alert state we are aware of our surroundings; we accept the situation and have energy. We do not spend time anxiously worrying and double-and triple-checking what is going on around us; we trust ourselves and our instincts, and we feel the energy inside us. In the stress condition, on the other hand, we deal with the frustration of the gap between where we are and where we intend to be. Stress is inherently negative since there is nothing positive about not being where we want to be; we feel exposed until we are back in the safety of our comfort zone. Stress comes from not accepting our situation fully. We might accept the need for a change, but not our own condition. So from an energy perspective one could say that under traditional stress we are bleeding energy, whereas in the calm alert state we are conserving or even accumulating energy. Those of us who have been stressed out occasionally know how the draining of energy can have an impact on other areas of our lives. As our energy drops we also find that some habits can be compromised; for example, do we speak as nicely as we should to others? Do we listen as well and seek understanding when we are stressed? The answer is probably *no* to both questions. Stress can be a culprit in breaking our good habits since it is a very common feeling in modern life in the Hyper-Volatile World. Stress is a kind of fear of accepting our situation wholeheartedly.

Most of us have probably felt what stress can do to us, but the opposite—feeling energized—might unfortunately be less familiar. The most well-known way of accumulating energy is probably simply having fun and laughing. Most of us are very familiar with the source of this energy, and it is also easily accessible, as we know where to find it. But sometimes this energy will also strike us when we do not expect it. It is probably hard to access this source in the circumstances in which energy is most needed. Another more likely source of energy is the feeling of flow, and some of us may have felt this when doing something that was hard physically or mentally, and yet we felt enjoyment of the situation.

Another good sign of flow is when we lose our sense of time when we are engrossed in doing something, and then we learn and excel step by step in the process. Elite sportsmen are very familiar with the experience of this flow, but they are far from being a small exclusive group. Psychologist Mihaly Csikszentmihalyi, who has been researching optimal performance for more than two decades, tells us that flow is something we can all experience. He describes a state of flow: "When the information that keeps coming into awareness is congruent with goals, psychic energy flows effortlessly."[49] In general, Csikszentmihalyi refers to the psychic energy as a prerequisite to finding flow; this is analogous with my arguments so far, if we consider psychic energy to be the state in which our three energies mix into the optimum execution of a habit. If we do so, the optimal experience is equivalent to what we experience when we are following our heart as well as keeping our thoughts in perspective and aiming for both our short-and long-term goals. So in other words there are no shortcuts to flow; we need be aware of ourselves in all three aspects of our brains, our current energy, and our situation in the environment, and we need to compile all this into a state of understanding where we have no fear.

In everyday life, we find that some situations are more enjoyable than others. In the enjoyable experiences we will have the opportunity to tap into our own calm energy. If we master this discipline, this energy, as opposed to the stress energy, we will be able to maintain a calm alert state in which we have the most capabilities. The stressed state wears us out psychically and creates tension in our bodies; the calm energy allows us to continue doing an activity effectively for long periods of time.

"Move with the cheese and enjoy it!" Such is the conclusion of Spencer Johnson's story "Who Moved my Cheese?" about the mice and the littlepeople. This short story is a very useful fable for understanding people's reactions when they are confronted with change; the failure to accept facts is fuelled by denial and fear of trying something new. At the same time, this failure deprives us of the enjoyment and rewards of adventure once we overcome the denial and fear. In short, Spencer's fable goes as follows. Two mice and two small people called littlepeople live close to a storage pile of cheese they have gathered. One day the cheese, which is the major asset, is gone. The mice react instinctively and start searching the maze where they originally found the cheese for new cheese—much like ants, by the way. However, the littlepeople, burdened with intellect, are reluctant to start searching for new cheese. They go through stages of denial and fear until at one point they start going into the maze without fear of getting lost and with acceptance of the necessity. They all succeed in the end, finding more and better cheese than they had before, and during the process they find themselves enjoying change.[50]

It seems that most psychological literature around change adds up to fun and enjoyment once we accept the need to make changes. And quite honestly, isn't that how life is? Have we ever encountered change in a situation and come out worse than before from a personal perspective? From my personal perspective, it seems that the job we have today is better than the jobs we had previously, the partner we have is better than the ones we had, and so on. Granted, the in-betweens can sometimes be frustrating and feel like a walk in the desert, but in the end it seems that change is what makes us who we are today—and most of us will probably agree that this is who we should be.

In a broader perspective, one could say that change is what made us climb to the top of the evolutionary ladder today as human beings. Being able to spot, understand, and even feel these patterns helps us accept and enjoy change. It is important to note that on the flip side of every change in the environment there are opportunities, and the faster we acknowledge this and start working toward the opportunity side, the faster we arrive on "higher ground" from where we were!

To find the flow and use ourselves optimally, it is important to understand who we truly are as individuals. Stephen Covey says the only things each of us can take for granted are our principles; everything else around us is subject to change. Defining our principles and understanding who we are might not be easy; all our principles might even undergo an evolutionary process as we go through life. Think back over your dreams when you were ten or twenty years old and compare them to the dreams and values you have today. Covey suggests that to find our true values and principles we should visualize our own funeral and "see" what our family, friends, and colleagues have to say about us; what would we like that to be? This visualization is a pretty good tool for establishing a lighthouse in the distance to guide us, or perhaps a "palm on the horizon," as I will explain later in this chapter. The only true asset we can count on is the human asset, since physical or financial assets are both unstable in terms of our retaining them, and most likely unimportant in the end. I very much like the idea that to define our own principles we need to figure out who we truly are, what core values we live by, and how we want to conduct ourselves through life.

Before we proceed, I would like to define my use of the terms *knowledge, skills,* and *talent,* as they tend to vary from author to author. In my opinion, the best definition is offered by Marcus Buckingham and Donald O. Clifton in *Now, Discover Your Strengths.*[51] They describe knowledge as either factual or experimental knowledge. Factual knowledge is what is referred to in this book as information, and experimental knowledge is information refined by practical experience in its application. Skills are a higher order of knowledge; structure is combined with experimental knowledge. It is at this level that we can excel based on our experience. Two people might possess the exact same amount of knowledge, but one will beat the other in performance since he has more experience—he has skills. On top of skills we have talent, and the boundary between skills and talent is unidentifiable if we consider two individuals at a given point in time. However, we will get an indication of talent over a time period by the speed at which an individual can acquire skills. If the person is gifted with a strong talent, he might be able to take knowledge and achieve a high level of skill in a much shorter time than a person with no talent. Therefore talent is important, as it will allow us to achieve skills with less effort, less energy. Obviously, we can develop skills in areas where we are not necessarily talented, but to achieve the highest level of skills with the least effort we should build them on talent. This is the only way we can reach the highest level of skills while consuming the least amount of energy.

One of the most amazing things about talent is that it appears that each of us has about two or three talents or skills that are entirely unique in comparison to the skills of any 100,000 other people. At least that is the conclusion of research carried out over more than four decades, involving more than 2 million individuals.[52] On the other hand this also means that if we choose something we are not that talented in doing, chances are that someone might be able to do it better than us; regardless of how hard we try we might never find flow. These unique capabilities are also part of the core capabilities that define us, and if we do not explore and use them we are not doing ourselves justice—we are not tapping into the potential flow within us.

Like Covey's definition of principles as the inner core of who we truly are, our values remain constant regardless of the changes in the world around us. If we consider these in combination with the skills we have, that are either built directly on talent or acquired through energy and discipline, we can sum up the core of a human individual's assets as shown in figure 5.1.

Figure 5.1 Our Core Human Assets

In figure 5.1, our individual human assets are shown as a symbiotic relationship of skills and principles. It should be noted at this point that we are not dealing with motivation and our inner wants, which can combine into habits; we are simply dealing with our basic potential. The idea of establishing this is to identify a place in which we can relax and gain energy. Having true knowledge of our human assets can be a remarkable state of mind in which we have no fear; we are not the prey in the jungle here, and no one can deprive us of the assets we have in this place. On the other hand these are the assets that we should hold ourselves accountable for. How well are we exploiting them day-to-day? These assets should be at work for ourselves and others on the quest for whatever one perceives as success. In other words this place can be the launch pad for any action, and the source of fuel for the full thrust with which we should be putting it into action. The best thing is that once we have felt its presence it can never go away!

Once we understand the presence of our core human assets, it is time to put them to work in the direction we perceive as the path to our success; or more likely it is time to align this path with them. The trouble here, of course, is that our lives are not necessarily aligned with the path to where we desire to be. There are many possible reasons for this misalignment. For instance, if we have not been truly aware of our unique talents in the past, we may have pursued a career where they are not truly put to work. Escaping this misalignment requires us to understand our talents, and in this context it is hard to give concrete advice on how to identify them to overcome this problem. However, looking back on what brought us the most joy, the most fun in our childhood, might not be a bad place to start. If we don't find any specific pattern there, we should move into our everyday lives because the answers might be very much around us, as if we were whispering them into our own ears, and all we have to do is just listen to ourselves. There's also a good chance that our talents will lie pretty close to things that give us passion, things we feel in our second brain: the heart.

I would argue though that one should not despair and seek the answers too far away from oneself, simply because by definition we carry our human assets inside ourselves. Perhaps the problem is that our mind is clouded by a set of everyday habits that have been shaped over the years by the environment, and these habits may have diverted us slightly from our inner core. To understand ourselves from a different perspective and frame of reference—a paradigm shift, as Covey would suggest—we can choose from many approaches, such as the funeral visualization mentioned earlier. Another way to explore our own personalities could be through an inquiry into values. Robert M. Pirsig, author of *Zen and the Art of Motorcycle Maintenance: An Inquiry into Values*, makes a compelling case for viewing quality through the eyes of a motorcycle enthusiast. What is quality? Is a life without quality worth living? Not that Pirsig answers these questions; he reflects on his own view of them. The questions should be answered by each and every one of us. The word *enthusiasm* originally comes from Greek and means "full of *theos*"—full of god—and Pirsig suggests that perhaps this word has lost some of its meaning in modern life. My guess is that we achieve excellence most easily in things or issues about which we are enthusiastic. Perhaps the best we can do is strive for what we as individuals perceive as excellence in our lives. Striving for excellence in life rather than seeking to fix specific problems could lead one to a more holistic view of life, since true excellence cannot exist within a narrow mind; therefore we need to break the barriers of our own narrow-mindedness. Perhaps excellence is really finding the quality, the human assets, inside us.

There will be days when our core principles are more clouded than others, when we're challenged on our principles or deprived of the opportunity to use our talents. I feel it is important to reflect during such times and recall what it felt like when we were equally challenged previous times. From such recollection we can find the energy to overcome the present challenges. There are also structured methods of mobilizing energy, such as active meditation, or passive meditation through sleep might serve us well here. There are also more simple options, like deepening and relaxing one's breathing, changing one's location or view, getting some sunlight, rebalancing one's posture and loosening up, sipping some ice water, enjoying a moment of humor, and so on. All these methods are valuable, but they are tools, so in my mind they should never get in the way of simply sitting down, relaxing, and remembering with a smile a past moment of true flow of our skills along the road guided by our principles.

In my mind, the most beautiful and simple principle is, "leave it a little better than you found it." Wouldn't the chance to look back on a life lived with this as a habit be worth living for today?

Energizing the Organization

Since I began living in the New York area in the midnineties, I have been fascinated by rap music; I am very much a text person with regard to music anyway, so I guess this text-rich music was bound to make some sort of impact. During the years, I have experimented with rap, not only as a hobby but also from a computing standpoint. I have created computer systems that can provide complex rhyme suggestions, and have also benefited from the Internet availability of tutors in the field. In this journey through rap music, I encountered freestyle battle rap firsthand during the summer of 2003 when I had the good fortune to meet a young MC[53] of half my age who called himself MC Sense. I later learned that he is one of the top Danish battle rappers. In his words, freestyle battle rap is about understanding the weaknesses of your opponent and exploiting them by improvising lyrics in which you address them. When your opponent attempts to rap about your weaknesses, you should counter every attack by turning his arguments against himself. While attacking and counterattacking, the skilled rapper will create intelligent rhymes where as many syllables as possible rhyme at the end of each sentence or within the sentence. For the rap literate, these types of rhymes are referred to, respectively, as "multies" and "double rhymes." On top of everything else, the talented MCs I have encountered will be able to do all these things so musically intelligently that the audience finds it amusing to listen to. Essentially, freestyle battle rap is a mind game that involves a lot of skills in terms of vocabulary, wit, and musical understanding.

My point in bringing the game of freestyle battle rap into play is that traditional games such as chess have commonly been known as strategic mind games; but as the world evolves into hyper-volatility and chaos, perhaps a strategy that involves thinking multiple moves ahead is not really what is needed. In many cases we cannot forecast our opponents' moves anyway, as we might not even know him, let alone understand the rules of the global competitive game. But we can face him when we see him; we can counter every attack when we feel it, and we can do these things successfully if we are able, much like the rapper, to channel our full energy and core competencies into every attack and counterattack.

If we accept the nature of the Hyper-Volatile World, we ought to at least consider changing the games from which we receive inspiration; for those who do not fancy rap music, perhaps tai chi, or other martial arts as mentioned earlier, can serve as inspiration. I am not suggesting that we disregard chess as a measure of strategic mastery. I am suggesting that we combine this game theory with elements of rules' being broken, or not even existing, combined with shorter reaction times and responses in multiple disciplines.

Successful reaction modes in a hyper-volatile environment can strengthen an organization. This is not surprising when we consider that mastery of practically any discipline requires experience and dedication, but it is worthwhile to note that when we feel threatened, it might indeed be our finest hour. Consider the time NASA was excelling and improvising to save the crew of Apollo 13. During this process the skilled technicians were applying their multitude of talents to resource and time constraints. Although the situation arose from an unfortunate situation, the learning and growth of the NASA organization during the process proved valuable later. Not surprisingly, we grow strength from resistance, and again I feel compelled to involve battle rap by quoting the lyrics of Danish Night Champion, MC Stroem: "Victory makes me proud, but the defeat makes me better."

Essentially, the approach of accepting the environment and applying multiple skills while reacting to opportunities and threats is the first key to preserving energy for an organization in the Hyper-Volatile World. The second key, which has the potential to increase energy, is understanding that actions against us are opportunities to improve and learn.

Part of strategizing, as suggested by the battle-rap metaphor, is also about understanding the opponent we face and the notion that any strength has a combined weakness; this goes for both individuals and organizations. For example, if an organization has a lot of resources in the form of people, it will probably be slower to reposition its strategy. As another example, a company with a large customer base might jeopardize its current position if it chooses to take highly innovative steps; therefore a successful company might lose its original entrepreneurial and creative spirit. These examples are just some of the weaknesses that can arise from seemingly beneficial circumstances, and regardless what position we take as an organization, there will be places where we are strong, but there will be just as many or perhaps even more areas in which we are weak.

These examples illustrate why it is imperative for an organization to organize itself to harvest its potential swiftly, before a new course of action is taken by our immediate opponent or another competitor. Maneuver warfare, which was first documented by Erwin Rommel in his diary from World War I, offers a lot of inspiration on the issue of timing.[54] Maneuver warfare involves seizing opportunities through continuously working to turn time to our opponent's disadvantage by breaking down a process into observation, orientation, decision, and action, the so called OODA cycle exemplified in figure 5.2. If one is able to have faster OODA cycles than the opponent, it is just a matter of time until victory is won.

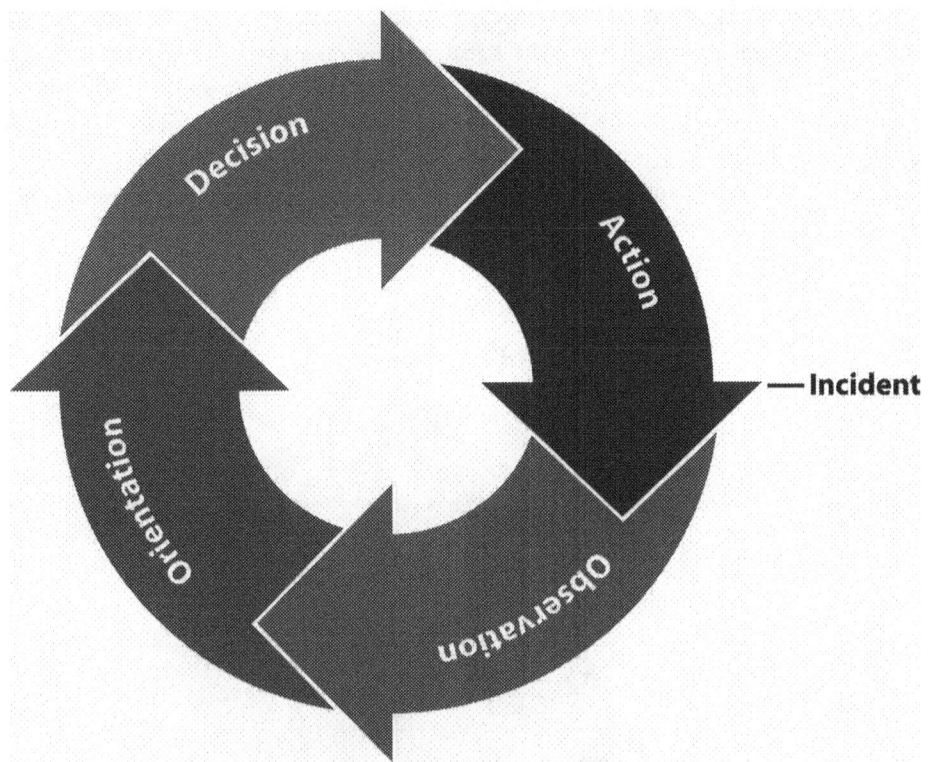

Figure 5.2 The OODA Cycle

A good example of successful implementation of this concept took place during the fight for airspace over Korea during the Korean War. In this fight, the American F-86 Sabre faced the Russian-built MIG-15, which in the accepted standards of the time was a superior plane, at least in terms of engine thrust and speed. However, the F-86 Sabre had an advantage in terms of a larger cockpit, which gave the pilot more visibility than the pilot of the MIG-15. Additionally, the F-86 Sabre had hydraulic steering, which allowed the pilot to execute moves more swiftly than the MIG-15. The Americans worked these two strengths and developed tactics that employed brake flaps to take the air combat down in speed and, by teaching the F-86 pilots to work the OODA cycle faster and more methodically than the MIG-15 pilots, they succeeded in improving their kill ratio significantly.[55]

If we look at a traditional strategy cycle of a larger organization, we find a fairly slow OODA cycle. This is typically because the company has had very focused strategies, and indeed the organization's very existence is testimony to that. Figure 5.3 shows the singular OODA cycle of a typical organization. The path from strategy to implementation goes through multiple layers that break it down to eventual action, a communication and breakdown process that consumes a very limited resource: time.

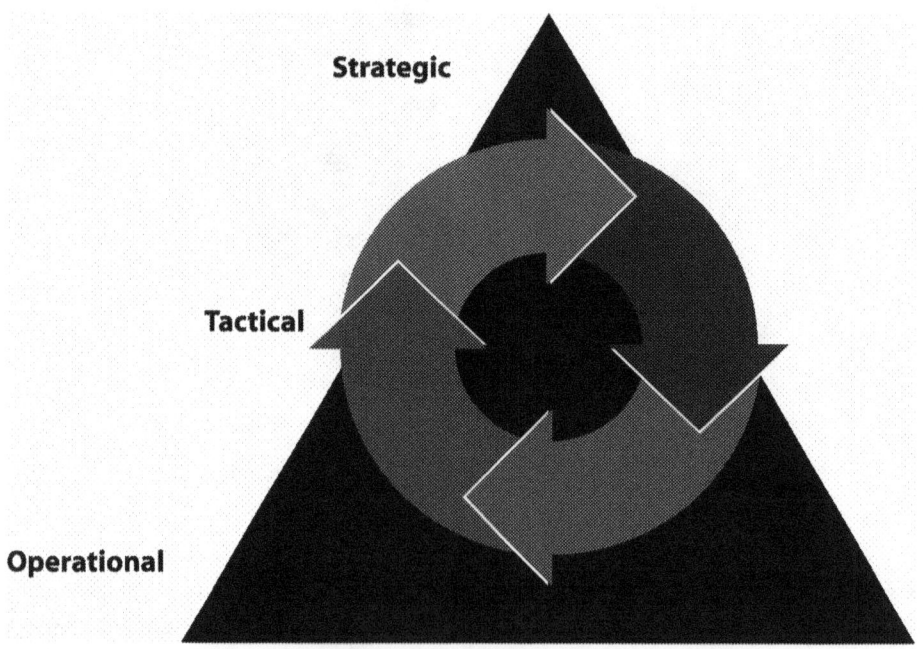

Figure 5.3 The Singular OODA Cycle Organization

Compensating for the inherent weakness of slow reaction times in large organizations by using multiple OODA cycles seems to be an intriguing idea. It would then be possible to at least mimic some of the velocity of a smaller organization. Inspiration for such arguments can be found in the modern-day maneuver warfare conducted by modern armies; the U.S. Marines, for instance, have employed such tactics. The idea is to combine multiple skills to create highly capable units with only mission objectives rather than specific plans. This leaves the leader on the ground with a high degree of liberty to use the various techniques as he sees fit. Since business strategizing originated in military strategy, why wouldn't a modern-day business do what its expert military counterparts do? In the article "Maneuver Warfare: Can Modern Military Strategy Lead You to Victory?" in *Harvard Business Review*, April 2002, Eric K. Clemons and Jason A. Santamaria suggested that learning from modern military can benefit organizations. Today they need to act and react more quickly on different issues because they are faced, as a consequence of global competition, regional instability, and vulnerability, with a business environment of rapid and disruptive change, fleeting opportunities, incomplete information, and an overall sense of uncertainty and disorder.[56] Perhaps a new breed of leaders who do indeed strategize based on learning derived from modern warfare will emerge from business schools.

However, we do not need to look ahead to find arguments for allowing a less planned and more goal-oriented approach that gives room for team and individual initiative. Marcus Buckingham and Curt Coffman's *First, Break All the Rules* presents an argument, anchored in twenty-five years of research, suggesting that managers should let go of detailed planning. The authors argued that a pre-defined plan for achieving any organizational objective will eventually fail. It is inefficient by nature, since it will not incorporate the unique talents of the individuals. It will also be demeaning by providing all the answers and thereby preventing the individual manager from perfecting and taking responsibility for his own style. And, last but not least, it will kill learning, because the energy for learning, namely choice and its illuminating repercussions, will be taken away.[57] In other words, it appears there is a sound argument for leveraging the organizational core competency that the business has already earned, by organizing teams and individuals such that they can exploit the benefits of more loosely coupled tactics toward goals derived from the overall strategy. Such an organization is shown in figure 5.4.

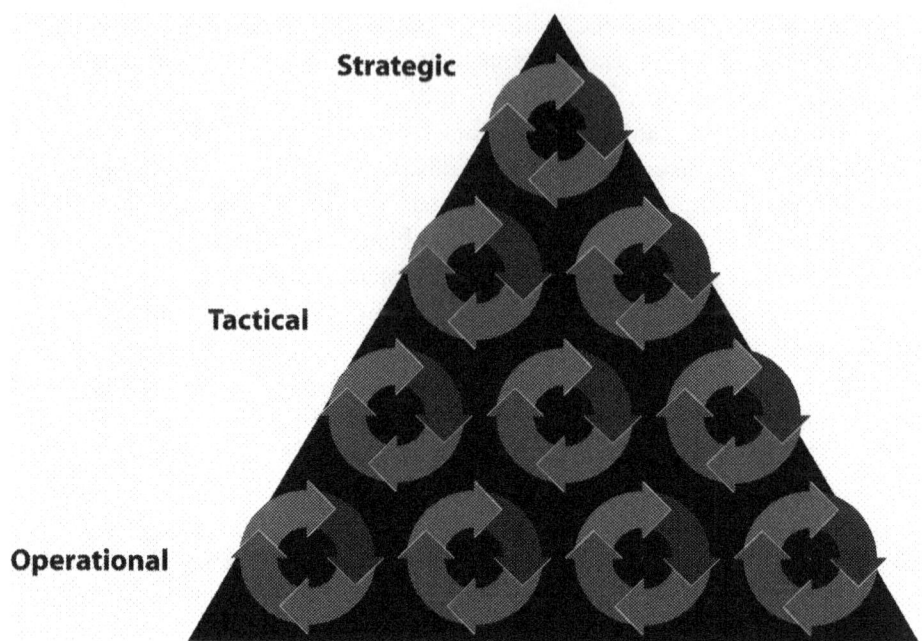

Figure 5.4 Organization with Multiple OODA Cycles

The proposed paradigm shift in the way we organize people in the Hyper-Volatile World is about leveraging core competencies in teams with synergic cooperation and empowering them to make decisions and take action appropriate to the achievement of a mission objective. These mission objectives are derived from the overall objectives of the organization, but they are indeed not stipulated as implementation plans derived from an overall strategy. Such organization brings into play the question of trust, not only among team members, but also the overall management team's trust in the collective teams.

If I were to say what I think it would take for someone to trust another person's judgment, I would say it depends on the principles and skills of the person in question. When we understand a person's principles and skills, we are able to define where we should place the limits on that person's autonomy in his job. However, in an organizational context we are dealing with a more specific part of people, namely their commitment to the organization's values and their contribution to the organization's core competencies. In other words we look at a subset of an individual's principles and skills. This is necessary, since the larger an organization is, the more unlikely it becomes that an employee will have a full overlap of organizational and personal values and principles, as well as a total overlap of core competencies and personal skills. My reason for stating this is simply statistics; as I mentioned earlier, each individual has two or three unique talents compared to 100,000 other individuals. If we were to create direct alignment of these two factors, we might not be able to recruit enough people. A direct consequence of this rationale is, of course, that the smaller the organization, the more probable it is that there will be a bigger overlap.

Another argument that indicates the problems of full overlap is based on the abstract eight personality types that can be combined from Jung's typology of four functions and two attitudes. We strive to cover most areas in order to build strength in a team, but creating such a team also means selecting people with different personal principles and skills.

An organization, as shown in figure 5.5, is a sum of human skills, and the core strength of an organization is its core competency. Obviously, the core competency must be based on the skills of the individuals in the organization, but the more individual talents these skills are built on, the faster the core competency of the organization will become excellent and the less energy it will consume maintaining this position as change occurs in the environment. It is equally important that the principles of the individuals in an organization are in line with the values of the organization. If this is ensured, each individual will automatically buy into the organization's purpose with emotional, mental, and most likely spiritual energy. These three energies in combination form the fabric of synergy within the organization, but it is important to note that, since the true principles of an individual are firm regardless of the environment, the only way to ensure organizational alignment is either by letting the individuals craft the values or by using the organization's recruitment processes to ensure that only individuals with principles aligned with the organization's values are on the inside.

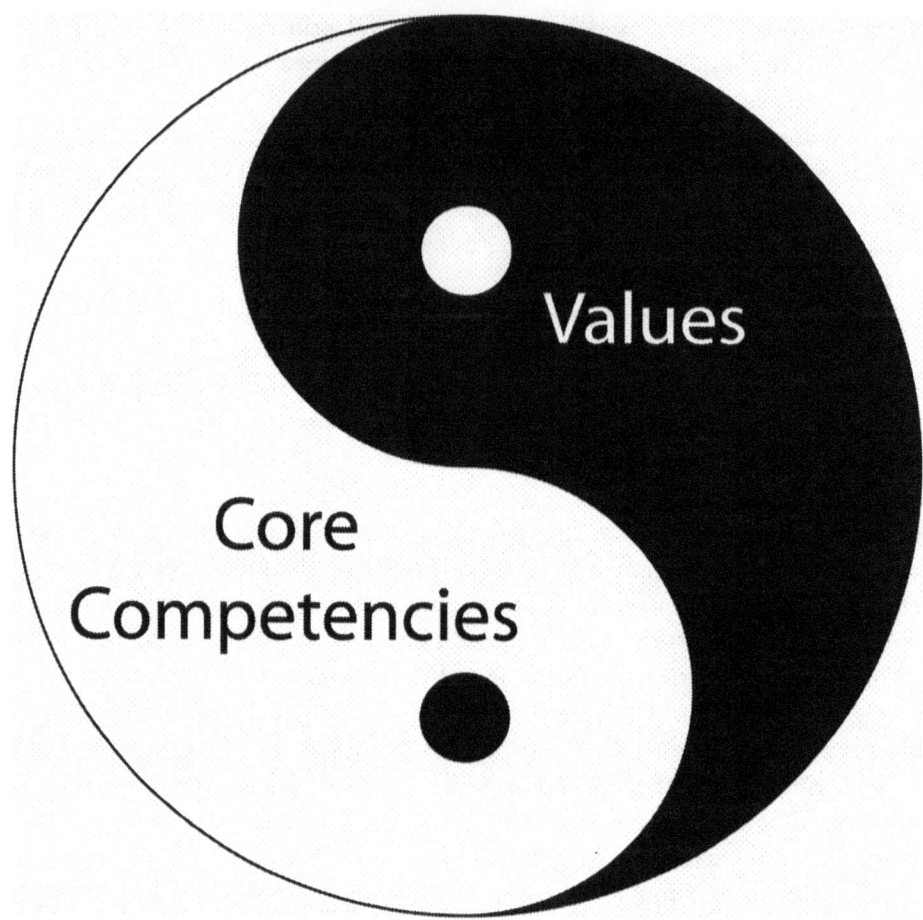

Figure 5.5 The Strength of an Organization

As the values and principles in an organization have to be aligned, another question one could pose is the extent to which the skills of the individuals should overlap or complement each other. Perhaps one would intuitively be compelled to say that the bigger the overlap of skills, the bigger the synergy between the individuals, because their understanding of intent would increase their trust. However, if we were to create trust in a situation where there was no overlap in skills, we would have the highest potential for knowledge collaboration, but in this case the values of the organization would have to be strong enough to create trust and synergy.

A leader seeking to delegate work to his trusted subordinates should ask himself, to what extent are the people I am delegating to personally buying into the organizational values, and to what extent do their personal skills match the core competencies, either present or required? If the answer to both questions is favorable, then there is absolutely no point in not delegating, and every hour of delay in delegating and empowering is a loss of energy for the organization as a whole.

To some conservative organizations that have been around for decades, such delegation might seem radical, but in elite leaders such as Jack Welch we find a lot of evidence that this mindset is already being used in some of the world's leading companies. In Welch's leadership secrets we find quotes such as, "Create a Vision and then Get Out of the Way," and, "Don't Pursue a Central Idea; Instead, Set Only a Few Clear, General Goals and Business Strategies."[58]

Henry Mintzberg's article "Crafting Strategy" is another good example of a decentralized approach from strategy to action, as well as a balance between top-down and bottom-up strategizing. Mintzberg approaches successful organization performance in the market from a learning perspective: learning is not just a matter of understanding and applying strategy; learning is strategy. Mintzberg's point, pioneered in 1984, is that strategy is really partly foresight and partly hindsight, in the sense that strategizing is not just done in the mind; it has to be materialized into implementation. These hands-on experiences are what Mintzberg labels *emerging strategies*. Mintzberg uses the metaphor of a craftsman who feels the material while adjusting it to perfection; he may have an overall plan and goal, but these are adjusted to reality in harmonic cycles of action and reflection on what works and what does not. Using Mintzberg's arguments, in the Hyper-Volatile World one can't simply invent detailed plans in the laboratory. We also need this process to state overall visions and goals. Mintzberg's advice is that to reach the optimum of both worlds, you need to have an overall vision and goal with no, or at best loose, implementation plans that have room to become emerging strategies.

If we manage our organization so it develops a culture of believing there will always be strength on the flip side of a weakness and there will always be an opportunity whenever there is a threat, then our organization will continually be learning and feeling the hyper-volatile environment. If we combine this with creating multiple OODA cycles throughout an organization, we will effectively create an organization that is aware of its surroundings and constantly feels and understands the strengths and weaknesses. It will be an organization that actively applies force with as much energy as possible against the weaknesses of its competitors. The hyper-volatile environment enables energy and resources to be shifted quickly. Decentralized awareness and empowerment will ensure we do not miss out on opportunities, and we will not fall victim to threats that occur as we will be able to counter them swiftly.

The keys to reaching this stage, from a leadership perspective, are trusting our organization and trusting its feelings. We should be able to do this if all individuals are aligned with our organizational values and core competencies; if not, we should reconsider the values and core competencies, not the employees!

Successful alignment will also mean more synergy in the organization, effectively making the organization a set of high-performance teams over time. This means that our organization will not only operate in the hyper-volatile environment with the least energy consumption, but it will gain energy as well, while it has the full potential for doing what Jack Welch suggests any leader should do: "Unleash the Energy of Your Workers!"

Let us now turn to the next chapter to find out how computers can leverage the assets of an organization and its individuals to a state of higher energy.

6

Computing for Energy in the Organization

Organic Thinking and Computing

Recalling the distinction between the emotional, mental, and spiritual energies for a human individual, let us consider this as a metaphor in an organizational context. If we take our human organism and decide to go in a certain direction, it will obey our mental commands. But if at some point we meet a challenge, such as stepping on a piece of glass on the way to our destination, our body will hurt, and we will probably step off the piece of glass and walk a different route to our destination. As we reconsider the route, the autonomous parts of our body are already exercising damage control in terms of seeking to stop the bleeding, prevent an infection, and heal the wound. If we look at the tasks undertaken in this organism metaphor, the strategic part in our brains formed a wish in the heart or a vision in the head to move to a certain destination, and our operation in the form of our body movements or actions started to comply with this image. At the point where we encountered a problem, our operation both informs our strategic layer that something is wrong, but more importantly it immediately starts autonomously to solve the problem locally. The rationale for the local solution is purely instinctive; it is a reaction based on the core competency of our body on a molecular level.

The reason for the metaphor of a human body is that this is probably the best example we will have in contemporary times of a unit that is highly adaptable and programmed for survival. So it is probably a good idea that leaders be inspired by the way our human body handles a situation when they are building organizations that must survive and evolve in the Hyper-Volatile World. This is especially true if we consider a human organism that is energized in the sense that it is not wasting energy unproductively on fear and stress but is functioning, as suggested

87

earlier, with the sentinels, factual knowledge, and wisdom supported by modern computing power.

Elaborating on this metaphor, we can relate the three brains in the human body to the organization. We could say that the autonomous nervous system, which involves the heart and gut, is in reality all the systems that energize the organization. This also covers the knowledge, wisdom, and values of the organization on the operational and tactical levels. If we turn to the brain in the head, the one responsible for the direction of the body, we could say that this is the strategic layer of the organization, the strategic mind.

Describing the organization from an organic perspective is by no means my own idea, as multiple authors have used the same metaphor. In *Business @ the Speed of Thought*, Bill Gates characterizes the knowledge age by the ever-increasing availability of information. According to Gates, the challenge for successful organizations is to make information reach the right people at the right time, and to accommodate this, the organization needs a digital nervous system. A digital nervous system brings the organization to life, in that it creates a constant awareness of the globally competitive environment in which the organization operates, and it transports the impulses to the right people, thus facilitating rapid situation assessment and reaction, or, as Bill Gates puts it, it is an assembly of advanced digital processes that allow the organization to make better decisions; to think, act, react, and adapt.[59] The idea that the organization's environment demands a digital nervous system as a means for basic survival is further supported in other best-selling books such as *Competing for the Future*, by Gary Hamel and C. K. Prahalad, which suggests not only an observational approach to the surrounding environment, but an actual probing of the environment to obtain new mega-opportunities in the global marketplace.[60] Such opportunities do not arise from the traditional operation alone, but require a more free and informal flow of communication and knowledge, which unleashes opportunities that arise from the organization's core competency rather than the rigid traditional organizational structure. In the next chapter we will deal more with probing and seizing opportunities, but for now let us simply note that the organic approach to organizations and the idea of an infrastructure that resembles a nervous system seem to be appropriate assumptions.

We now consider the individual tasks in an organism and note the distinct differences in what our stem cells evolve into from our conception. To be functional, an organism consists of multiple highly specialized fields that are able to operate either in the context of conscious and deliberate actions or autonomously; and in the energized organism everything is in harmonic and synergic cooperation. Think of it another way: how stressed out would we be as masters of our bodies if we were to be mentally involved in every heartbeat, every breath, or even every cell replication? So it makes sense to organize such an organic operation around a high degree of autonomy within the specific areas of core competencies; in an area of core competency, it is really just a matter of the expert in the field acting and reacting habitually. Again we can comfort ourselves with the knowledge that others appear to be in agreement, as similar recommendations can be found in *The Power of Now*[61] in which Vivek Ranadivé stresses the need for real-time information throughout organizations. Importantly in this particular case, Ranadivé suggests that leadership is a matter of leading by being led, as this will unleash the full potential of the organization through the individual skills within the organization. However, in order to do this in an overall effective way from the organization's standpoint, the mission and values need to be very clear.

So there we have it: if we organize properly by empowering the individuals with core competences in the context of our vision and mission objectives, we are doing what appears right from both an organic and a literary standpoint. However, in order to reach this point we need to truly understand the core competencies, or talents, of our organization and its individuals. If we succeed in applying the core competency from the right individuals in every action, the entire organism will flow through the environment and achieve greater things with less effort. In other words it will husband its resources in such a way that it will be able to convert its highest potential into action and success.

Full understanding of the talents of the individuals is a prerequisite to organizing them effectively within an organization. There are basically two computing concepts that can assist us in understanding these talents, namely key performance Indicators and an individual energy journal.

In traditional performance measurements, we assign a number of key performance indicators, KPIs, to an individual, and from there we monitor the person's level of competence in them. This approach will obviously favor those who are talented within the areas monitored by the KPIs, thereby refining the collective organization's ability to reach an accumulated set of KPIs. If implemented intelligently and tailored to each individual, such a system would in many ways work very well. However, the weakness of this approach is the origin of the KPIs; what if a person has talents that are not part of the KPIs simply because the management does not realize they even exist? To handle this problem, we might be even more successful if we build on the first solution and extend it to include psychological profiling. Psychological profiles have been widely used for decades, and from a generic perspective they are pretty efficient; they would be able to give indications of the potential strengths and weaknesses of an individual and would therefore allow better tailoring of the respective individual KPIs. I am not necessarily suggesting that managers of an organization should monitor their employees. These systems can be used just as well by individuals for self-assessment and to build on their own strengths. The only point is to identify the areas in which computers are able to assist and enhance the search for individual talent, which is by no means entirely clear for everyone throughout a lifetime.

If we assess our current performance in KPIs at a given level, we can then start to monitor progress using the data we might already be collecting in the context of developing habits and wisdom as mentioned in Chapter 4; we can start monitoring the learning progress. Additionally, such journals and track records in either structured or unstructured forms can be used to identify trends in our learning progress. If we identify directions in which our learning accelerates, chances are that we are either within or close to a talent. Such monitoring may seem trivial, but in detailed journals that are updated over the years, most of us will find we have had avenues of opportunity that we did not pursue, only to experience them later as fun and rewarding under different circumstances. Some of these trends or patterns are easier to identify and learn from if we have kept detailed journals. However, we might be able to do better than simply monitoring progress in existing KPIs as an approach to discovering talents. There are a number of different applications, in the form of personal computerized tests resembling psychological profiling, that can assist in this process. One example is Gallup's StrengthFinder, which guides the participant through a series of 180 questions in which the participant is asked to prioritize two statements. From this input, a top-five selection from a pool of thirty-four generic talents is identified. Using such a process allows talents that we are not necessarily using today to emerge, and from these, new KPIs can be identified.

Having identified either new talents or talents emerging from performance, the individual energy journal will enable the individual to monitor learning and the effects of pursuing tasks that are in line with his talents, or enable him to be more aware of when he is operating within the boundaries of talent.

To avoid the pitfall of getting even the slightest misdirected angle in the application of the organization's thrust, we can use computing to understand the organization's core competency relative to the continuously evolving hyper-volatile environment. When we were computing against fear, we deployed sentinels in the boundaries of our internal knowledge space. These pieces of information are generally the same ones we can use to feel the environment and our impact on it. It is important that we think of tuning the organizational positioning as a continuous process in this context and not as an initiative against a specified number of competitors. The reason for this is that the basic energized organization should not only be able to address the competitors we know, but should also be able to sense and react to any threat that arises. One could say that, in theory, the energized organization has its defense closer to its heart and therefore allows any enemy to get in a little closer, but the closeness means that it can see and understand the enemy better, so when it reacts, it does so with wisdom and thrust. Therefore there is no risk in letting the enemy in closer, and as a general benefit we do not waste energy on potential threats that do not become a situation requiring action. Additionally, we are able to counter any attack, not just those of a select few competing initiatives. It should be mentioned that we shall look into specifics on how to identify new positions for the organization in its environment in Chapters 7 and 8. In this context we begin to use more intelligence about areas and competitors that are out of sight of our sentinels, but at the current point we are only dealing with an energized organization that is able to stay on the heading of a given mission and strategy in order to reach its objectives.

In the sentinel approach, the speed and transparency of the nervous system that allows individuals to react is critical. The faster the nervous system, the faster the reactions in the OODA cycles throughout the organization, as shown earlier in figure 5.4. The more transparent the nervous system, the better observation and orientation we have as a foundation for decisions. We turn now to the knowledge we hold inside the boundaries of the sentinels. This should of course also be current and transparent to the same level as the information from the sentinels, but historical relationships between the information within the boundaries and information from the sentinels will allow us to review our past experiences. The balance between internal and sentinel information over time, combined with the actual current status, is the foundation that makes up the decision in the OODA cycle and leads to a given course of action. Now, it is important that we do not stop the computer support at the point of action; computers should assist us in executing the action: *computerized operational deployment*. This would first be a matter of communicating the specific mission objectives, followed by monitoring the objectives until they are either met or are deemed impossible to meet. At this point we would have completed a full computerized OODA cycle as shown in figure 6.1.

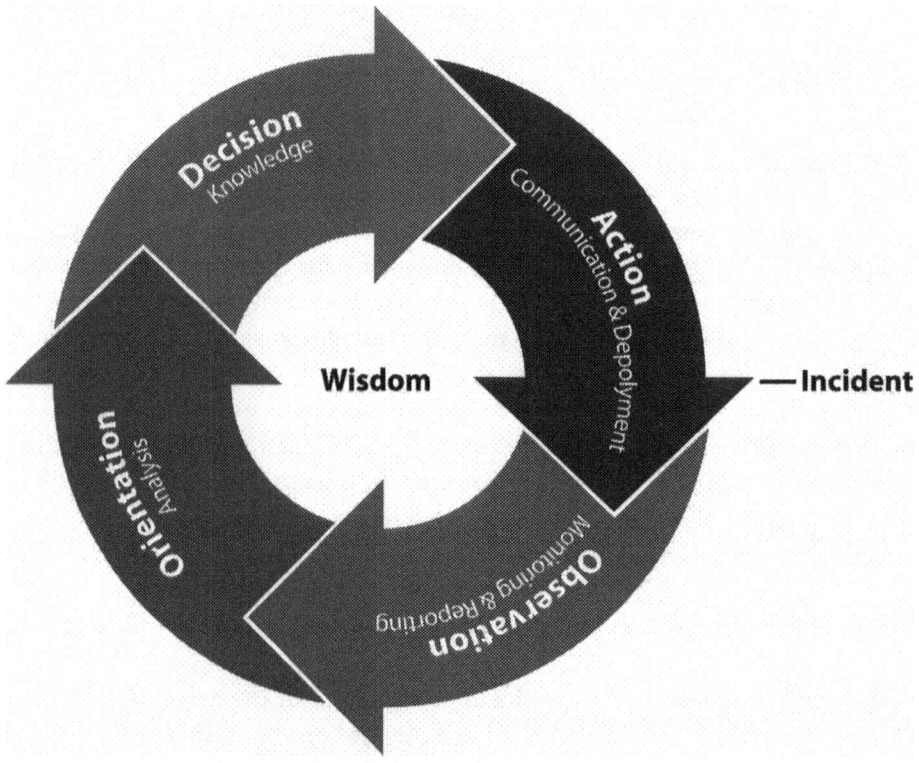

Figure 6.1 The Computerized OODA cycle

Obviously, the individual who has completed one or more OODA cycles will have a history of successful and less successful cycles that have provided valuable experience for further developing skills, and, more importantly, the accumulated track record of OODA cycles for the entire organization is testimony of the organization's core competency at a given time. The organization can use this information to monitor the trends in the core competency as it evolves, but it can also use the knowledge to enhance its core competency by regrouping the individuals so that their skills are employed where they have the greatest impact on, or best support from, the desired core competency. In effect, the core competency in the computer-energized organization will improve noticeably, actively crafted by the leadership of the organization. The organization will therefore resemble an organism that is continuously adapting itself to its environment by consuming the least energy possible while moving itself in the direction its mind has told it to go.

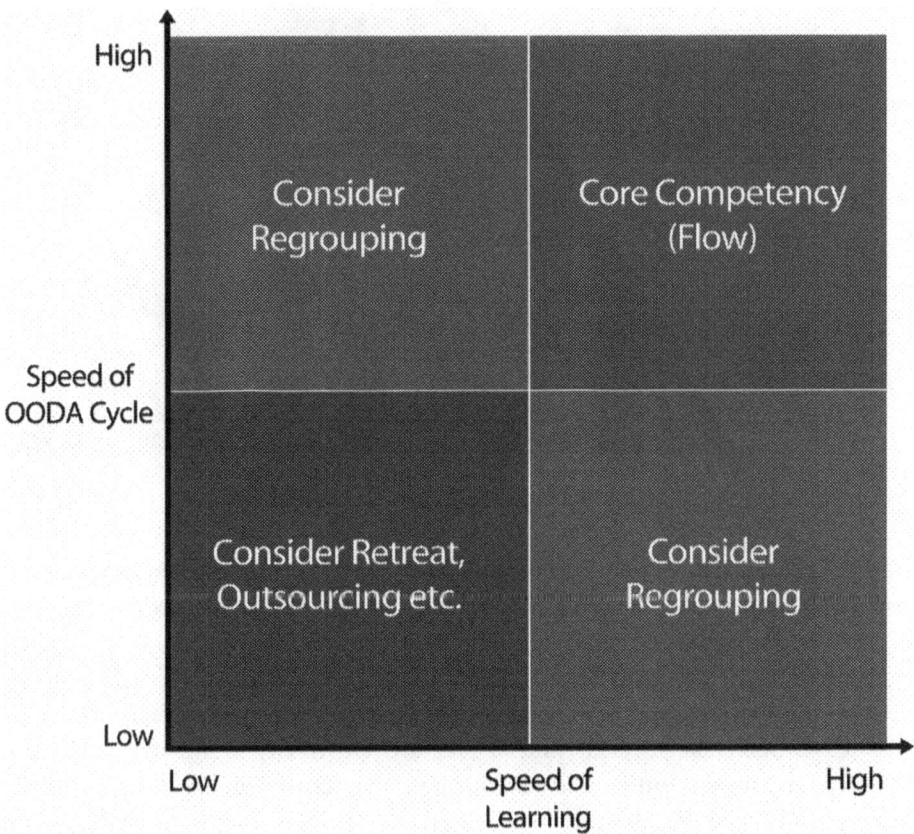

Figure 6.2 Core Competency Assessment of OODA Cycle

Using the matrix in figure 6.2 is an easy way to assess whether the potential of the OODA cycle is likely to be a core competency. When this *core competency computing* is applied to the OODA cycles throughout the entire organization as shown in figure 6.3, a pattern will emerge and give the leaders and managers an understanding of the areas in which there should be adjustments to either the desired core competency or the resources.

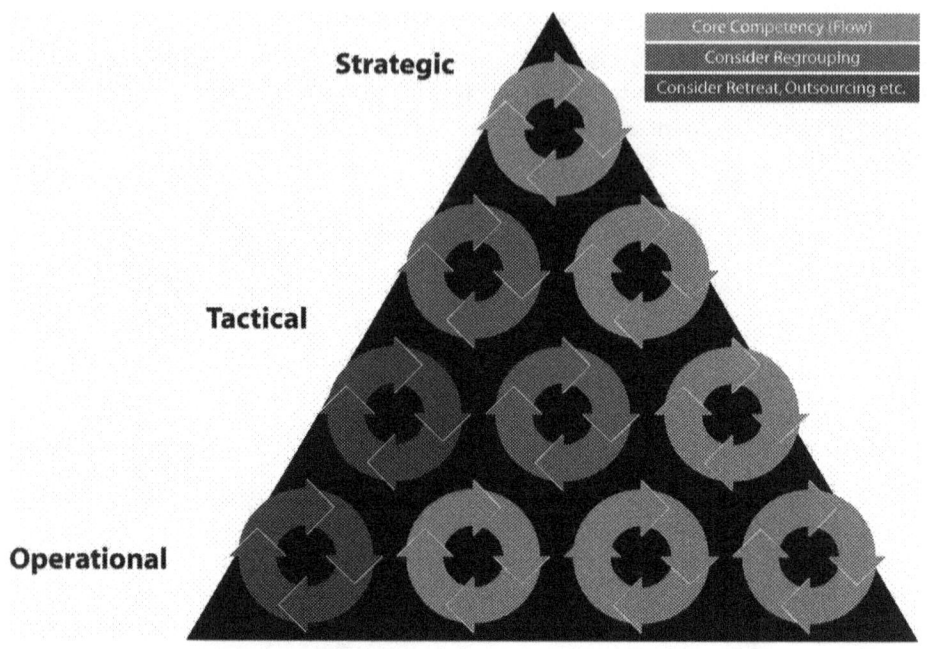

Figure 6.3 Core Competencies Revealed

If we go beyond the conventional approaches and look into applications that can influence our personal energy level, we find various forms of meditation. This may sound somewhat alternative, but remember that sleeping is, to my mind, also a form of meditation. Recent research into power naps, short sleeps during the working day, suggests that they significantly improve performance during a day's work. Specifically, researchers at Harvard University found that volunteers who slept for sixty minutes midway through a series of grueling tests improved their performance dramatically compared to their counterparts who stayed awake.[62] Perhaps a less radical alternative to power naps is simply to plan our decisions to allow for a night's sleep between the impressions we receive and the time when we make a decision based on them. This has been commonly accepted wisdom for ages, and from a neuroscientific standpoint it makes sense, since it seems that in sleep we consolidate impressions from the visual cortex and transfer the impressions to other parts of our brain.[63] The individual effects of using either sleep or power naps could easily be captured in notes in the individual energy journal. Using the notes and subjective evaluation, the individual can find the mixture that best suits him. Progress from experimentation with meditation could also be monitored in the individual energy journal. The readily available multimedia capabilities of computing can easily provide the stimuli needed for meditation, so guided meditations or meditation music and sounds available over the existing information infrastructure in an organization could be a more advanced and perhaps even more effective tool than power naps. We will refer to steps like these as *computerized meditation techniques*. Research suggests that using music and other sound stimuli can enhance the meditation process by stimulating certain patterns in brainwaves and thereby provide focused states of consciousness.[64]

If we step into a not-so-different future, we might find that the traditional psychological discipline has evolved into the field of neuroscience. *Harvard Business Review*'s February 2004 issue includes an article proposing that technology such as MRI scans, which can track bodily reactions, including brain patterns, to stimuli, might very well be applied as mainstream technologies as widely as traditional psychology has been used for self and organizational development. *Harvard Business Review* deemed "Business on the Brain"[65] one of the top ten breakthrough ideas for 2004, and why not? Since we adopted psychology in the field, why not the hard-and software that will shortly be affordable as mainstream technologies? These advanced technologies will open a host of new ways to analyze and understand our reactions. Some of these technologies may be much more efficient in discovering our true energy flow in difference situations in which we have our talent in our favor. Please bear in mind that these are the same technologies that gave rise to the discoveries supporting the three brains as more descriptive than the classic view of the brain as being located only in the head. In the short term, the broad availability of these technologies seems to promise both more understanding of humans and, in slightly longer terms, better individual understanding for self-development.

It seems highly likely that in this not-too-distant future we will be able read at least certain states of mind directly into our computerized energy journals. This would be a more effective way of maintaining the individual energy journal, so it would probably be updated much more frequently. Furthermore, the individual's judgment in maintaining the journal would be eliminated, so the individual journals could be accumulated into an organizational energy journal. Computerized direct reading of the individual's state of mind would also lead to development of better personal-planning tools for using computerized meditation techniques and power naps. My favorite idea in this context is enhancing computerized meditation techniques by having a computer select the appropriate meditative stimuli based on their effects on the individual using them. This meditative feedback loop with meditative stimuli could perhaps create an entirely new and powerful meditation technique in which we could achieve meditative synergy with the computer. All we would need to do to tap into this potential source of energy and inspiration would be to use the findings of meditation research conducted over the past three decades and combine these findings through software with either new and affordable fMRI technology that monitors neuron activity in the brain in terms of blood and oxygen flows or, perhaps even better, EEG[66] technology that monitors electrical impulses from the neurons more directly.

We turn now to the organizational energy journal, which in theory could be an aggregate of the individual energy journals. We do not need to wait until we have a fancy solution promised by the development of MRI, EEG, or the combination of them into MEG.[67] The organizational energy journal could be an assembled registration of learning in either document or more structured analytical forms. Such journals already exist in customer relationship management, CRM, as well as in human resource systems. For the latter type of applications, structured monitoring of individual, team, and organizational learning and progress could be added to the organizational journal. Finally, simple surveys of employee satisfaction, talents, and their utilization could be conducted and aggregated into the organizational energy journal.

Currently, we can easily apply the knowledge from key performance indicators to create individual and organizational energy journals, allowing an organization to build on each individual's talents and strengths. If this knowledge were combined intelligently into an organism so that all talents complemented each other and even collaborated to an extent we could call synergic cooperation, then logically this organism would have a high potential for acting effectively irrespective of what it faced. On the other hand, if we do not understand the collective talent or core competency of this constellation of individuals, then we are potentially at risk of not applying the full potential of available energy in any given situation. Any slight twisting of the angle of application of the organization in the hyper-volatile environment such that the core competency is not directly aligned with the application to its challenges would require more energy than if the application were fully aligned with the core competency. Therefore, if we do not have

100 percent understanding of the collective core competency, we can never be sure how to harness the benefits and full potential of the organization. In the worst case, a wrong application by an organization could be fatal in the sense that it would have absolutely no effect at all, simply because the organization would not be strong enough to maximize its core competency to fight the competition. Worst of all, this could happen even if everyone within the organization unleashed his or her full energy. In such a worst-case scenario, the organization would burn out from the inside out, consuming all of everyone's energy, yet accomplishing absolutely nothing. Please note that an organization in this dreadful situation was initially correctly applying its energy in accordance with its goals, but the hyper-volatile environment simply shifted to an increasingly divergent angle, neutralizing the effect of the organization's efforts.

CALM @ Work: An Example of OODA Cycle Optimization

In the early 1990's I was working at Maersk which is the biggest company in Denmark as well as the biggest shipping company in the world. During this period, Maersk was pioneering a new computer application called LOG*IT, which was a mainframe based system that allowed customers not only to ship containers, but to ship individual purchase orders from the point of production to the point of sales. Such an application would for example allow large retailers in the United States to plan backwards from the time of a given promotion to the time of production in China, and by planning this process efficiently they could limit the time in the logistical pipeline, which meant greater operational flexibility based on market demands as well as the fact that less money was tied up in orders in transit. From a Maersk standpoint it would mean that more information was available earlier about customers' need for shipping, and by knowing in advance what would come out of the factories and where the orders would go, a more efficient planning of container capacity could be conducted.

The system itself was very visionary; not only was the system supposed to handle a much larger volume of data than any other application in the organization at the time; it was also designed to operate the entire logistical flow of goods with few resources. The system was operated by an intelligence that was planning in advance at the time an order was placed what was expected to happen all the way from the factory to the retail store; this meant that the staff that were supposed to operate the logistical pipeline only needed to react when something unexpected happened, they were, so to speak, "Managing by Exception". In other words, the cycle of observing, orienting, making decisions, and actions was enhanced from a resource utilization standpoint as fewer people were needed to operate the pipeline; and more importantly, whenever their decision and action were needed they were prompted with exactly the problem they needed to solve.

Using the global LOG*IT system in logistics at the time was unique and proved successful over the next decade. A success which was only possible since Maersk owned and operated the world's largest privately held computer network at the time and used some of the biggest computers available from IBM back then. Today the cost of computer capacity has declined and the internet has become available, which means that an infrastructure which can facilitate a system such as that pioneered by Maersk a decade ago can become available to practically any organization.

—*Consequently, the tools are available to the CALM leaders and managers, and all that needs to be done in order to effectively improve the OODA cycles is to apply these tools appropriately to an organization through software.*

Stopping the Bleeding

Much like a child at play, the energized organization cannot avoid getting bruises in the hyper-volatile environment. Therefore, the organization's focus should metaphorically be on stopping the consequential bleeding. In practice, this means we will see things happen from time to time in the OODA cycles of learning that are not necessarily advantageous, or that are perhaps even wrong. In these situations, we rely on the immediate reactive response of the organism to solve the problem actively at the local level; this is important even though the strategic mind, the leadership, of the organization is aware that something is wrong. The computerized approach to this is, as already mentioned, an availability of knowledge that supports the OODA cycles, and this knowledge is, as already stated, a balance between internal and sentinel information over time, combined with current internal and sentinel information. The presence of the information constituting this knowledge is not the issue, simply because, by definition, the boundaries between what information we have and do not have is guarded by sentinels. Sure, we might desire more information, and we might choose to expand the scope of the available information by moving our sentinels even further out. But the point is that at any given time, we will have a combination of internal facts and sentinel information available, so the problem we all too often experience is that this information is simply not present at the time it is needed. The trouble is not that it does not exist. The problem is merely a virtual logistical problem of getting the right information to the right people at the right time, pretty much the same problem as stated two decades ago by James Martin in "The Information Manifesto."

This logistical exercise plays a critical role in success. It is, much too often, a problem for organizations today as suggested by Larry Bossidy and Ram Charan in *Execution: The Discipline of Getting Things Done*,[68] so it is even more disturbing to find that most organizations have not found a solution to this problem. Granted, the problem is complex in the sense that, in principle, it involves the same types of trust needed when we are aiming for synergic cooperation between people. To reach a state we can refer to as synergic computing, the computer needs to be trustworthy in the eyes of the person using it, and this person should also see a potential return from the investment of effort in using the computer for the task. Synergic computing is, however, the only solution to competing in the Hyper-Volatile World simply because computers are shaping the environment and, in many cases, *are* the environment as well. So, since there are no shortcuts around them, how do we manage to reach their full potential in synergic computing?

Consider the following problem of computers being trustworthy. In a weekly performance-review meeting, a sales and a financial person are comparing two different reports that both tell them something about the trend in sales figures. The breakdowns of the figures are different, as the sales person has a report with the figures broken down into individual salespeople, whereas the financial person has a breakdown on geography. Both reports show a decline in sales performance, but there is also another problem: the sales figures appear to be slightly different on the two reports; they show the same trend, but the totals do not equal.

From my experience as a speaker in business intelligence, I know that this is a very likely scenario, and it happens a lot. The real problem is not that it happens;

it is the effect it has on the extent to which we choose to rely on computers and the data behind the pieces of information. The typical consequence is that the organization will be paralyzed by the poor quality of the information in this example. The data behind each of the reports may be correct, but the time the reports were produced or the criteria by which they were created are probably different. This is an example of poor information quality in its most common form: the information does not add up and is therefore not transparent. Surely, the data behind the reports could also be faulty, meaning that the problems in terms of computers are even bigger, but again, the consequence of poor information quality is a paralyzed organization. In effect, the organization continues to bleed while the internal systems are being scrutinized. Therefore, information of poor quality is even worse than no information at all, since having no information would lead us to do something intuitively and remain focused on the actual bleeding rather than lose this focus and channel our energies unproductively inward.

If we were to try to solve this first challenge of "untrustworthy" computing, we should look very closely into the data fabric to ensure data quality. This has been the mantra in computer-systems design for ages; we want to avoid the "garbage in—garbage out" scenario. However, this task appears to become more and more trivial as time progresses. First of all, organizations' information systems are becoming more and more standardized, so the databases they produce have thorough documentation available. Additionally, people throughout an organization are becoming both increasingly dependent on, as well as daily users of, the systems, meaning that more eyes are looking at the actual data, and if the system was cleverly implemented, data is only entered once and used many times. From a purely statistical perspective, any given system would gain a higher degree of data quality in general from these factors. If an organization does have a data quality problem, it will be very obvious to the organization, and every effort should be put into solving the issue before even considering any of the steps suggested so far in terms of addressing fear and energizing the organization.

From this point on, let us assume that the data is of acceptable quality. This leads to a problem that to my mind is much more relevant in today's organizations, namely information quality. The core problem with information quality is in reality that only a few people in an organization know the databases and how to extract information from them correctly. The irony of this problem is that broad availability at this step has a paralyzing effect on an organization, since multiple people access the data in different ways; this means that they are actually spending energy doing the same things in parallel, and while doing so they are even further bleeding the energy of the organization.

The solution for both unleashing the energy tied up in redundant work and for securing homogenous and adequate information quality is to have a few highly skilled people undertake the task. The typical organization would have a few people who could team up to do it. If no one with relevant skills is available, the task ought to be outsourced so that skilled people undertake it. It is the key to reaching an energized state, and even better, if we have a few people preparing the pieces of information for many other people, then the inevitable initial questions about the reliability of the information can be addressed swiftly and for everyone's benefit. I have seen a few systems over the years, and what puzzles me in this context is why some organizations do not attempt to take the information quality to its highest possible state; many organizations let their users navigate on the data level rather than the information level. They might choose to make the individuals' tasks easier by letting them work on a set of metadata, as contemporary business-intelligence literature on data warehousing by gurus like Ralph Kimball suggests.[69] Metadata are basically a set of data that describes the data, often referred to as, "data about data."[70] However, even though metadata is a step in the right direction, in my opinion we could take it much further if we were to work with terms like metainformation or perhaps even metaknowledge.

My point is inspired by the concept of lean manufacturing, in which one seeks to have a product's significance define itself at as late a stage as possible. The product in this case is information and knowledge. We should work toward producing them in one single line and not branch them into tasks for individuals until absolutely necessary. This makes sense in terms of resource utilization, but it also makes a lot of sense from a pragmatic standpoint. Consider the number of pieces of metainformation in an organization: earnings, revenue, account balance, profit, employee headcount, and so on. How often does a new measure like these appear? Probably not very often. Typically, we would look at the measure "revenue" for different periods, different customers, different products, and so on, but the measure "revenue" remains only one measure. So if we were to define the pieces of metainformation from a centralized standpoint, having a constant number of measures would most likely not be a bottleneck from the individual user's perspective, as new pieces of metainformation are generated at a fairly slow pace. On the other hand, the pluralism of different types of decisions based on either analysis or reporting escalates dramatically when we look at the processes that turn metainformation into knowledge and wisdom throughout an organization.

The step from metainformation to knowledge generates pluralism in an organization, because if we want to energize through multiples of OODA cycles, we have to consider two factors that result in this. First, not all individuals or teams are doing the same thing; some are handling sales, while others are involved in production, finance, and so on. Second, the further we move down the organizational hierarchy toward the operational layer, the more changes need to be made to the knowledge over time. Whereas the first factor is pretty evident from any organizational chart, the second is slightly less obvious. However, if one considers any organization working toward an objective, continually learning and improving, one realizes that more changes will occur in operations since this is where things are being applied, whereas the strategic objectives are much more static, as they change only when the strategy changes.

To exemplify this, consider an organization that has a production facility in which a total quality management (TQM) program has been initiated to improve quality. From a strategic perspective, the overall objective is zero defects, and a report is produced daily with a breakdown of the figures in production lines. However, the managers of the individual production lines need additional information to understand what is going wrong if the production line within their area of responsibility is producing low-quality products. The managers need to be able to analyze the individual production lines to identify the problem. The analysis produced by the manager is the information he needs to find the cause of the problem so he can eliminate it, and if he is successful, this problem will not recur. The next time he experiences poor quality it will be caused by another problem somewhere else on the production line. Therefore there will be more changes to the analysis conducted at the production line than there will be to the overall report of the daily status on conformance to goals, since it is not the same machine breaking down time after time; if it were, it would not be an operation of continuous improvement, Kaizen,[71] which was in place at the facility. By the way, consider the timeframe the manager is working within to get production up and running at the operational level. Not only do requirements change more often, but there is also less time to meet the demand for the changing requirements!

Since the pluralism occurs not just from the number of different areas of responsibility and their OODA cycles, but also from increasing frequency over time as we travel through the organization toward operation, any centralized initiative to turn information into knowledge will eventually reach an equilibrium, since people employed on this task will eventually find themselves maintaining and adjusting the application of information—the analyses and reports—to the continuous changes demanded by the organization as it is continuously learning, as shown in figure 6.4.[72]

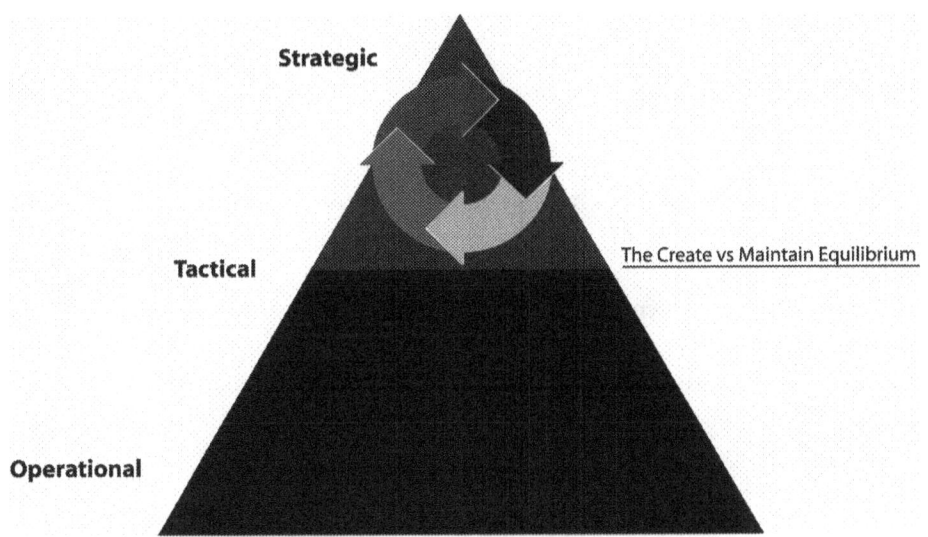

Figure 6.4 The Create vs. Maintain Equilibrium

A State of "Being"

The reason for even trying to solve the problem of pluralism from a centralized standpoint might have arisen from the statement from some business intelligence vendors[73] that the mixture of reporting and analysis can be described by the 80/20 rule, meaning that 80 percent of all people in an organization only need predefined standardized formatted information with limited flexibility, whereas 20 percent of the people need analytical flexibility. However, what is the reality we experience? In my opinion, whenever we receive a report with standardized information, we are doing so to get a general overview of a situation, but if one figure is not what we expect, do we want to analyze that into details? Most of us probably would, and so reports result in a demand for analysis throughout the organization. On the other hand, if we encounter a significant issue during an analysis and we want to dedicate future attention to it, we probably create a report or at least a standardized analysis to monitor the issue. Therefore analyses result in reports being demanded by the organization. With these arguments, I would say there is no distinction between analyses and reports; in fact they are both part of the process of circling through the OODA cycle, refining the available information into knowledge. If we do not provide the individuals in this process with the flexibility to ask new questions as well as monitor progress, we will miss out on reaching the stage of wisdom in the cycle. James Martin stresses that in his experience managers don't know what they want until they see it.[74] This comment draws attention to the fact that management too is a learning process, and flexibility is even more significant in it than the actual number of changes brought about by changes in the hyper-volatile environment. Taking into consideration that Martin wrote this statement two decades ago, why do we think managers would know more in an even more volatile world? And if managers in those days did not know it, why would we think empowered employees would today? In my opinion there is no doubt that flexibility and learning are the key elements to facilitating OODA in general, so an organization that seeks to define the tactical and operational layers rigorously will miss out on unleashing the full potential of both individuals and the entire organization. Far worse, in the short term the organization will lack the flexibility to put an immediate stop to the inevitable bleeding of energy in the hyper-volatile environment.

The idea that analysis and reporting should complement each other is actually taken very seriously by an organization such as TARGIT. Our recent development has been narrowly focused on this aspect of the MetaMorphing process, mentioned earlier, and some of our latest development and patent claims actually cover technology that allows a user to turn any report into an analysis instantly. The analysis is based on the user's own preferences, since it is generated through artificial intelligence based on the user's own analytical behavior. Time will of course show the extent to which such technology breaks through, but it is a product of a firm belief in the findings that lie behind this book, and as such it is testimony of my commitment to walking the talk of analytically empowering the multitude of individuals in an organization.

Accepting that we need flexibility and learning is far from having it, but to get to that point we need to reconsider the centralized approach to computer systems development by creating transparent systems that utilize methodologies like

MetaMorphing, as described in Chapter 4. We also need to ensure that the pluralism, for instance generated by MetaMorphing, is sufficiently reliable to generate knowledge and wisdom. The initial footwork needs to be done, as suggested earlier, by centralized skilled IT professionals. They refine the data into information, but from this step all the way to OODA knowledge and subsequent wisdom, the empowered individual in the organization is alone. He has the flexibility of analysis and reporting, but he needs reference points to be able to relate his exploratory learning process in the information back to the initial information. Therefore it is imperative for him to be able to trace a clear path from information to knowledge, for example by keeping track of the actual criteria applied to the initial information in order for the knowledge emerge. For such a trail of the learning process to be effective, it should ideally track both the criteria applied and the sequence in which it was done. By maintaining a clear path we are always able to relate the initial status of an analytical process to the findings, but even more importantly we are able to share the findings and learning among individuals. If we make computer systems that provide flexibility of learning in the OODA cycles and share the learning, we have gone a long way in terms of not only stopping the bleeding of energy but also of preserving and synergically exploiting the energy.

Ultimately, we should be able to reach a state in which individuals in an organization accept changes without fear as they move through their OODA cycles, refining knowledge to wisdom. This means that an organization will reach a state of "being" in the Hyper-Volatile World; it will continuously refine and be aware of its core competency, and it will be able to apply it in accordance with an overall strategy consisting of a series of objectives. If we update the list of computer systems from Chapter 4 with the additions from this chapter, we find the systems of the energized organization as shown in table 6.1.

CALM Components	Fear	Energized
Trustworthy Shared World View: Facts and Sentinels	√	√
Autonomous Information and Knowledge Refinement; e.g. MetaMorphing Analysis and Reporting	√	√
Computerized Communication and Collaboration; e.g. Time-Stretch		√
Computerized Operational Deployment		√
Individual Energy Journal	√	
Computerized Meditation Techniques		√
Individual Simulation	√	
Organizational Energy Journal		√
Organizational Simulation		√
Core Competency Computing		√

Table 6.1 Computer Systems to Energize

In the energized state, the organization is now ready for successful ventures as directed by its leadership in the hyper-volatile environment. In the next chapters we will explore appropriate strategies that take advantage of the hyper-volatility of the environment as well as the opportunities afforded by computing that can aid the leaders and managers in materializing visions and goals through action.

7

Strategic Direction and Focus

Approaching Strategy

To win one hundred victories in one hundred battles is not the acme of skill.
To subdue the enemy without fighting is the acme of skill.

—Sun Tzu

The Danish philosopher Søren Kierkegaard said, "To dare is to lose one's footing momentarily. Not to dare is to lose oneself." I feel this is a strong argument for sometimes accepting that the heart and guts have a sense of direction that our rational mind does not; at least that is how I perceive Kierkegaard's sentence. However, we should not venture too far down the path of guts and hearts if we find no clues that confirm the path as right. When I founded my first company in 1996, which aimed to benefit companies in decision making, I used the slogan, "spotting a palm on the horizon will lead you to the oasis." I imagined how nomads would navigate through the desert from oasis to oasis, using palm trees as beacons indicating water. I imagine such a voyage between beacons would feel like losing one's footing, yet still being within the boundaries of reason and experience. Another interesting aspect of this metaphor is that if we do not move to a new beacon regularly, we will empty the reservoir where we are now.

But even with a desire to choose and act, we might still not see the "palm tree" to aim for; perhaps it has not grown high enough to see yet, or it is too far away to be visible on the horizon. In this case what can assist us to make the right choices? Referring to the previous section, ideally we should take the path that requires the least energy. This may sound cheap at first, but think about flow—if we engage in activities that require less effort to excel and that might even give us energy while doing them, we will not only get there, but we will learn and grow while we are on the move. In other words, if we do not see a clear objective, we should simply excel at what we are doing now and follow this path of incremental improvement. The path I am proposing is similar to what Covey describes as moving along the production/production capacity line. On this path we build on talents and skills while focusing on taking the next step. Even though we might not see the long-term goal on the horizon, at least we will be moving, aligned in all three brains, and once we spot one or more beacons of opportunity on the horizon, we will be ready to steer the organization toward the one that is best aligned with our organizational gut, heart, and mind.

So far we have been concerned with the organization's reaction to its environment and its survival. The metaphor of a nervous system is very apposite for the collective system that ensures swift and effective reactions to threats to its survival. The metaphor is even better when we consider that our own human nervous system is autonomous, and yet it reacts intelligently in every environment we find ourselves in. If we now look from the autonomic nervous system to the decisive brains in our heads, and use that metaphor in an organization, we find ourselves strategizing in the context of the organization's vision and mission.

Strategia is Greek for the art of what generals do in war, and though some of my arguments against detailed planning might have indicated that strategizing is going to be obsolete in the Hyper-Volatile World, this is not true. However, we need to update our method of developing strategies, and if we still use the military as a source of inspiration, we arrive at the contemporary methodologies like maneuver warfare. In maneuver warfare we find that there is an overall strategy, but the main difference compared to traditional strategic execution is that the individual unit is more empowered and has greater autonomy. Additionally, there are more capabilities in the individual unit, compared to units in traditional strategic execution; this means that a wider range of disciplines in skills and weaponry, such as infantry, artillery, and engineering, are combined in smaller units. Finally, the main strategic factor is that the leaders of the units are given mission objectives rather than specific plans. This means that the leaders of smaller units have a clear objective to achieve, but they have the flexibility to choose the tactics they see most fit as the battle unfolds, and thereby can make the best use of the unit's capability, improving their chances of reaching the overall objective.

If we bring this into a broader scale as an organization in the Hyper-Volatile World, we find that the strategic process is more a matter of setting objectives than of making tactical plans. Therefore we should not simply take a strategy process and divide it into tactics and operation. Ideally, we should divide it into tactical objectives for the employees and teams so they can apply their skills as freely as possible, yet in accordance with the organization's overall objectives and strategy.

Perhaps "the balanced scorecard," the brainchild of Robert S. Kaplan and David P. Norton, could be the solution to such an implementation of strategy. Essentially, the balanced scorecard is a balanced measurement system derived from the organization's strategy.[75] It therefore looks at an organization as a holistic system. The balanced scorecard is balanced in three ways: it is balanced in time—long-term and short term; it is balanced in internal and external processes; and finally it is balanced in causes and effects.[76] Since its conception in 1996, the balanced scorecard has earned a well-deserved good reputation, as it marked a revolution in traditional financial reporting at the time. However the potential devil in the system is in its implementation. The scope and the intentions are good overall, but if the measurements are implemented too specifically they become the equivalent of detailed strategic implementation plans. On the other hand, the balanced scorecard can be very good since it deals with measurements of objectives rather than specific plans, and an organization using the balanced scorecard framework is sure to generate objectives and corresponding measurement systems around them that are holistic, lessening the risk of an individual objective getting too much attention. The balanced scorecard mindset gives balance to the objectives, but it does not necessarily help us identify the initial objectives.

In *Competing for the Future*, by Gary Hamel and C.K. Prahalad, the idea of action in the environment is simple: innovate or be overrun. Companies like Caterpillar, IBM, and Xerox all had good reputations and track records, but they found themselves threatened by the companies Komatsu, Apple, and Canon, respectively. These latter companies all had strategies that leveraged innovation along the lines of the organization's core competency. The point here is that the incremental improvements in an organization's nervous system simply do not counter long-term structured innovation; these bold innovative moves do not stand a chance without the continuous cycles of improvement. The key to solving this problem is probing, which is a process where a less mature product, the probe, is sent to market in order to test the market. If the probe tells us that there is something positive happening, then the cycles of continuous improvement, the OODA cycles, take over. In other words, the brain of the organization should consider where to go in terms of product and market innovation and then channel them to the nervous system by using a market probe to expand the reach of the organization.

Through this dual action-reaction strategy between the strategic level and the lower layers in an organization, we can succeed in seizing business opportunities, and at the same time never risk the strategy's becoming misaligned with the operation. The probe, if successful, is simply a directional marker for the organization, which moves at its own pace in the direction of the probe. If we consider Mintzberg's crafting of strategy in this context, the OODA cycles throughout the organization can also be considered learning cycles, and the fact that the organization is not moving faster than its inherent pace of learning means that the strategy is being crafted while the organization moves toward the probe. In reality, the actual strategy that is crafted emerges from the force field between where we are today and where the successful probe is. So the brain and nervous system metaphor will take us all the way to the best practices in objectives and measurements as well as in organizational involvement and learning.

This having been said, there is of course a way to improve the speed of the organization if we increase the speed of the continuous OODA cycles; the faster the cycles, the faster the movement, and thus the faster the strategy is executed. Of course the pace of the OODA cycles depends on the time spent in each of the observation, orientation, decision, and action stages. The time spent in each of these stages depends on the values and core competencies of the person or team that is traveling through the cycle. To elaborate a little further, in the core competencies we have the skills and talents of the individuals combined with the systems to support them. If these are optimized, the time for observation, orientation, and action will decrease. If the employees fully embrace the values of the organization, then the basic reaction pattern will be in accordance with the values, and therefore the time needed to understand what a decision should be under given circumstances will be reduced. There are of course overlaps of the four OODA disciplines with core competencies and values, but the point is that the better the integration of the two, the faster the reaction throughout the organization, and therefore the shorter the time from strategy to action and learning. In other words, the collective brain of the organization is aligned through the strategic objectives, and its heart and gut are aligned through core competencies and values. Its autonomic nervous system supports the brain. The organization metaphorically, and the individuals literally, will survive and subsequently succeed in the Hyper-Volatile World through the continuous collaboration of the three brains.

Defining Leadership and Management

At this point we have studied the computer aids available to harness the energy that would otherwise be spent unproductively on fear and stress, and convert it to productive action throughout the organization. The organization should now be ready for the leader to take it for a voyage in the Hyper-Volatile World. Much like a seaworthy ship, the organization at this level is able to handle the environmental challenges, including the weather conditions, and remain steadily on course. Obviously, there are a few limitations to the challenges an organization can undertake. It would be unwise to attempt to transport crude oil in a yacht; after all, some ships were designed for different purposes, much as organizations plan their growth in different types of core competencies. However, if we set our sails for a voyage from one strategic position to another, the energized organization will remain stable en route to its objectives while building on its core competencies according to changes. Therefore the organization will be able to withstand practically any environmental condition in the hyper-volatile "waters."

In other words, as the commanding officers of this fine ship, it is now up to the leaders and managers to set the course. I feel it is reasonable to distinguish between leaders and managers, since in my opinion computerization so far has been of greater benefit to managers. Consider the distinction between the two disciplines offered by Abraham Zaleznik in the *Harvard Business Review* article "Managers and Leaders: Are They Different?" The managers are portrayed as detail oriented and concerned with control, whereas leaders are described as almost mystical pioneers who break new ground and are able to inspire and motivate people to follow them. The psychological profiles also differ. Managers are very attached to the people in an organization; they need people around them to discuss and approve their actions. Leaders on the other hand are detached from the organization; they may work in an organization, but they never belong to it.[77] Leaders dare to lose their footing momentarily!

Perhaps leadership is, as Max DePree suggested, an art; great leaders share many of the intuitive and flow experiences with great painters and musicians or, perhaps a more appropriate analogy, with orchestral conductors. However, losing one's footing, as Kierkegaard suggested, is perhaps a vital part of leadership, at least letting go of control. DePree views the organization as a group of inspired individuals whose exploration and self-realization through individual talents and trust are the keys to success. In this context he describes the tasks of leadership: "The first responsibility of a leader is to define reality. The last is to say thank you. In between, the leader is a servant."[78] Recalling Jack Welch's leadership secret, "Create a Vision and then Get Out of the Way," it is not hard to see the pattern in what great leaders do.

So, while we employ computers to store detailed information that allows managers to monitor and control the details of an operation, and perhaps also communicate among their peers, we also need computer systems that allow leaders to work actively with their gut feelings in choosing the avenues down which the organization will venture. Leaders need computer systems that enable them to define reality, set clear visions and objectives, and subsequently turn them over to the talented and skilled individuals in the organization so they can pursue them independently, but with the leader's support and guidance when necessary. If we have an organization that is energized in the sense that we have computer-supported OODA cycles throughout the organization, we are already at a stage in which the leader is able to set overall objectives, and the organization will be able to pursue them swiftly, learning as it goes along. So to my mind the ideal place to exercise the art of leadership is in a computer-energized organization. In such an organization the leader still has full knowledge of the processes that are going on, so one can of course argue that he is not actually losing his foothold. However, harmony between the individuals and the teams throughout the organization will enable them to deal with facts to overcome fear and improve their speed and learning in their OODA cycle, so it is a prerequisite for the leader's success, and the computer systems already discussed in earlier chapters will support this.

On the other hand, if we do not have the basic computer systems in place to facilitate leadership at this stage, the organization might even be doomed to become a ghost ship, drifting rudderlessly around in the Hyper-Volatile World. Luckily, the computer-energized organization will steer us clear of the ghost ship scenario.

Turning now from the leader to the manager, let's look at how we can optimize the manager's insight into and control of the operational processes. According to business guru Peter Drucker, decisions should be "made at the lowest possible level in an organization and as close as possible to where the outcome will be executed." Therefore, in principle, either the managers should be as close to the operation as possible, or we should redefine the term *manager* as the self-management part of each empowered individual in an organization. There is already a trend toward this; the bureaucratic manager of the past, who did nothing but exercise control for the sake of communicating and enforcing a strategy, is becoming obsolete. Management has to add more value than simple communication and control; these disciplines have long been exercised more effectively through computing. The organization that does not exploit computing effectively will not be energized. Communication, information, shared knowledge, and wisdom should flow effortlessly in the organization, without a manager acting as a bottleneck. However, the manager can redefine his classic task of communication to a continuous process of refinement of the information, knowledge, and wisdom that flows through the organization, and thereby create the environment for synergy to add value to the energized organization.

In addition to managing the refinement process, managers are often physically present when things get done. Managers should add value not only by refining the information, but also by refining the employees' skills. In Marcus Buckingham and Curt Coffman's *First Break All the Rules*, successful managers

1. select people based on talent and skills,

2. define the right outcomes,

3. motivate people to focus on strengths and not on weaknesses, and

4. develop people by helping them find the right fit in the organization rather than simply promoting them to the next level.[79]

Perhaps it is worth noting that these statements are not just suggestions or mere management philosophies. These statements are findings that surfaced during a Gallup survey of more than 100,000 individuals aimed at identifying what great managers do differently from average managers. A great manager in the energized organization is primarily a catalyst, rather than a piece of the machinery. He stimulates the OODA cycles as well as defining them, but he is not an active participant in the specific operation. During the operation, the manager is just as much a servant as the leader.

I should point out that I am leaning somewhat toward Buckingham and Coffman's finding and suggestion: "People don't change that much, so don't waste time trying to put in what was left out. Try to draw on what was left in, that's hard enough."[80] Therefore I would say that from an energy consumption stand-point, as well as a pragmatic one, it makes sense for a manager to build on exist-ing strengths rather than attempt to fix weaknesses. However, in this context I am not disputing the antideterministic thoughts of Stephen Covey that it is indeed possible to reprogram our habits in even very extreme ways, meaning that we can choose our own destiny and reprogram our habits.[81] There might also be a num-ber of restricting habits, such as fear of change, which we dealt with in Chapter 3. Such "habits" are obviously not positive qualities, so they should be shed by appropriate self-discipline and coaching.

A manager should, however, respect the individuals in the organization and meet them where they are—as what they have become—so a manager is not responsi-ble for developing them. Should an individual successfully reprogram his habits, it is of course the role of the catalyst to harness all the individual's positive strength and turn it into organizational energy. Therefore the manager should remain aware that people can change but should not expect them to, let alone assume they will change or plan to change them.

It should be noted that the distinction here between leaders and managers is to some extent abstract, as a clear dividing line between leaders and managers may not be evident in our daily work. However, the reason for making the distinction is to allow a more specific identification of the role of the computerized CALM components. I would suggest that if one finds oneself in a very grey area between being a leader or manager, one should bear in mind the concept of building on talent. Since it appears unlikely that one would have equally effective leadership and management skills, perhaps this transitional state is an opportunity to seek some more focus in one's life.

Visioning by Sending the Mind Ahead

Great leaders have great visions. Consider for example John F. Kennedy's launch-ing a vision to land a man on the moon and return him safely to Earth within the 1960s. Another example is the strength of Dr. Martin Luther King Jr.'s vision for a future where a black girl and a white boy could drink from the same water fountain, sit in the same classrooms, and walk hand in hand down the same street.[82] Perhaps these great visions of the past are taken for granted today, but each of these visions was extreme at the time.

Bearing in mind the greatness of such leadership, the power of vision and the mind cannot be underestimated. Things that are imagination today are facts tomorrow. Indeed, our very world and our existence are products of events that, by conventional logic, were impossible, and yet they happened. A funny thought to consider when things seem impossible is to try to name one single example from human history of a thing or achievement that has been proven absolutely impossible to make or do. On the other hand, it is not hard to find remarkable achievements that required great and visionary leadership.

So far we have taken an organization's overall strategic position for granted and assumed that energizing the organization was the strategy. We will now look into the possibility of using computer applications in crafting strategy for the Hyper-Volatile World. As leaders and managers, we already know that change is inevitable, and we know that with every change there is an opportunity; therefore we have nothing to fear. We also have an energized organization that can seize the opportunity, so it is now time for the strategic mind of the organization to set the course and go for it!

Setting course deserves some attention since we subsequently want to dedicate our full potential to the direction we come up with. It has been said that maturity is the right balance between courage and consideration, and I'm very much in agreement with that. Another way to put it is that all our three brains need to be aligned; the spur of excitement in our gut along with the passion in our heart need to be aligned with rational thinking based on the experience we store in our head. Maturity is balance.

If we were to introduce the cycle of change as well as optimization of our core human assets into an environment of continuous change, we would find ourselves in a continuous cycle of accepting new circumstances and taking the appropriate action. To cycle this effectively with high speed, we need to use our energy and core human assets efficiently. We have only touched upon this from a spectator's perspective. Now it is time to synergize our three brains and decide the direction in which we want to focus our efforts.

Motivation is a force that can work both for us and against us: it can guide us in setting our priorities and thereby be an effective partner in dedicating our energy to the right tasks, but it can also blind us to reality by deceiving us into thinking that there is always a straight line between our current location and the next oasis. This can leave us frustrated and stressed, since the only constant is change in the Hyper-Volatile World, and at the same time humans are by nature reluctant to embrace change as described in the cycle of change.

That being said, we still need to think of planning, but we need to be aware of and understand the workings of the hyper-volatile environment in which we are using the plans.

Few successful management books would dispute that selecting the right task is to "put first things first," meaning that short-term, urgent, and important tasks need to be given a higher priority than short-term, unimportant tasks. However, even in the field of traditional time management we will find less room for the long-term important tasks than for short-term tasks. With this in mind, Covey argues that the fourth generation of time management should make us consider spending more time on tasks that are nonurgent but important in the long term, such as interfacing with other people and seeking inspirational learning. We should also remember to reserve a time to reflect and energize ourselves. In my opinion, this type of time management will certainly lead to more efficiency than just simple prioritization of tasks, and it will leave room for building the personal skills and relationships that are highly important in the long term but not urgent.

Prioritizing tasks takes into consideration only the tasks we have at hand. What about those that would become relevant if we had the courage to take a step in another direction? These types of tasks begin outside the scope of management. They start with personal leadership! Leadership is, to me, the true source of tasks—or it should be—because if we are not leading ourselves and actively engaging in the world around us, we will miss out on the potential momentum of change and fall victims to the impact of other people's choices. This is especially important for leadership in the hyper-volatile environment. So we need to dare to choose, or the choices will make us!

We need to step a little away from ourselves and visualize the different types of mindset we have had in the past when selecting a beacon: our current job, our partner, or a great exciting project. What were the drivers? Are we working on what I would take the liberty to label a Western-style revolutionary change or an Eastern evolutionary path of change? I am not trying to voice any preference for either of these ways, but my reason for the labels is merely that I found the inspiration for my work with decision-making software throughout the world. Western business leaders aim primarily for fairly quick fixes or remarkable results and breakthroughs, whereas business leaders from companies with an Eastern philosophy, like the Kaizen circles, are seeking more long-term prosperity through continuous improvement. The Eastern approach to change is actually one of my strongest arguments for the wisdom of being extremely cautious in disregarding ancient Eastern medicine and practices for well-being. If Kaizen has carried such ancient practices from generation to generation for thousands of years with commitment and discipline, some of these practices must be successful to some degree.

Well, whatever our pattern of change, I think it is important for us to understand our reasons for the choices we make, solely because we have to maintain the acceptance in the cycle of change. If we impose changes on ourselves at a pace that is too fast for us to have time to react and feel the environment around us, we will lose touch with reality, and over time we will go off course. We need time allow our intuition to help us select the right palm trees to guide us. To manage such time effectively, it appears that Covey's fourth-generation time management could support us. The continuous circles of improvement will ensure that we do not lose touch with reality, but they may fail to stimulate us to harness unused potential outside the circle. A Kaizen circle revolves around a more-or-less defined goal, and over time the circle will gain more and more momentum, while at the same time it will become rigid as we become set in our beliefs and aware of our talents. However, when Kaizen manages to skip a generation and live through the scrutiny of a descendant generation, I believe as an incarnated westerner that it should be taken very seriously. Therefore both reflection and appropriate learning cycles can be tools for allowing our minds to change appropriately in response to our environment.

When dealing with the circles of change and the circles of improvement, I cannot help thinking about the samurai warriors who dominated Japanese history for 700 years. These great warriors may have been slightly more ruthless and violent in reality, perhaps due to the idleness between wars, than the romantic heroes they are portrayed as in movies. Nevertheless, they managed to leave their imprints on Japanese culture for several hundred years, and, perhaps most remarkably for contemporary times, they inspired the principles that allowed Japan to rise after World War II. Understanding Bushido, meaning "way of the warrior," is the beginning to an understanding of the samurai mindset. Interestingly enough, if we consider the first part of this chapter, the philosophy of Bushido is "freedom from fear." It meant that the samurai transcended his fear of death, which gave him the peace and power to serve his master faithfully and loyally and die well, if his death was necessary.[83]

> *I have no strategy; I make the Right to kill and the Right to Restore Life my Strategy.*
> *I have no designs; I make seizing the Opportunity by the Forelock my Designs.*
> *I have no miracles; I make Righteous Laws my Miracle.*
> *I have no principles; I make Adaptability to all Circumstances my Principle.*
> *I have no tactics; I make Emptiness and Fullness my Tactics.*
>
> —An excerpt from the samurai creed [84]

In the excerpt above, we find a lot of evidence of striving to accept "the now" and the situation as the fundamentals of action. Effectively, the samurai would seek to deprive himself of feelings on the eve of battle in order to be constantly in the positive half of the cycle of change.

Eckhart Tolle, author of *The Power of Now*, also addressed the pitfall of not accepting "the now." His book deals with the gap between what our mind "wants" and our history, meaning that if we are fixated on either desires that we want to achieve in the future or things that have happened in the past, we do not grasp the moment we are in right now. This gap between the "now" moment and the thoughts in the mind is where anger, frustration, fear, stress, and any other undesirable feelings reside.[85]

I would think that the brain in our head is more powerful than our feelings in many cases. If this were not the case, it would not be possible to reprogram our habits of stimuli responses as mentioned earlier. But in order to create an intelligent balance with the other brains, it is important to understand empirically the roles our gut and heart play whenever we make decisions with our brain in the head. Such knowledge enables us to use our experience to tune our behavioral patterns. It may very well be that in some cases we will find that the gut is a better judge than the head, and vice versa, but the Bushido can still teach us valuable things about accepting change. We also need to understand that to get into action once we have decided on the direction, we need to have all three brains aligned. We should regard each of them as important.Luckily most of us are not battling every day, so, unlike the samurai, we will have plenty of time to complete the exercise of visualization, which can take us to the stage of focusing and unleashing our full potential in the direction we choose.

At this point, If we think of a situation that has taken us through the first two phases of the cycle of change, the input we received has traveled through the gut and the heart and on to the head brain. At this point, we have assessed the circumstances and decided on a course of action. The combined synergy of our three brains is what I will label the mind, and it is now time to apply this mind power to proceed on our journey.

Elite sportsmen and other top performers use visualization to focus their efforts. Dr. Charles Garfield became fascinated by peak performers while working with a NASA program, and he studied the characteristics of peak performers for his second PhD His research showed that almost all world-class athletes and other peak performers use visualization. They see it; they feel it; they experience it before they actually do it. Stephen R. Covey puts it this way: "They begin with the end in mind."[86] So if such a powerful source is available to all of us, why shouldn't we all seek to use it?

First of all, visualization is a great tool for aligning our three brains. Once we have created a mental image of the desired outcome of an action and have focused our mind on this situation, we can start involving our heart and gut. We can do this by closing our eyes while focusing on the feeling of having accomplished what we are setting out to do, and from this point interpret the feelings we have in the heart and gut—what do we feel? Chances are that if the outcome would be beneficial and in line with our principles it will feel great. We can almost taste it. At this point we should be very much underway in Walt Disney's terms: "If you can dream it you can do it."

Some might even suggest going past the point of simply visualizing. Dare to say it out loud, which is the recommendation of Napoleon Hill in *Think and Grow Rich*. He suggests that there is an almost magical power in saying things aloud as opposed to "just" thinking them. Allegedly, great men throughout the past century, such as Andrew Carnegie, Thomas A. Edison, Henry Ford, Dr. Alexander Graham Bell, and many others, used such techniques.[87] Shouldn't we accept the potential for Kaizen in these techniques?

Napoleon Hill argues that "thoughts are things,"[88] and I have to agree. If we recognize contemporary science, we will agree that the human body is made of billions of atoms that are in constant movement. Whether we think of the brain in the head as either a reflection of our soul or merely as meat and fluids, any thought of a bad experience or an error we made will be a collective vibration of a constellation of atoms. Even though we are very far from being able to see more than the areas of activity in a brain, it is not hard to imagine that thinking very hard and focusing on a situation would create a more aligned and therefore more powerful collective vibration. Since everything around us is also made up of atoms, the vibration would have a medium to spread from our brain as rings in water. How far would these rings go? Would they be able to penetrate another person's brain and create a similar vibration and thus the same thought there? Would these brainwaves be able to travel even much further out in the world and be the first step in materializing the situation? In Chapter 6, I elaborated further on the potential association of mind waves with computers; however for now we will leave this thought experiment.

Energy to succeed comes from visualization; it comes from letting the mind wander ahead and show the direction and the feelings and perhaps manifest the desired situation in words as well. The involvement of our mind and heart as motivation, in combination with our core human assets, is exactly what Stephen Covey refers to as a habit in *7 Habits of Highly Effective People*. In Covey's definition, a habit is the combination of knowledge, skills, and desire. One of my favorite American phrases, which I picked up while I was living there, was, "walk the talk." It is a great habit, because it means you will be true to yourself and others, but I would argue that if there is "no talk" there will be "no walk"—"no talk, no walk." I truly believe that we have not yet realized the potential that lies in being able to use our mind as more than a guideline for physical movement; for what is the mind anyway?

In great leadership there is great vision—the thoughts that stimulate the realization of impossible dreams. For the CALM leader, the ability to harness thoughts into focused visions is a key human competency, and it is a discipline in which humans surpass computing; the inability to visualize, think, and dream is the computer's inherent weakness. Therefore, if the leader focuses his energy on visions, thoughts, and dreams, synergic computing will mean that the best human skills compensate for the computer's greatest weakness.

Strategizing by Feeling the Environment

> *To be certain to take what you attack is to attack a place the enemy does not protect.*
> *To be certain to hold what you defend is to defend a place the enemy does not attack.*

—Sun Tzu

Sun Tzu[89] was the father of the oldest military strategy guide known in history, and the somewhat extreme statement above makes much sense in my mind, even though battling is in many cases inevitable. My point, however, is that an organization obviously consumes much less energy winning without direct confrontation than through confrontation. Consider again Jim Collins' fable of the fox and the hedgehog that I mentioned earlier. Did the fox and hedgehog feel they were in "battle" during the same periods of time? Most likely not. The fox was constantly planning an attack, but the hedgehog was going about his normal business and simply reacting to the circumstances. Their very perception of battle was different, even though they were indeed fighting the same battle.

Therefore, to avoid ending up as the fox in Jim Collins' fable and spending all our strategic energy on thinking, we can use probing. Much like in a military situation where a reconnaissance platoon can be dispatched to gather intelligence, we need to have people on the ground to get the true feeling and intelligence on enemy troops and the terrain. Using this metaphor in organizations, it simply means that we need to launch initiatives in order to know for sure how they will work. Probing is energy efficient, allowing us to launch an initiative on a small scale and gradually increase the energy we dedicate to the initiative once we know that we will get a return on our investment of energy. This process of probing has indeed been used in the last few decades by successful companies such as Canon, CNN, and Wal-Mart. Gary Hamel and C. K. Prahalad mention this in their book *Competing for the Future*, so the strategy of stretching for the next level through probes seems to be proven.[90] However, the most important thing about this concept in relation to computer-aided leadership is that probing does not require any changes to the way we operate, and the computer supports the energized organization; the systems, core competencies, and values are the same. This means that probing is automatically fitted into the rest of the routine operation as a natural part of the energized organization. Some probes will succeed, become operational, and gather momentum as OODA cycles and learning pick up, but some probes will fail and will naturally be discontinued because once we know we are in a blind alley, we will revert to the status quo ante and explore a different road. Reverting to the status quo ante can only be a problem if the probe is a product of a diversification strategy, and therefore the probe has no historic previous status in the organization. Only in this case will active leadership be needed to terminate the initiative.

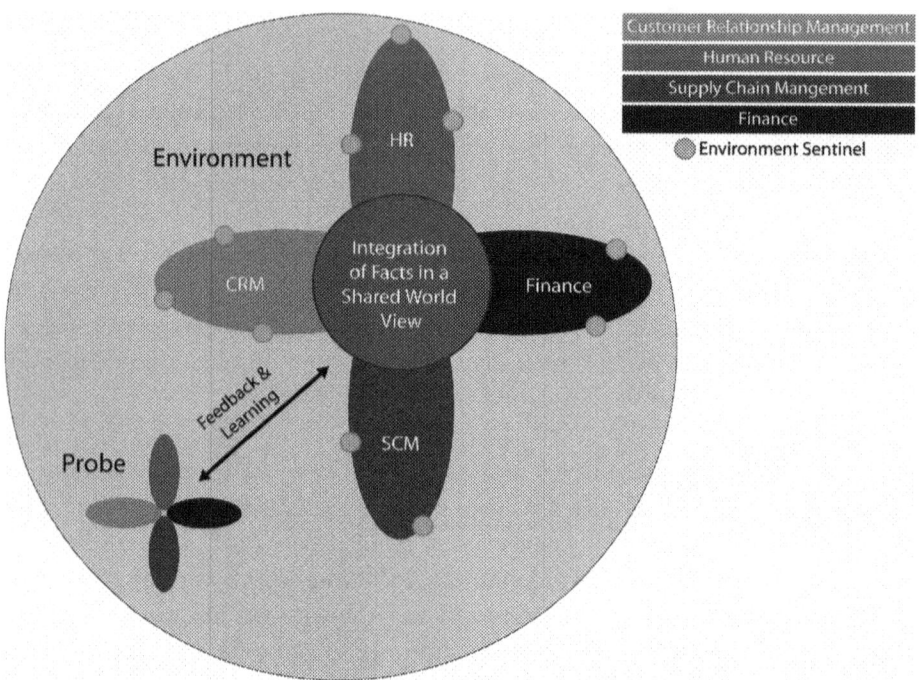

Figure 7.1 Example of Probing

In figure 7.1, a probe is illustrated as a more elaborate version of the example in figure 4.1. The probe is shown as a subset of what the organization is already doing, so the existing systems supporting the organization also support the probe. Had the probe been a significant diversification, a meaningful subset might not have been possible. An entirely new set of systems might then have had to be developed. Therefore it is obvious that if a probe has synergy with existing systems, it is of course directly interrelated with the organization's core competency and requires less energy in systems development for the organization to pursue the direction of the probe. Moreover, it makes sense from an energy perspective for the organization to use much of its existing knowledge and wisdom to work with the probe. These factors make for greater understanding and more effective handling of the probe, including the evaluation of its success and viability as a marker for the strategic direction of the organization.

Leaders can employ probing to use the organization's energy to set new courses effectively, while at the same time ensuring that a new initiative does not become a liability to the organization. The leader can measure and monitor the progress of the organization through the same channels that any other empowered individual in the energized organization would use. This probing process takes into account the chaos of the Hyper-Volatile World, and it is a feasible and fail-safe way to distinguish between the initiatives that will actually fly and those that will not. Probing also has the advantage that the leader can act on his gut feeling and can prove it wrong or right without consuming much of the organization's energy. The leader is of course also supported by the same tools as the remainder of the organization and can therefore also monitor and enhance his exploration of his gut feeling in accordance with the learning and experiences he has gained from the probes. This enables him to take new leaps in visionary directions at minimal risk.

An organization that allows or perhaps even nurtures skunkworks is highly mobile, as it can launch probes rapidly. Skunkworks are projects that are not really part of the official strategy and portfolio but are pursued by employees based on gut feeling and interest. This happened to Microsoft when it realized its proprietary approach to the Internet was losing ground to Netscape and other companies. In this case, there were actually a number of skunkworks going on that could be combined into the product Internet Explorer, which was the first initiative for Microsoft and marked one of the most rapid shifts in strategic direction for a large organization to date.[91] 3M as an organization even recognizes the benefits of skunkworks to the extent that employees are expected to spend a certain percentage of their time doing them.[92] In general, a probing process can be used without skunkwork, but recognizing and nurturing this line of work possibly stimulates the employees' innovation. Therefore a skunkwork that is suddenly put into real action will most likely have the organizational layers already aligned with it. My personal experience in TARGIT suggests that there is a high chance of a given skunkwork's being congruent with the organization's current product portfolio. The simple fact that some work and experimentation has already been done means that the time to market for the probe will be much shorter. Therefore skunkworks "bends time," as it were.

There is of course also room for classic scrutiny and assessment of the situation so that we become "luckier" when launching the probes. If we take Igor Ansoff's four generic growth strategies[93], namely market penetration, market development, product development, and diversification as shown in figure 7.2, we can seek to limit the risk of a probe. Analyzing the information we have gathered by surveying the market is the only choice in a diversification; or we can use the information we already have if we choose to keep either the market or the product constant in the organization's scope of operation.

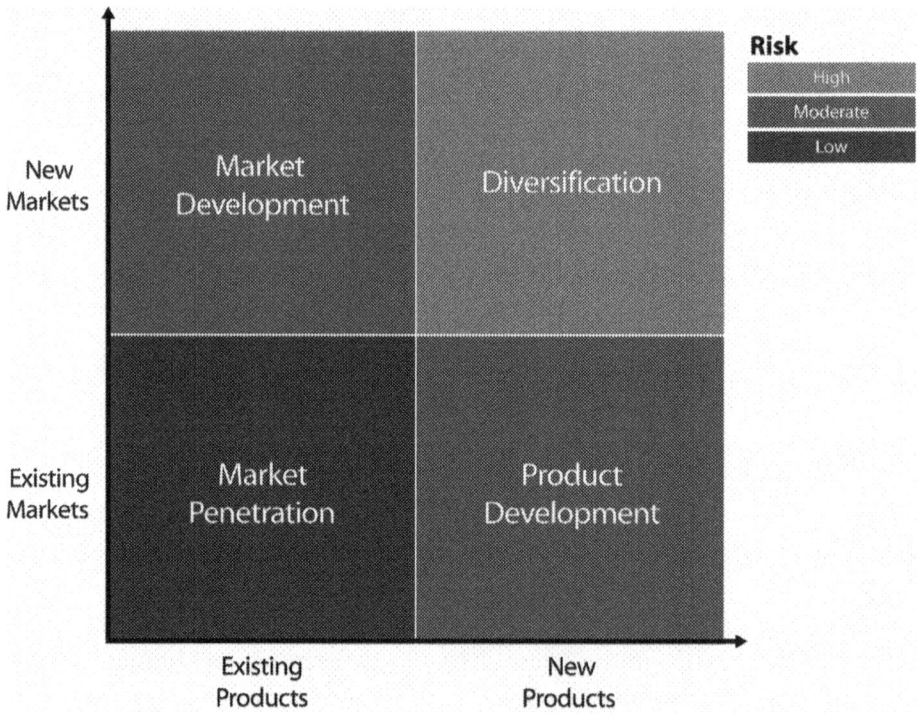

Figure 7.2 The Ansoff Matrix

It is obviously less risky to hold either a product or a market constant, as more internal knowledge and perhaps wisdom is available. The methodology for these two least risky strategies are straightforward for an energized organization. It is simply a straightforward OODA cycle that the leader will circle, and during this process he will be supported by the facts and sentinels. In such a situation the weight of the analysis is most likely to be put on the sentinels, as a new initiative is less likely to be covered by internal facts. The OODA cycle can then be supported by additional analytical information gathered directly from the market in the form of *customer surveys* and *competitor assessments*. Such information would be the only information available if we were to go with a diversification strategy. In this context, I am stressing the word *information* rather than true knowledge, since the information does not contain any associated track record of organizational experience and learning. Therefore if all three strategies are available to the organization, the least risky strategies are perhaps more desirable because in these cases we have both knowledge and information.

Building Core Competency on Talent

Strengthening an organization by allowing it to utilize individual talents widely and appropriately requires some thought on the inherent workings of the human brain, specifically the emotional and rational parts of it. From the workings of our autonomic nervous system in the gut and heart, combined with the limbic system,[94] which is the part of our brain in the head that deals with emotions, we might find that it is sometimes hard to motivate ourselves to undertake some tasks, although they are important. When this happens, we need to work with our neocortex, which is the site where rational thinking occurs. It will probably be able to help us in undertaking a given task that does not have emotional appeal to us. It is the part of us that allows us to reprogram our habits even though the undertaking might initially seem either scary or hard. The strength of the thoughts and visions materialized in the neocortex will keep us going and eventually get us to succeed. The more we do a certain thing, the more it will become a habit. In fact, it appears that the synapses that carry impulses from neuron to neuron in the brain will become broader. This means that we can use our neocortex to rewire our brain to operate more efficiently. Although it seems hard at first, the more we do it, the better and more spontaneously it will happen until it becomes an established habit. Except for the neuroscientific explanation, this is hardly news to us, but my point is that we need to exercise discipline and courage to exploit and develop our brain in these areas. We need leaders and managers to coach individuals in challenging themselves and developing the skills needed to meet the demands of both themselves and the organization.

This means that leaders and managers should be able to set the right goals as well as identify and develop the right skills. The word *right* is actually a challenge for leaders and managers themselves, since *right* in this context means aligned with the organization. This is alignment of the values of both the individual and the organization; the values must be congruent. If they are not, the individual is basically unsuited to the organization, as neither of them will be fulfilled. The individual will suffer from an emotional, mental, or spiritual gap that he will have to fill through excessive energy consumption. This inner energy consumption means that both the individual and the organization will suffer from the effects of low potential. The most crucial task for leaders and managers is therefore the recruitment of the crew, because without the right crew, there would be limited synergy, and therefore no or at best limited potential to unleash. Gallup surveys confirm that the casting of the right crew is one of the tasks great leaders and managers deem a high priority.[95]

Having recruited the right people for the jobs, the next priority is to determine the area the empowered individuals and teams should focus on. If we again consult the methods of great managers according to Gallup's research, we find that the most successful leaders and managers spend most of their time with their best-performing employees, as opposed to with those who are less successful.[96] We already know that these leaders and managers select and build on skills and talent, so perhaps the reason is that they simply do not believe in fixing errors, but prefer to explore the greatness of the highly talented individuals. Therefore they don't have the task of coaching people who are not performing well due to lack of skills and talent. Underperforming employees are relocated to positions in which their skills and talent are needed, or they do not remain part of the organization at all. The successful manager is perhaps not disputing the antideterministic perspective of Stephen Covey and contemporary neuroscience that skills can be developed through personal discipline even though no initial talent is present. However the great leaders and managers simply economize on the energy. They recruit the best fit in skills and talent, and only exercise discipline where necessary. This means that the best leaders and managers can focus their attention on enabling their employees to excel within their areas of skills, talents, and interests. This priority makes even more sense if we consider the theories of Mihaly Csikszentmihalyi in which we perform optimally in a state of flow by working in a continuous process where we are competing against ourselves and balancing between the known and the unknown, as shown in figure 7.3.[97] If we focus the organization and the individuals in it according to goals where possible, we benefit from the highest potential of talent and its future development through flow.[98] Another clue to the focus of great leaders and managers is that they never set goals based on the average performance of members of the organization. They set goals based on the individuals, and they work with the individual who is competing against himself.[99] This focus further enhances the flow scenario and unleashes his potential to the benefit of the individual and the organization.

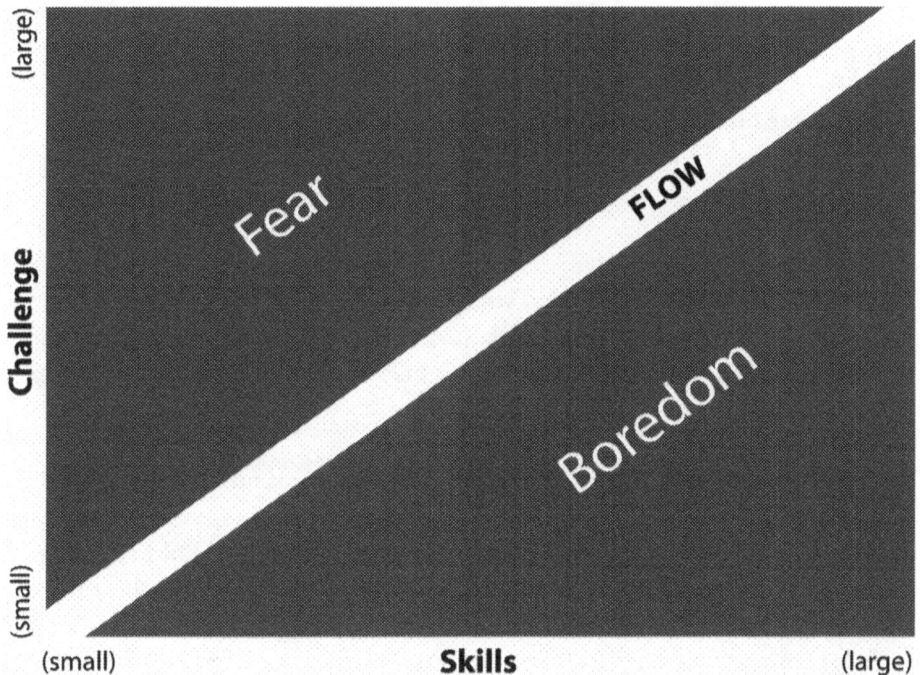

Figure 7.3 The Theory of Finding Flow

We have dealt with the ideal scenario in which we align and focus the organization toward the flow of skills and talents, but reality often proves this picture too romantic. Leaders and managers in particular must exercise discipline over the employees to ensure that important but slightly more trivial tasks are carried out. Priorities need to be set wisely to ensure that these tasks are undertaken.

In "The Common Denominator of Success," Albert E. N. Gray identifies one denominator that all successful people share; he concluded that "the secret of success of every man who has ever been successful lies in the fact that he formed the habit of doing things that failures don't like to do."[100] "It is essentially not because they like doing these things, but they recognize their purpose and therefore subordinate their dislike."[101] In other words, success depends on the discipline to do things that are important even though they are not necessarily within the boundaries of flow. Danish management guru Siegfried W. Andersen, for two decades a highly respected coach for the most successful companies in Denmark, such as the A. P. Moller group, set out to explore the appropriate balance in strengths and weaknesses. His question was, to what extent should one focus on eliminating a weakness as opposed to building on a strength? After reading an article about the Danish decathlon legend in the late 1980s, Lars Warming, Siegfried contacted him to learn his views on strengths and weaknesses. Since no one could be excellent in ten different disciplines, certainly a world-class athlete from this field would be able to shed some light on the matter. By talking to Lars Warming, Siegfried discovered that his focus was on building strength, but he was able to see what an average performance was in a given discipline by monitoring the competitors' performances, which were fairly publicly available. If he was able to meet the average in all his weak disciplines, then he would not invest more in the weaknesses, but dedicate the rest of his energy to the disciplines in which he was strong.[102]

There are other strategies than Siegfried's discovery for limiting the potential for weakness to cause failure. Marcus Buckingham and Donald O. Clifton, in *Now, Discover Your Strengths* suggest, among other things, that one could partner with someone with strengths in one's weak areas, and simply not do the things in which one is weak.[103] However, the idea of at least being as good as average or, as Buckingham and Clifton put it, "getting a little better at it" appears to be a strategy that is in line with Gray's persistence of successful people: strengthen the weakness until it serves the purpose; then focus only on strengths.

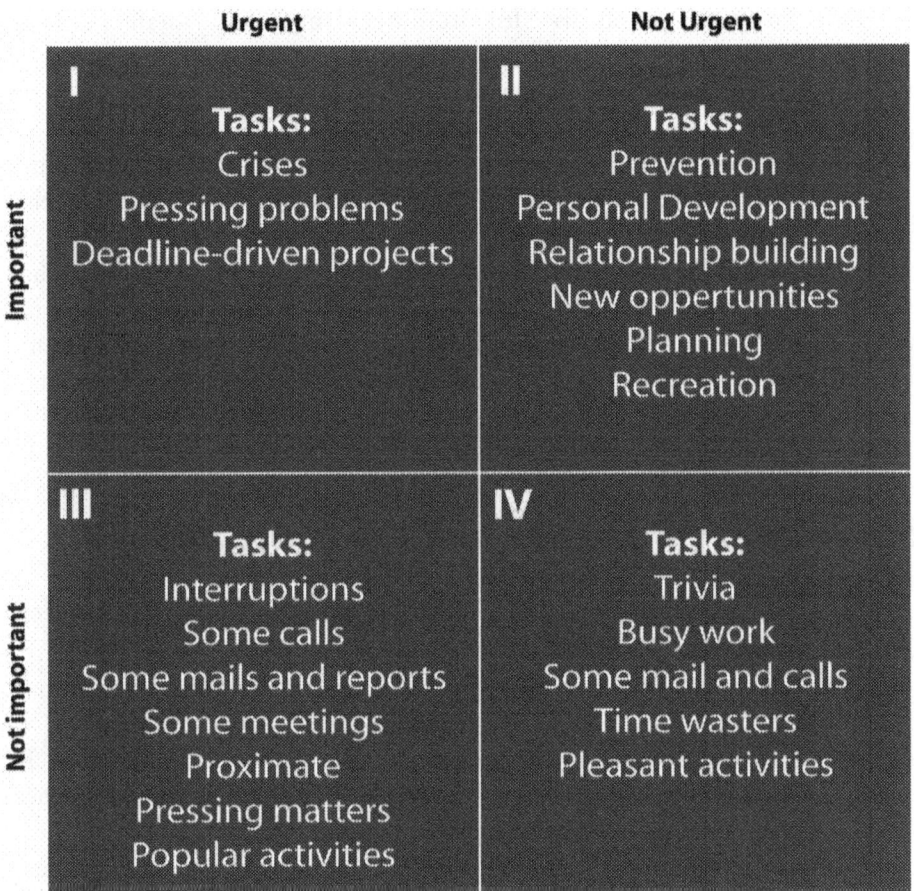

Figure 7.4 The Time Management Matrix[104]

Exercising the discipline suggested by Gray could also be viewed from a time-management perspective. Stephen Covey's third habit for highly effective people is, "Put First Things First," which describes a principle of personal management where tasks are distributed in four categories based on the dimensions urgent/not urgent and important/not important, as shown in figure 7.4.

According to Covey, there is a tendency for an individual to drift from quadrant II to either quadrant III or IV. However, if we look at tasks related to the external environment, such as a business opportunity, it will drift from quadrant II to quadrant I if we are lucky or if an opportunity turns into a problem or crisis.

However, sometimes it may also drift from quadrant II to quadrant IV, in the sense that it simply does not matter any more. We lost the opportunity because we were not there to seize the moment.

When we unite individuals into an organization, it is the task of leaders and managers to ensure that the quadrant I and II tasks are undertaken. In a CALM-energized organization, we do not need to worry as much about quadrant I as we do about quadrant II, as the organization is empowered with the autonomy to handle crises and pressing problems as well as to move toward objectives. The leaders and managers need to exercise both wisdom and discipline to find the appropriate mix between quadrant I and II and focus their attention on ensuring that the tasks necessary to achieve goals are undertaken on the organizational and individual levels in the optimal way to meet both short-and long-term objectives.

Stimulating Motivation and Creativity through Objectives

Leaders and managers are both servants and catalysts; however we should not neglect the classic disciplines of aligning and focusing the organization. Although their primary objective is to unleash potential, aligning and focusing the unleashed potential is necessary for the overall efficiency of the organization. For example, the employee will not have an overview of the organization as a whole, so although he may have the best of intentions, his efforts to develop his own potential may actually hinder or inhibit the development of the full potential of other employees. The result for the organization would then be less than optimal. This challenge typically arises when a supporting area such as IT or administration is overdeveloped at the expense of other sections of the organization. Additionally, some objectives are too narrowly defined. For example, a manager may believe in full documentation of all an employee's tasks, but the documentation would need to be updated regularly as the hyper-volatile environment changes. This could create a problem similar to the equilibrium of analysis and reports discussed in Chapter 6. The solution to this problem is to describe fewer objectives but make sure that the objectives are holistic while at the same time providing enough room to allow the employee, team, or business unit to unleash its full potential. This problem is also likely to decrease over time, if employees in general seek win-win outcomes and trust each other enough to share their challenges. Nevertheless, it is the role of leaders and managers to define objectives that maximize potential and eliminate potentially conflicting objectives.

Some inspiration for the idea of decentralization and motivation through broader objectives can be found in *Business @ the Speed of Thought*. Bill Gates states that he considers meetings with more than four participants a sign of an organizational problem, making the additional point that his meetings are based on solid analysis and produce actionable decisions.[105] Why? Because Microsoft hires creative thinkers; such people should be empowered with a seamless flow of the information they need through a digital nervous system. Gates does not argue the case alone. As early as 1956, William H. Whyte, in his *The Organization Man*, described bureaucracy and orders as killers of creativity and initiative. Mihaly Csikszentmihalyi describes the state of flow as follows: "When the information that keeps coming into awareness is congruent with goals, psychic energy flows effortlessly."[106] In other words, excellent performance and employee satisfaction occur when there are no disturbances or frustrations such as a rigid organizational structure might impose. Ensuring that employees feel the impact of empowerment and excellent performance is becoming more and more part of the employee/organization contract, since the number of creative people as a percentage of the entire organization is rising.[107]

The broader objectives that allow the organization to adapt to its environment are not only a matter of survival and operational success, as we found in Chapters 5 and 6. They also stimulate creativity on the individual and team levels. Moreover, they are part of the motivation that is expected by the talented employees for which organizations are competing.

In general, CALM leaders and managers are challenged to unleash the potential of humans and computers in their appropriate organizational context to ensure the organization's survival and success. The basic role of the leaders and managers is to apply the appropriate CALM components mentioned in previous chapters to eliminate fear and stress within the organization and provide the systems and lines of communications that create an energized and adaptive organization.

The CALM management team should ensure that the organizational core competency is built on talent, and that the synergic computer and human potential is maximized to enable the organization to reach its goals and ultimately its strategic objective. From this standpoint, CALM leaders can set the organization in motion toward visionary new horizons directed by strategic objectives that are continuously met by the organization, and at the same time the organization is crafted by the learning of the voyage.

In the following chapter, we look into the specifics of how to apply computing to these areas of responsibility and opportunity.

8

Mastering CALM

Computing for Visions

Thoughts are Things

—Napoleon Hill

Vision is a crystallization of human thought, and a strong vision allows us to see it as a "palm on the horizon," a clear marker of direction, under any conditions we are faced with in our environment. Therefore it is essentially the strength of our thoughts that allows a vision to be materialized in reality. A vision is clear thought that guides action and other thoughts; in other words, it is a "thing" in the human domain if we use Napoleon Hill's statement that "Thoughts are Things." Therefore the leader's mind, rather than a computer, is the womb in which a great vision is conceived and gestated until a strategy is born that develops into actions and ultimately success.

If we add Mihaly Csikszentmihalyi's research on creativity to the equation, we find that great ideas usually come to us outside the normal working environment, when we are at ease and not necessarily focusing too hard on the problem. Therefore, to stimulate the visioning process, computers need to accommodate a natural human thought process and allow a form of unfocus that enables the individual to get more peripheral information and inspiration rather than specific information within his normal area of expertise.

In the Internet era, the availability and amount of information that can inspire has increased significantly; information of reasonable quality on every subject is available globally, so the visionary leader can easily use the Internet to stimulate thoughts with additional information, as well as to get information about external political, economic, social, and technological factors that influence a vision.

However, the weakness of traditional Internet access in this context is that the person seeking information needs to be aware of some specifics about what he wants to know, and secondly he needs to be actively working with a computer to access the information, effectively tying him to a familiar environment. This is the case even if we consider handheld devices that could perhaps be taken to the top of a mountain. Although we would most certainly improve inspiration from this change of view, our thoughts would still be tied and constrained by the way a computer works today, requiring us to seek information actively.

The agent concept is a computerized solution that could allow computing to overcome these weaknesses by making the computer the human's assistant rather than his tool. A *personal agent* is essentially a program with the individual's preferences for content in terms of subjects. The agent travels the Internet and perhaps also other sources to find information related to these subjects and tells the individual where any interesting pieces of information it finds can be accessed. Perhaps adding some personal demographics and some artificial intelligence will make it possible for the agent to use the factual information and behavior of the individual to advise the user of associated new subjects of which the leader was perhaps not aware. Agents could help us receive new pieces of information at random times and thereby give them the characteristics of inspiration. Additionally, the agent will perhaps inspire us by bringing subjects of which we were unaware—subjects beyond the horizon of our knowledge—to our awareness.

The Internet already has agents working. For example, Amazon.com has an agent that knows our reading habits and suggests additional books that might be of interest. Most of the agents I know of are embedded in self-service applications on the other side of the counter, as in Amazon.com. However, these intelligent applications can easily be deployed to become personal tools, since the only changes needed to these applications involve the data it uses. An agent has been embedded in most of our Web browsers, such as Microsoft's Internet Explorer, which allows us to track changes on Web sites with content or interest criteria. Therefore the computerized agent that inspires and informs a CALM leader is most likely just around the corner.

Delving even deeper into how ideas emerge, we might consider the wisdom found in the writing of Descartes and in ancient meditation techniques and stimulate our mind even further through computer-assisted meditations, as suggested in Chapter 6. The benefits of these approaches are that we not only receive inspiration, but we gain more access to our deeper wisdom and our own capacity. Since visioning is perhaps the most human aspect of the entire CALM concept, the idea of not simply stimulating our thought process as we use it regularly, but perhaps even using it in a more effective way makes a lot of sense from both a personal-development as well as a pragmatic capacity-utilization standpoint.

A leader can initiate a learning process by experimenting with inspirational agents, meditations, and his ability to utilize his capacity. Like everyone else in the organization, the leader can use an individual energy journal, also discussed in Chapter 6, to facilitate this learning process by monitoring his progress and aligning his personal values with those of the organization. This is obviously even more important for the leader than for his subordinates in the organization, since the leader needs to be fully aligned personally with the values of the organization. The leader does not only need to buy into the values; he needs to live them.

A successful CALM leader is able to live the values of an organization and has the mental strength to unleash the energy to materialize visionary ideas into strategy. For a CALM leader, this energy is equally strong in pure thought, computerized communication, and knowledge, as well as in actual physical implementation. Computers can assist and actively participate with us on the electronic and physical levels, but on the level of thought they can only serve as channels of inspiration. Therefore a wise CALM leader will achieve synergic computing when he develops his strengths along the lines of visionary thoughts.

The closer we get to the materialization of the vision, for instance developing the strategies that are derived from it, the more appropriate a computerized approach becomes. A technique that was used by my friend Pat Robinson, who has been pioneering computer applications to marketing research for almost five decades, was based on the notions that "humans are not as good as computers at predicting future scenarios based on time series" and "computers are worse than humans at visualizing outcomes and anticipating possible scenarios." The idea is to use a "backcasting" process to stimulate thoughts of possible future scenarios, essentially by using hindsight to strengthen a vision. In reality this process is carried out by looking back for a historical period of the same length as the future period in which we desire to materialize our vision. By looking at the past we can answer these questions:

-What did we do then that we are glad we did?

-What would we have done differently in hindsight?

We can use these "backcasting" experiences to identify different scenarios with outcomes that might be likely given different courses of action. Additionally we can identify what we might do to influence these outcomes. The scenario with the most desirable outcome is selected, and the courses of action and influencing factors that are part of the scenario can then be used as guidelines when formulating and executing the strategy that should ultimately lead to realization of the scenario.

In such a process, the computers can assist us greatly in the backcasting process by providing the actual facts. They can also assist in the generation and evaluation of scenarios to select the most desirable scenario. By distributing human and computer capacity in this way, we get optimum synergy. In general, it seems that the closer we get to putting our thoughts into action, the more the computer can get involved in the visioning process.

Computerized Strategic Probing

With the computing potential available to us today, we can even enhance the strategic process more radically than by simply using historical knowledge combined with human wisdom. By using structured approaches to innovation, computers can assist us in finding new venues of opportunity that we might not even have thought of. There are basically two processes that come into play. One is computer support of an engineering approach to innovation: *computer engineered probes*. Another is the computer utilization of massive empirics to generate probes: *massive empirics probes*. The least radical of the two processes is the engineering approach, which is basically getting computers to support the traditional stages of innovation. Such stages can be in the design and testing phase of products and ideas where we can use computer applications to outline a new product using tools ranging from spreadsheets to CAD applications.[108] These techniques have been available to us for the past two decades, but the extensive use of them in more than the traditional engineering of products remains to be seen. We have discussed the idea of a structured process of innovation to some extent, but the structured process of innovation seems particularly applicable to larger organizations that are at risk of choking the creative spirit of entrepreneurship, since the bigger the organization becomes the greater is the potential for becoming rigid as processes are optimized. According to John Seely Brown, former director of

Xerox's Palo Alto Research Centre and author of *Research that Reinvents the Corporation*, the research of larger organizations need to undertake more and more tasks such as process design and new-product design.[109] Therefore, the structured innovation process that is optimized by computers would be something that would allow the organization to keep up with the increasing demand for innovation.

A structured innovation process could be something as simple as looking at all the factors we take for granted in a product, for example its unique features, its price, the way we market it, and so on, and then changing the factors one at a time to see how the outcomes would change in the different scenarios. One example of such an innovation process could be the invention of unleaded gasoline; lead was taken for granted based on the need to control the combustion. However, removing the lead and adding an alternative created a new product with the same effect, but with more environmental appeal.[110] Based on this approach, a number of options will be generated and then used to simulate different scenarios based on the combinations of the different options, enabling the experimenter to identify the most desirable scenario.

The simulated world in which we apply the changed scenarios can be created mostly from the information we already have as facts and from the sentinels, but it can be adjusted through the application of organizational human wisdom and perhaps even customer surveys. The idea here is that magic or miracles are part of the innovation process. It is a structured process in which computers can assist in generating, presenting, and evaluating the likely impact of various scenarios. I use the word *innovation*, but it might as well be called strategizing or envisioning, as we are indeed going through the same process whether we are designing or repositioning a product or an entire organization.

Launching probes in this way can also be used in areas other than product development. The "What If?" types of analysis are examples of this. In practice they are done by building a simulated world in which the computer generates answers describing the scenario in response to questions such as, "what would our organization look like if we had ten times as many customers?" Such computerized probing will allow us to uncover issues of lacking organizational scalability in the form of bottlenecks in the operation, and it will perhaps give us the necessary insight to focus on the right areas in order to meet our objectives with the least energy consumption even though a number of factors are fixed. When operational conditions are more or less fixed, this type of probing becomes even more effective, since the simulated world will then look very much like the real world. Therefore it is a relevant tool for managers who are operating under the constraints of the strategy; their world is somewhat more defined, as it is derived from the overall strategy, and yet they are still expected to meet their objectives with the highest efficiency.

Turning to the more radical massive empirics probe, we can benefit from the computing powers that have evolved in accordance with Moore's Law as well as the continuous growth in computer-network bandwidth. In massive empirics, we let the computer search for solutions autonomously. In principle we just feed it with data for inspiration and knowledge to let it search for solutions based on a set of desired objectives. The computer conducts everything empirically. The idea of this as a serious means of getting inspiration in an organization originates from the saying that "10,000 monkeys at 10,000 typewriters will eventually type out the entire works of Shakespeare."[111] The interesting part of this is that simulating the 10,000 monkeys in a reasonable timeframe and identifying the relevant information is not such a big problem anymore, and it is getting progressively easier as computers evolve. There is of course a huge difference in this empirics approach compared to traditional human research empirics, in that the latter is guided by inspiration and gut feeling as well as common sense. However, since computers have an ever-increasing advantage over humans in the sense of being able to handle massive amounts of data, perhaps massive empirics is a feasible approach to solving some problems. The computing power to conduct the massive empirics is additionally increased by the fact that we do not have to rely on the individual computer evolving alone; new developments in parallel processing over the Internet or grid computing will facilitate an even more rapid growth in computing power.[112] The interesting aspect of these techniques is that perhaps an innovation process needs some human interaction, although not to the extent of traditional research. The interconnected computers on the Internet would provide a resource where an unprecedented number of people are available. These people could easily be stimulating the computers in parallel via the Internet, which means that the human interaction with computers can support the rapid growth in computing power that comes from parallel technologies such as grid computing for instance.

If we consider the strengths suggested by Pat Robinson for this process, we should note that humans should deploy the computerized massive empirics in simulation areas as wide as realistically possible in order to get the maximal benefits from it. People's strength is still in getting the ideas to form visionary scenarios, and computing powers could either be limited to a constrained space or put to work in infinity with little chance of ever finishing the task if humans don't create the appropriate initial conditions of the massive empirics.

The massive empirics computing processes can be enhanced even further to arrive at desired scenarios faster than simple random generation of scenarios and trial and error through the use of methods such as data mining and evolutionary algorithms. These techniques are already proven, and certainly more and more of these enhancement techniques will follow. The more intelligent we make the computer, the more it will work empirically in ways that mimic human behavior and thought processes. These massive capabilities of computers lead me to believe that the empirically operating computer is by no means unrealistic today, and once leaders understand how to tap into these capabilities and harvest the benefits, survival and success in the Hyper-Volatile World will be dependent on this ability simply because our competitors will be competing by using it as well.

In its ultimate form, massive empirics is applied as a problem-solving mechanism on the individual level in the OODA cycles to assist in crystallizing knowledge and to stimulate learning of further lessons. Massive empirics can be used on strategic levels for new organizational and product initiatives. However, I think one of the most intriguing areas in which we are already applying methods of massive empirics is in solving or at least gaining some insight into some of the big questions in life. Consider the SETI@home project, which is a scientific experiment that uses Internet-connected computers in the Search for Extraterrestrial Intelligence at Berkeley University of California.[113] To me, the utilization of massive empirics to search for intelligent signals from outer space might very well just be the beginning; how about applying massive empirics to some of the ancient methods of medical practices to identify their true worth? Once we are able to build a physical simulator of the human body that allows us to test the effects of various practices all the way down to the genome level, there will be unprecedented potential for computers to identify and test new methods. Perhaps in a decade computers will be able to engineer drugs and methods of treatment we have never thought of; or perhaps in two decades computers in nanoscale will be able to apply various techniques that are tailored to our individual bodies through massive empirics. It seems justified to anticipate these applications. It is just a matter of time before they become reality. However, if we raise the bar just a notch higher, why not start utilizing massive empirics to discover some of the relationships between our emotional, mental, and spiritual energies? Massive empirics offers almost unlimited possibilities to accelerate research and thereby the generation of knowledge and wisdom. All it will take is to build a simulation of the environment, and although this is a complex undertaking, the promises of innovative solutions to the challenges of change seem worth the effort.

Perhaps in a few years a simulator of the hyper-volatile environment can be built, and computers will be able to refine the suggestions in this book. If this should prove to be the case, at least this paragraph should not be rejected.

Computers can not only help us understand how a proposed initiative, a probe, will behave in the market, but they can also help us directly to engineer, suggest, test, or even autonomously develop the probe. At this point in the process, it is time for the computer-aided leader to take action. It is important to note that we are not able to gather true knowledge until we launch the probe; only at that point do we know how the market's customers and competitors will react. The hyper-volatile market is chaotic and unpredictable, and we have to face the fact that we cannot count on the reliability of information outside the boundaries of the sentinels we have in place. Therefore we should rely on what we actually have rather than seeking new sources on the fly. At best, these sources can only be at the information level—nothing more. We can familiarize ourselves with the most likely scenarios, but as leaders it is important that we get to the point of launching the probe. If we use information from the market to argue that no probe should be launched, we are generating a dangerous self-fulfilling prophecy that will propel us into oblivion. Worse, if we are not probing, we are not unleashing any energy from the organization; everything is in fact going on in our mind, but nothing is happening in terms of action. As leaders we need to accept that we do not know enough to not launch a probe; we should indeed do as Kierkegaard suggested and risk losing our footing by launching probes and let the opportunities the probes identify guide our way as palms in the desert.

We should observe that even though a leader is a true revolutionary in the sense that he does not have the time to launch a probe at all, the CALM organization will still be highly fit for any initiative a leader might decide on in the Hyper-Volatile World. The reason for this is that it offers the best chance of survival in hostile environments. The CALM organization is much like a cat that will always sense its environment in every cell and seek to make the most of it, landing on its feet when it falls and regaining its stability quickly. Moreover, once the CALM organization has landed, it will continue to adapt to the leader's direction and goals; the learning will be cumulative, shared efficiently, and applied effectively. Therefore, even though a leader might not want to probe at all, the CALM organization will still allow him to fulfill his dream and reach the organization's objectives.

Computing for Talent

Building an organization on talents requires some additional attention to the domain of managers. A manager can benefit from tools that allow personality patterns to emerge in the recruitment process. These patterns can tell him about an individual's psychological profile and ability to relate to others, and assist him in finding areas of potential strength and talent to build on. Both the ability to relate to others and the ability to build on talent are necessary for true synergic cooperation within the organization. There are a number of tools for psychological profiling already available, and perhaps as Gallup's research results are becoming more widely accepted, a new systems such as their StrengthFinder will also become more widely available.

Having identified and recruited a number of individuals with the right talents, it is the manager's role to assemble the teams and arrange them into a lean, agile, and, most importantly, energized organization. This process will be ongoing for the organization, and for this purpose, the manager can find assistance in the information that resulted from learning throughout the organization. Through the patterns of individual's and team's excellence and failure in terms of their ability to meet their KPIs, he can gain insight into which areas of core competency are present and thereby align the core competency with the organization's strategy. The ability to monitor the core competency is partially a matter of organizing individuals in teams that operate in autonomous OODA cycles, and from there monitor and analyze their performance over time, as suggested in Chapter 6. A manager can also benefit from analytical findings in an organizational energy journal, which comprises all journals in different legacy systems such as CRM as well as an aggregate of the individual energy journals. From the information of actual performance and individual and organizational learning, the manager is able to rearrange the organization by empowering and stimulating individuals and teams where talent is emerging and reassigning individuals and teams where it isn't. The ultimate goal of this crafting process, based on talent, is to align talent fully with the organizational core competency.

As mentioned earlier, simulation can accelerate the learning process. By playing games that are extreme in time or context we can force talent and individual and organizational learning to emerge. In this context I must mention a game I designed to work with talent and core competency in TARGIT: "The Coup d'État Game."

The game was inspired by reading *Coup d'État*, by Edward N. Luttwak, which is a practical handbook on seizing control in a country through a coup.[114] In my opinion, the abstract problem of executing a coup seems to apply to businesses, especially smaller businesses with scarce resources. They could learn from these tactics, since they aim to win over the sympathy of the people as well as focus their efforts on key objectives in the hostile world surrounding them.

In the game, two small teams consisting perhaps of half a dozen individuals with different individual skills are given the challenge of planning to seize power in the country over a twenty-four-hour period. It is up to the team to decide when to initiate the plan, but it has to be detailed, giving the activities and location of each individual during the coup. Obviously, it is virtually impossible for a small team to seize power in a country. Therefore preparing the plan is an extreme goal. The team members need to think creatively, and they need to accelerate every effort they make using the "forces of nature" in the environment. This means they should understand the trends and stability of the society and seek to exploit these. Ideally they only need to invest little energy wisely in areas where other people will be accelerating it, either from sympathy or simply because the society is extremely dependent on certain cornerstones, which thereby gives modification of these cornerstones extreme impacts. Once they have completed their plan during a certain amount of time, perhaps four hours, a copy is handed to the game master who reviews it and identifies different areas where things will not go exactly as planned. The game is then played over the twenty-four steps outlined by the team. Both teams travel through each of the twenty-four steps, with the team that is not active serving as the jury for the other. The idea is that for each step, the individuals involved in a task should present it to the team serving as jury, which subsequently rules whether it believes the individuals are capable of the task. There is room for argument, as the active team can argue its case, explaining why it believes it is competent to carry out the planned action, but the game master, who initiates each step, makes the final decision on the success or failure of a task. The game master also puts in unforeseen obstacles in some of the steps, and communication between the individuals on the team is limited to realistically reflect who is present at a given location, lines of communication, and the like. Again the jury and game master decide whether the action at that step of the plan is successful.

The point of this game is first of all to set an extreme goal, a goal that is unrealistic yet sufficiently plausible to get the individuals to start reflecting on their competencies and talents. During the execution of the plan, the team and individuals receive feedback from colleagues on their perceived competency; this means that a dialogue can take place in which the individual argues perhaps undiscovered competencies and then receives feedback from his colleagues' perception of whether he will be successful in carrying out his plan. During the game, the teams also learn about the individuals' reaction patterns when confronted with the inevitable changes the game master makes to the plan.

This game is designed for teams of people who are already very familiar with each other, the aim being to take the knowledge of each other's talents and mentality to a more insightful level. Receiving feedback on actions in an extreme and unrealistic scenario will lead to feedback on failures and wins that are extreme. This allows a clearer pattern of talent and perceptions on an individual and interpersonal level to emerge.

Using games such as the "The Coup d'État Game" can unveil new talents, but most importantly it will reveal a pattern of individuals' perceptions of their colleagues. Using such information, *talent computing* allows managers to team people together for optimum synergy based on their talent and enables the individuals to gain experience of working in a changing environment in which resources and energy are scarce. Even though the game itself doesn't rely heavily on computers to crystallize the patterns of talent and perception, computers should be used for both planning and recording what is learned during the game, as this information is a natural part of the organizational energy journal.

Computing for Autonomous OODA

There is a lot of room for computer support to assist the manager in his role as a catalyst in achieving the four generic objectives. The most common belief in traditional measurement is that a balanced scorecard is an appropriate way for the manager to succeed in his role. In theory, the balanced scorecard is a good way to monitor the organization, as it provides a balance not only in time, but also between internal and external processes, as well as between causes and effects of different actions and situations in the environment, as mentioned earlier. The balanced scorecard approach will seem intriguing from the manager's perspective since it promises insight and control of the execution of the organization's strategy. However, we must understand that the flip side of the balanced scorecard is that in the worst case it can be devastating for an organization, as it can slow down OODA cycles throughout the organization and decrease its ability to adapt to changes in the Hyper-Volatile World.

The challenge with a balanced scorecard is that it provides valuable insight, but in order to get this insight we need to measure performances and compare them to specific goals. If we fail to provide room for the individuals in an organization to work creatively around the OODA cycle, the balanced scorecard can suddenly turn the organization into a singular OODA cycle type of organization with the associated disadvantages, as we saw in figure 5.3. In this context, please bear in mind that the balanced scorecard was conceived in 1996, when the hyper-volatile environment had not picked up to its present pace; however the principles of balance that the balanced scorecard pioneered are highly relevant in the energized organization. So the trick is that the manager must ensure that the balanced scorecard is not too rigid. In practice this means that the manager should create mission objectives for the OODA cycles and give the individuals a lot of freedom within these cycles. In effect, the organization's operation will be a series of *autonomous OODA cycles*. If we monitor the organization as a set of autonomous OODA cycles that interact, rather than as a number of functional departments, and apply the balanced scorecard in this context, we should be able to succeed. However, please also note that there is a risk that the application of a balanced scorecard even at the OODA-cycle level could be too rigid and perhaps also too costly, much for the same resource-limiting reasons as with the implementation of analytical and decision support tools for the autonomous OODA cycles as shown in figure 6.4.

Another problem with the balanced scorecard is the setting of standards. If we derive a number of measurements from an overall strategy, how do we deploy the ideal score for that measurement? If we set overall objectives and unleash the individuals' energy and ingenuity, we will perhaps arrive at entirely new ways of doing things and thereby new standards for the measurements. If we had defined a standard to begin with, we would have prevented the organization from reaching the stage where it could unleash this potential. This problem is fuelled as well by the idea that autonomous OODA cycles evolve over time as the organization is subjected to the changes of the hyper-volatile environment.

Indeed, getting a deep holistic perspective on an organization is a very healthy exercise, but there is a risk of killing initiative and potential as well as creating an organization that is not agile. One way of harnessing the best of both worlds could be by creating the balanced scorecard on the autonomous OODA cycles. It might also be wiser to monitor the trends rather than set specific standards for performance. Inspired by Kaizen, we can measure ourselves against our own progress. Seeking ways to optimize our performance would give valuable insight to assist us in our learning processes in the OODA cycles. Additionally, the overall learning trend could be assessed to identify the autonomous OODA cycles where the teams learn faster than others. Such measures would help us identify and understand the development of the organization's core competencies.

So the balanced scorecard is a nice *tool*, which if applied properly can be an energizing factor for the organization and a way for the manager to use his energies as a catalyst. The challenge is in not creating a rigid system that causes friction in the organization's agility and thereby consumes energy. One could say that the balanced scorecard itself can only be used successfully in a balance of three factors, namely energy, leadership, and management.

As we seek to make information available toward the operational layer, the refinement to knowledge throughout the organization may prove to be a challenge. Much as I described earlier with the pluralism of analysis and reports, as changes to these need changes at a faster pace due to the nature of operation, the historical data available at any given time is limited. On the other hand, the more we are able to measure throughout and on the periphery of the organization the more data will flow into our databases. This problem of being able to generate more data than we are able to store has a similar impact: we need to complete OODA cycles that are based on incomplete information. Computers can help the manager get a more complete picture by providing him with more detailed information and control. The problem is simply that the data streams in faster than we can store it. When this happens, computers can establish trend patterns and models based on the data to reduce its size in individual numbers by turning the data set into mathematical formulas. These models and trends may be extremely complex, but the processing power of computers will probably overcome the problem, especially if we use techniques such as grid computing as mentioned earlier. Once we have the models in place, we simply dispose of the data that created them, and we are left with information compressed to a manageable size. In the other scenario—too little data—we can complete the picture artificially by using similar computerized techniques, building the model based on similar abstract situations to approximate the missing pieces of information. Such techniques are already being used to sharpen the focus in pictures, optical scans of text, and the like.

It is inevitable that we will have to base judgment on incomplete information in the Hyper-Volatile World; this is simply the nature of chaos. However, through the methodologies of creating and associating models of trends, we can solve this problem through computers. In essence, this is also how we ourselves learn. We don't store all the details of the information behind the lessons we learn; we store the lessons themselves.[115]

We can take this first step in computer aiding the manager even further. If we process the information to a higher level of knowledge, we have an excellent field for simulation as well as the platform for creating computer systems that can cycle the OODA autonomously. These systems are already widely used in the fields with traditions for simulations; think about the autopilots in commercial airlines. They are being adopted rapidly in other computerized environments. Consider the autonomous antispam or antivirus programs that we trust to scan our e-mails for unsolicited mail or devastating viruses and destroy them. Both of these electronic menaces are highly destructive and can in some cases cause significant losses to an organization in the Hyper-Volatile World. Or consider the guidance of a Patriot Missile, which was trusted as the most effective countermeasure against enemy missiles during the Gulf War. These missiles used advanced artificial intelligence based on a combination of fuzzy logic and neural networks as guidance for their flight to locate and destroy another missile in midair.[116] We trust computers to protect our organization or even our lives. How long until we trust them to make semiautonomous commercial decisions? Some would say that we already do, as the computerized stockbrokers have been around for decades; but for the computer-aided manager, the application of such systems could energize the organizations of tomorrow even more. In this context it is interesting to note that as early as 1967, Patrick J. Robinson, Paul E. Green, and Peter T. Fitzroy conducted research on the human ability to make decisions in a simulated marketing environment under uncertainty. They found in experiments that people were less successful at making decisions that maximized profit than were computers using the mathematically based Bayesian approach to decision making.[117] Findings such as these suggest that we should consider whether it makes sense to assume by default that humans make better information-based decisions than do computers.

The manager with the wisdom to understand the potential applications of computing will be able to "grow" his own specific applications in greenhouses of information, simulation, and automated testing, and deploy them in areas where accelerated OODA cycles are desired. Obviously, there will be limitations to these techniques. They will be different from human intervention, but, much like massive empirics, they will have advantages over the human OODA cycles, as well as disadvantages. The computer-aided manager will be able to balance the application of techniques to make the organization as energized and agile as necessary to face and succeed in its hyper-volatile environment.

Consider a future experiment with autonomous systems that complete OODA cycles intelligently, with speed and focus, constantly reacting to and acting upon the attacks and opportunities of the environment. I believe that a lot can still be learned from the battle rap as a metaphor for modern strategizing. My dream is to commence a project, when I have finished this book, in which a supercomputer is able to battle with a human. Such a system would need to be able to compose sentences that rhyme, address the weaknesses of the opponent, and defend itself from the opponent's attacks. This system would need to be able to understand attacks in words and counter them intelligently, so building this computer would be a more sophisticated version of chess computing. One could say that suddenly the outcomes would be limited only by an entire language rather than by the permissible moves on a chessboard. Once the system is ready for testing, I will have it battle great rappers, like Deep Blue played world chess champion Gary Gasparov. In computing nature, the system I design will perhaps not beat the opponent at first, but with every loss it will gain in strength. By pure computing advancement, it will be a matter of time before it can beat a skilled opponent, and I am confident that valuable lessons in both artificial intelligence and speech synthesis from this project could then be used in other areas to assist in computerizing autonomous OODA cycles.

Time will show how that project takes off, but managers aided by computers will gradually be able to turn over some of the OODA cycles to computers and free up more human energy for other tasks. The organization will gain in agility and speed since the length of the computers' OODA cycles will be reduced, and they will continue to be reduced as computing evolves.

If we combine the challenges of alignment and focus for practitioners of CALM, we find that even though computing will facilitate tasks such as swift execution of autonomous OODA cycles, it is in the selection of appropriate human skills and talent through recruitment as well as in the alignment of human and organizational values and goals that the CALM practitioner needs to exercise human judgment and wisdom. Computing will unleash much human energy that has been tied up in other tasks, and this energy should be channeled into these talent selection, alignment, and focus activities. It is the human knowledge and wisdom in these areas overall that, through the application of CALM, will make organizations succeed or fail; therefore the human skills and talent needed to undertake these tasks are paramount for leaders and managers practicing CALM.

CALM @ Work: An Example of Computerized Probing and Autonomous OODA Cycles

At the time of writing, Google is the world's most used search engine for the internet, as more than 80% of all users on the internet use this service. Thanks to its position, Google is not only a successful organization solemnly focused on delivering services that are purely virtual in terms of bits and bytes; Google's position also means the company knows a lot about what more than 80% of the users on the internet search for. Obviously, such knowledge can be used by Google for developing new products that can be made available to users on the internet, but most interestingly they succeed in doing so in a development and deployment cycle that does not involve humans!

The service that succeeds in this is called Google AdWords. It is a service in which a customer, typically a commercial enterprise, can create a campaign for a product or service by reserving a number of keywords during a period of time. From a CALM perspective, what's smart about AdWords is that the pricing as well as the configuration of the product that Google sells is done autonomously by computers that reach into Google's knowledge bank, which is based on experience from 80% of the internet's users. A customer will simply select a number of words he would like to assign to his promotion, and the Google computers will estimate the traffic that specific keywords will generate to the customer's website, based on this traffic (as well as the attractiveness of the keywords) the customer will receive a quote and is able to buy.

From a CALM perspective, this is a remarkable example. Google sells a product that can only exist in computers; it is defined by computers, priced by computers and sold by computers without any human intervention. Effectively, not only is the OODA cycle completed by computers autonomously; the products are also "developed" and prized autonomously based on customers' demands. This means that eventually a Google employee manager will be able to see in hindsight which keywords products are the most successful and how much they generate sales, but all this will be after the fact that computers have developed and sold whatever products the market demanded.

It might be easy to disregard the Google example by its unique 80% market share of internet users' searches; but as CALM leaders and managers we should realize that such solutions are only the beginning. Within our own organizations' areas of operational expertise there is most likely knowledge that can give us parameters for which we can create new product variations and test them against customer behavior based on experience; when we are at this level, why not add in real customers to the equation and have them buy the new products? Finally, the most important question at this stage: How much human intervention is still needed in a given development or sales cycle...?

—CALM leaders and managers will harness the power of computers and knowledge to continuously refine products and services to meet the demand of the market. As humans we have the responsibility to continuously question whether we should be part of the cycle or simply benefactors of the output.

The Edge of Computing

Ultimately the role of the CALM leader and manager is to understand the boundaries between human and computer capacity to an extent where he is able to apply them appropriately with the most synergy. The systems proposed so far are all possible with the existing technological level that is widely available today. The capacity and opportunities are continuously expanding, but in the short run computing will only be used in the domains that require the raw power of computation. Therefore intelligence in the sense of computing should only be described as artificial.

Give the computers the jobs that the humans do poorly.

—Pat Robinson

Recognizing this, the CALM leaders and managers should be able to team human capacity with computing so that computers can use unique capacities in terms of inspiration, intuition, and human chemistry. On the other hand, tasks that require human capacity in the form of logic, applied to either procedures or mere calculations, will be undertaken by computers over time. Computers will displace human capacity from some parts of the mental domain, but are still very far from becoming relevant in the emotional or spiritual domains. This knowledge is exactly what the CALM leaders and managers should use in a continuous process of selection and learning; the more the humans of an organization focus on the emotional and spiritual domains, the more the organization can achieve synergy with computing to support its success.

At this stage let us sum up the computing techniques supporting the masters of CALM:

CALM Components	Leaders	Managers
Personal Agents	√	√
Individual Energy Journal	√	√
Computerized Meditation Techniques	√	√
Customer Surveys and Competitor Asessments	√	
Computer Engineered Probes	√	√
Massive Emperics Probes	√	
Talent and Core Competency Computing		√
Autonomous OODA Cycles		√

Table 8.1 CALM for leaders and managers

This concludes the journey through the computing techniques within what I call the CALM components. In the following chapter we will look into the practical implementation of all the components of the CALM concept as well as establish some feel for the trends that are likely to influence CALM in the future.

9

CALM in the Future

Implementing CALM

In the previous chapters we examined the challenges for organizations in the Hyper-Volatile World and identified computer components that can assist organizations to turn these challenges into opportunities and successes. The CALM components we found are described below.

Trustworthy Shared World View; Facts and Sentinels

This is the foundation for CALM. To achieve it, we organize the data we already have in an organization in a computerized environment so that it can be used by everyone in the organization. The data are transformed into information by a few skilled individuals so that they are reliable, and as everyone ultimately gets information that originated from the same systems, any decentralized approach to this process would waste energy. We divide the shared world view into facts and sentinels so that we have information about the organization internally as well as indicators about its surrounding environment. The initiative for this process has to come from the leader of the organization, and the decision to launch the CALM concept in the organization is the first decision a leader would have to make.

In practice, the trustworthy shared world view will be a database that is centrally administered to ensure data availability, quality, and security. The appropriate data availability and quality will be a constant iteration and enhancement process that is undertaken by skilled centralized individuals for the benefit and efficiency of all other users. The database technology could be supplied by Microsoft, Oracle, IBM, or any other provider that has technology available that supports the creation of analyses and reports. At present these technologies will most likely be referred to as relational or multidimensional databases depending on the provider, but there is already market evidence of a trend for these various techniques to merge.

Autonomous Information and Knowledge Refinement

This is the first level at which we start to harvest the benefits from having created the CALM infrastructure. By allowing the individuals in an organization to get insight into the KPIs of their performance, we allow them to eliminate fear by facing facts and thereby cycling the cycle of change faster. We also energize the organization as the empowerment of the individuals, which will allow us to have multiple OODA cycles throughout the organization. Information can be refined with analysis and reporting tools into knowledge and wisdom in the OODA cycles and made available to everyone. The OODA cycles will therefore improve in quality and speed, and the multiple OODA cycles will enable the organization to adapt quickly to its environment.

The approach to reaching this step should be selected carefully so that it is able to cover pluralism in need without creating a centralized bottleneck. Individuals should be allowed to adapt the information and knowledge refinement process to their own situation, using as little energy as possible. Letting the individuals work in intuitive and familiar metaphors minimizes the energy consumption. Very intuitive user interfaces with the business terms individuals know, for example the MetaMorphing process described in Chapter 4, could be used. The users at this stage need general business intelligence applications, from analysis and reporting to various more complex types of simulation and forecasting. It is essential to realize that it is not the complexity of the individual application but the fact that the entire organization can be covered that is the true key to success.

The process that refines information into knowledge and further into organizational wisdom is started and continuously enhanced by the empowered individuals throughout the CALM organization.

The specific technologies in this process are software applications, specifically tools to support analysis and reporting, that allow the users to access the information stored in the trustworthy shared world view. For specialists, I should note that I consider the term *analysis* to cover both data mining and forecasting. There is a multitude of applications for the purpose, and I have to admit that I am not unbiased in mentioning TARGIT as one solution. My slight justification for bringing TARGIT up is that the software is specifically engineered to support the CALM concept. It is about bringing synergy to both analysis and reporting throughout the entire organization. There are of course many good applications in the business intelligence arena that in many cases complement each other; these are offered by vendors such as Microsoft, Cognos, Business Objects, SAS Institute, and others.

Computerized Communication and Collaboration

This is a natural part of the process. Perhaps these steps have already been implemented in the organization's current computer systems. I am not aware of any company that does not use e-mail, but the actual automation of workflows for these organizations might be falling slightly behind. Even if automation of workflows are already in place, I would still urge leaders to revisit this area while implementing CALM, as the mindset during the implementation phase might not have been that of the CALM organization.

The intention of this step is to "bend time" through computers to reduce employee stress in the organization and thereby allow them to focus more of their energies on their tasks. The computer support of the operational communication and collaboration between individuals will accelerate the pace and stimulate the employees to improve the quality of the OODA cycles.

The typical tasks related to computerized communication and collaboration are the development of interfaces between existing computer systems, as well as a revising of operational procedures to assess whether some steps can be eliminated by computer aid and so on. The goal is to make the interfaces transparent and so efficient that data needs to be input by human hands only once and from there is reused by all systems. This process should be initiated by the senior management team.

In practice, these systems are the traditional e-mail and intra-and Internet components, but the level of collaboration and synergy probably depends mainly on people sincerely attempting to use them rather than falling back on the more familiar person-to-person communication, when using these technologies would make more sense. The operational systems in an organization might be enhanced with more seamless procedures through computerization, such as computerized document workflow systems and the like.

Computerized Operational Deployment

The operational processes that couple human involvement loosely with them in time to be more energy efficient can be further enhanced if we add computerized deployment of operational initiatives. This will speed up the pace of the OODA cycles, enabling the organization to react more quickly to opportunities and challenges in its environment.

Depending on the operation of the organization, operational initiatives can range from delivering a CAD design to a robotic production line to the updating of pricing in an ERP application, but the process we must follow is exactly the same. We ensure that all the deployment scenarios of operational initiatives can be started by an individual with a computer. No more human energy will be used, as the initiation process does not have to be repeated and communicated. Once we initiate a process, it should start up and run quickly and efficiently without further intervention. This will improve the pace of the OODA cycles, as it ensures that new initiatives are carried out swiftly and with the least energy.

The review of processes and their computerization should be in the hands of the management of the organization.

In practice, the implementation of computerized operational deployment will require the organization's operation to be fully supported by computing. A computer should be used everywhere it could make the operation more effective or efficient. The applications are typically systems for service, production, sales, and the like. Once the organization's operation is fully supported by computing, this component is about tuning the parameters of the operation—making changes in procedures, pricing, and so on. Ultimately, computerized operational deployment can be done autonomously by computers. If the computers are already running the OODA cycles autonomously, computerized operational deployment is inevitable as well as highly effective in terms of high speed and low energy consumption.

Individual Energy Journal and Individual Simulation

This component is intended to relieve individuals of unproductive fear of change by allowing them to understand themselves in different situations, and simulation is more powerful than a journal since it will allow the individual to gain confidence in areas outside his normal comfort zone by making extreme situations familiar without risk and in a comparatively short time.

As well as relaxing the inherited habit of fear of change by either keeping a track record of experiences or directly simulating them, this component also enables people to recognize their talents and skills, strengths and weaknesses. With understanding, people are more confidant and motivated to set and achieve personal goals, and less afraid of change. The Internet-based StrengthFinder application is part of the book *Now, Discover Your Strengths*, by Marcus Buckingham and Donald O. Clifton. It is yet another way to show how computing is reshaping traditional knowledge by adding a dimension of a Web site that is available to readers of the book. Its purpose is to help the individual discover his own personal strengths.[118] The StrengthFinder works pretty much as a psychological profiling test. The individual's input data is matched against the thirty-four strengths identified by Gallup's research profiles, and the output is a profile describing the specific strengths he is most likely to possess. Such a tool is a beginning, but a much more individual profile based on a personal journal of experiences would be better, as it would be possible to give more specific guidance based on personal talent, not just generic strengths.

Finally, the journal can be a track record for an individual's ability to achieve his goals and the lessons that were learned in reaching these goals. Such a journal does not have to be related to work only. It can be used equally well in one's personal life as suggested by Stephen Covey in *The 7 Habits of Highly Effective People* or other authors that coach personal development. Covey suggests that reaching personal victory is a prerequisite to reaching public victory,[119] and the process and learning related to seeking our personal and public missions and goals can easily be recorded in an electronic journal.

The actual systems supporting this process could be simple journals in either text or multimedia form; in my experience, the more senses that can be associated with a situation, the better and faster we can relate back to it. However, something as simple as text and figures in a journal could also be effective. A more advanced version of such a journal could be a combination of journal and goal setting. The application PlanPlus, for example, was developed in cooperation with Stephen Covey.[120] It integrates Covey's seven habits for personal greatness into a familiar environment such as Microsoft's Outlook product, where planning and priorities are also made in other contexts. The existence of this product suggests that personal productivity tools for personal growth will be developed over the next decade, and I believe more authors and software companies will follow suit.

For a more advanced simulation, knowledge and wisdom can be gained by adding the history in the organizations' trustworthy shared world view into the individual energy journal. This combined information will put personal progress and learning into an organizational as well as an environmental context. The software for these simulations in the various fields of operation might be available; if not, perhaps we need to create our own simulations based on the desired objectives and habits.

The initiative for these journals or simulations should originate from managers or leaders; but it must in effect be an individual initiative. Everyone should buy wholeheartedly into the process of working with his habits; such a buy-in can only be assured if individuals are confidant of a personal gain. As some individuals might distrust this process, it is important to start small and allow people to become familiar with it. They will trust it when they become more familiar with the positive effects. Eventually, all fear of this process will be eliminated once people realize that we cannot program a habit we do not want.

Computerized Meditation Techniques

Experimentation with sleep, power naps, and meditation are closely linked to the energy journal, which can be used to monitor progress and experiences with the various visual or sound-stimuli techniques. It is easy to make various multimedia computer applications available, such as a series of guided meditations or meditation music available over the existing information infrastructure in an organization.

The actual systems that provide these techniques could be mp3 files stored on an organization's intranet. For more advanced applications such as the meditative feedback, special programs will need to be developed to create vision, sound, and perhaps other vibrations based on hardware such as a "helmet" that can read the electric field around the head while it relays the stimuli to the person using it. These types of applications are not, to my knowledge, commercially available yet.

Personal Agents

Personal agents that can monitor updates on Web sites are already available today in web browsers. Additionally, many Web sites have notification services that allow various alerts to be sent when content on a subject of interest is published. Software for more advanced behavioral tracking and intuitive correlation is expected to become available within the next decade.

These agents are in practice programs that run on either the organization's server or on the personal computer of the person using it. The characteristic of the program is that it is able to capture an individual's preferences rather than actual requirements. This preference information allows the artificial intelligence of the agent to seek and provide content that the individual might not have though of, or might not have had time to seek.

Organizational Journals and Simulation

This component can address the fear that prevents synergic cooperation in an organization. It can also give the entire organization some time-collapsed learning similar to the learning achieved with individual simulation. The key lessons that can be derived from an individual perspective of these types of simulations are identification of skills and talent as well as awareness of other individuals' intent. The organization gains from employees' synergic cooperation, as people trust themselves and others more and seek win-win situations as the intent of both parties is visible. The organization also learns about the behavioral patterns throughout the organization, the presence of core competencies, and the performance of OODA cycles. It can then use its understanding to refine the lines of communication.

The journals that are already present in some operational applications, for instance the customer dialogue journals in CRM systems or the ability to comment on certain incidents in the analytical and reporting layers of the shared world view, are the simplest supports for this component. A track record of organizational surveys that assess employee satisfaction, talent utilization, or perhaps even a direct aggregate of the individual energy journals will allow the organization to summarize the journals of individuals into the organizational context. An available and easily accessible organization or team journal of learning is a great knowledge asset even in its simplest form, but the more structured and unified the measurement instrument, the more transparency. Therefore the more structured it is, the more potential there will be for organizational knowledge and wisdom.

So in general, the information and knowledge as well as the applications needed originate similarly to the applications for individual simulation. However as the entire organization is more complex than the individual OODA cycles, the building or acquiring of such applications will most likely be more costly in the short term. Even so, the effect will be worth it in terms of true synergic cooperation! If we look into the trend with personal productivity tools, it is not at all unlikely that the applications that already assist us in operational efficiency and effectiveness will allow us to have journals readily available when we operate within our area of responsibility in an organization. In the long term, these journals and the learning in relation to missions and goal setting will be the next natural step if such application emerges in the tools that allow personal productivity. Much like the PC evolved into the Internet, so could personal alignment tools in the personal productivity space evolve into tools that promote organizational synergic cooperation. However, at the first level these applications will most likely be in journal form as we already find them in CRM, but ahead of us is an interesting prospect of synergizing more with computers through simulation and perhaps even computer autonomy.

This component cannot live without a buy-in and a true expectation of win-win outcomes for the individual and the organization. Used successfully, this component can address practically any fear that is creating friction in the organization, and with a true intention of win-win, the track record of the initiative will create trust incrementally, and the effects will permeate the entire organization.

The initiative for organizational simulation relies heavily on the catalyst skills of senior management.

Talent and Core Competency Computing

This is an iterative learning process in which the OODA cycles as well as organizational simulations are monitored in order to rearrange and stimulate the process of building on talent and skills throughout the organization. This process is iterative because the hyper-volatile environment is continually changing, shaping the organization and the internal learning of it, which again shapes the need for core competency over time. Computing can also be applied to games and simulations in which talents and skills are discussed and revealed, including dedicated applications such as the StrengthFinder from Gallup. By its nature, the energized organization will continually attempt to adjust, stimulating the management's catalytic action. Although not as operationally involved as the managers, the leaders of the organization will also be able to benefit from insight in the overall status of the core competency when developing strategies.

The information and knowledge from this process is found by using the trustworthy shared world view in the organization, in particular by studying the OODA cycles' performance in terms of cycle time and learning curves. Additional information for gaming, simulation, and profiling can be gathered from the relevant dedicated applications.

Redesign or reassignment of skills and OODA cycles is a management task. However, this component is very important from a leader's perspective as a process of overall continuous assessment of the organization's capabilities, strengths, and weaknesses.

Customer Surveys and Competitor Assessments

This component is an external supplement to the trustworthy shared world view, as it can give a better understanding of the opportunities in and threats from the environment. However, it is important to note that we are dealing with information on factors we do not control, so such information should never be trusted more than the knowledge and wisdom that can be refined from the trustworthy shared world view.

This supplement is a relevant stabilization of organizational perceptions and a sanity check against the real world and can be a substitute for multiple probes if they consume too many organizational resources. The findings are only relevant briefly, as the rapid changes of the hyper-volatile environment will soon outdate them.

The surveys and assessments should preferably be conducted directly on the organization's information infrastructure such as the Internet or intranet, and the information should also be available for analysis without too much preparation. This both limits the resources needed to conduct them and ensures that the data do not become biased information. The data should speak for themselves, allowing patterns and clusters to emerge, because if too much time is spent grouping and categorizing data before the actual analysis, there is a risk that the purity of potential knowledge and wisdom will be polluted by biased data.

These external surveys and assessments are tools that leaders and managers can use whenever needed.

Computer Engineered Probes or Massive Empirics Probes

When we have all the previous CALM components in place, we can use this component to take action in the environment. This component is the leader's tool for setting the course and applying the thrust of the energized organization in order to reach its strategic objectives.

It is not a "fire and forget" approach like a heat-seeking missile, but a continuous strategizing process in which the organization evolves and adapts to the environment, heading always toward markets where its core competencies are most relevant. The computer support of this process can aid significantly in reducing the cost and time needed to develop the probe, and in the case of massive empirics it can even facilitate the discovery of effective courses of action that are not immediately obvious.

The actual applications for creating probes will probably be on the organization's servers. This is desirable, as it maximizes the available computing power and makes the process of sharing the results from a probe easier. The actual software can be CAD, or it can be simulations that either output blueprints for actual products or suggestions for marketing scenarios. In practice, organizations may find that there will be no standard software to support the simulation process, and indeed this makes sense since the organization's very core competency and market proposition are probably unique. This development task therefore needs experience in development and might require significant skills, but there are database and simulation platforms that can assist in this development.

Autonomous OODA Cycles

The OODA cycles are the power tool of the manager in an organization. The organization's energy and flexibility depend on the number of OODA cycles throughout the organization. By monitoring the OODA cycles, the manager has a tool to catalyze OODA cycles efficiency by applying the right mixture of core competency, computer support, and human resource.

The management mastery of this process keeps the organization alive; the pace and quality of the OODA cycles is the competitiveness of the organization, since it is here that it beats the competition in being the best fit for any given situation in the hyper-volatile environment. The management must ensure that maximum effect and speed are achieved with minimal energy consumption. Computers can eliminate friction by empowering individuals. Management should have the competency to apply computing in the way that generates synergy between human and computing potentials. If these potentials are applied wisely, they can be harvested in full. Depending on the process, the OODA cycle will in some cases be completed without human interference at all, and in others the OODA cycle will have significantly more human involvement. The manager needs to review each OODA cycle and evaluate whether human interference is really needed. This makes sense since organizations today are more collections of humans than computers, but computers are gradually displacing the human core competency needed in some OODA cycles.

The actual applications that run the autonomous OODA cycles are most likely modules that are plugged into the applications that already run the organization's operation as either standard components provided by existing vendors of the operational infrastructure or developed components within the environment provided by the vendor. The vendor or traditional business procedures might limit the availability of such autonomous OODA components, so for an infrastructure best positioned for today's and the future's hyper-volatile environment, it is important to think this step through before acquiring or updating operational systems.

The application of this component is a continuous process and an extremely important one for management in present and future organizations.

Mastering CALM through Balancing Energy, Leadership, and Management

If we think of the organization as an organism, the roles of the leader as a setter of the course and the manager as a catalyst are perhaps analogous to the conscious and unconscious processes that go on in the human body. Neither of them is more important than the other, and in their symbiosis they both have equally important meaning. Arising from this symbiosis is an amount of energy that can be used for any given purpose we decide upon; this purpose is traditionally first a matter of survival, and secondly a desire for success.

The role of leaders and managers is to identify the objectives for the organization that represent the biggest opportunities that can be reached with the least energy consumption. In practice, this means we should first understand the nature of the human and computer potential within the organization, and then decide how best to create the processes that will use the potential of both people and computers synergistically. Finally, we should identify the ideal objectives, the objectives that generate the most success for the organization with the least energy. This is the art of computer aided leadership and management, CALM.

It is important for managers and leaders to understand that CALM is a balance, since management is mostly about creating the environment to maximize organizational potential, and leadership is channeling the resultant energy where it will create the most benefit. Management and leadership are interdependent, because you can't channel energy until you have it, and unfocused energy will not achieve an objective.

Figure 9.1 is a summary of the CALM components and the suggested ownership in an organization.

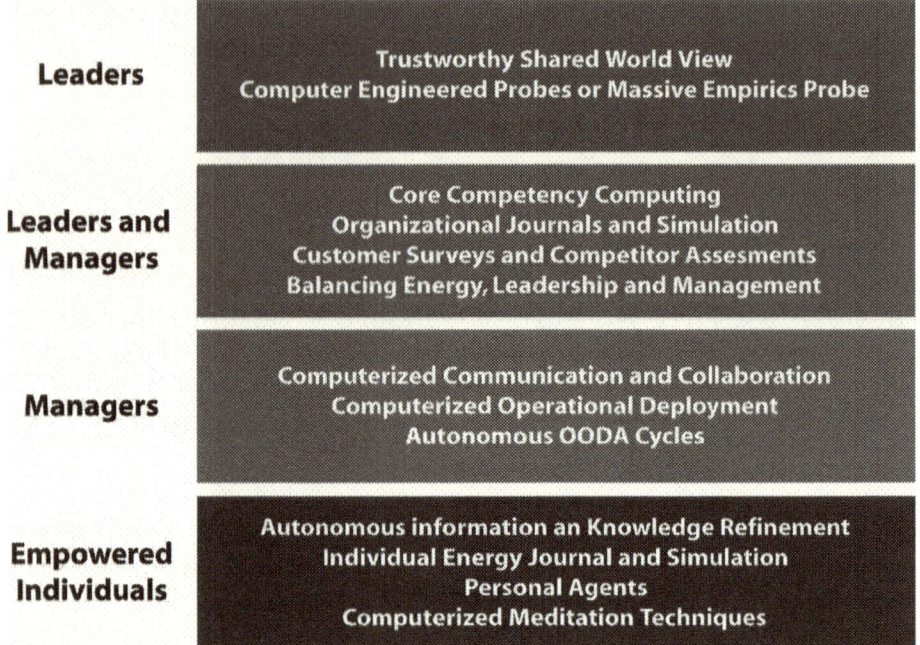

Figure 9.1 CALM Components and Their Ownership

When implementing CALM, one should be aware that whenever we are able to choose between a fully or partially computerized process, we are perhaps reluctant to choose the fully computerized process since we do not truly trust computers. However, playing safe and leaning toward human involvement means we are only going to benefit from a potential that develops in parallel with our human efficiency as opposed to the computer efficiency that develops exponentially. Therefore, to receive exponential gains by using the computer's full potential, we need to have the wisdom that will enable us to find synergic cooperation between computers and humans. This is a critical task for leaders and managers of organizations in the hyper-volatile environment. The only universal truth at the moment seems to be that the hyper-volatility of the world and the computing potential will grow. Therefore success or failure will be based on an organization's ability to use the computer and human potentials synergistically in a competitive environment.

Once the CALM components and their respective ownership have been identified, these components must be put to work in the organization. CALM is a symbiosis of visioning, computer systems, and culture; the culture is the hardest to change but by far the most important, since this is where we energize without fear. One cannot implement CALM overnight. It is a process in which synergy gradually displaces fear as people learn to trust the organization's computers. Implementation of the CALM process can, however, be divided into fundamental steps and subsequent benefits as well as steps that require more synergy between humans and computers, therefore requiring more trust. Taking these factors into consideration, I would divide a CALM process into the three steps as shown in figure 9.2.

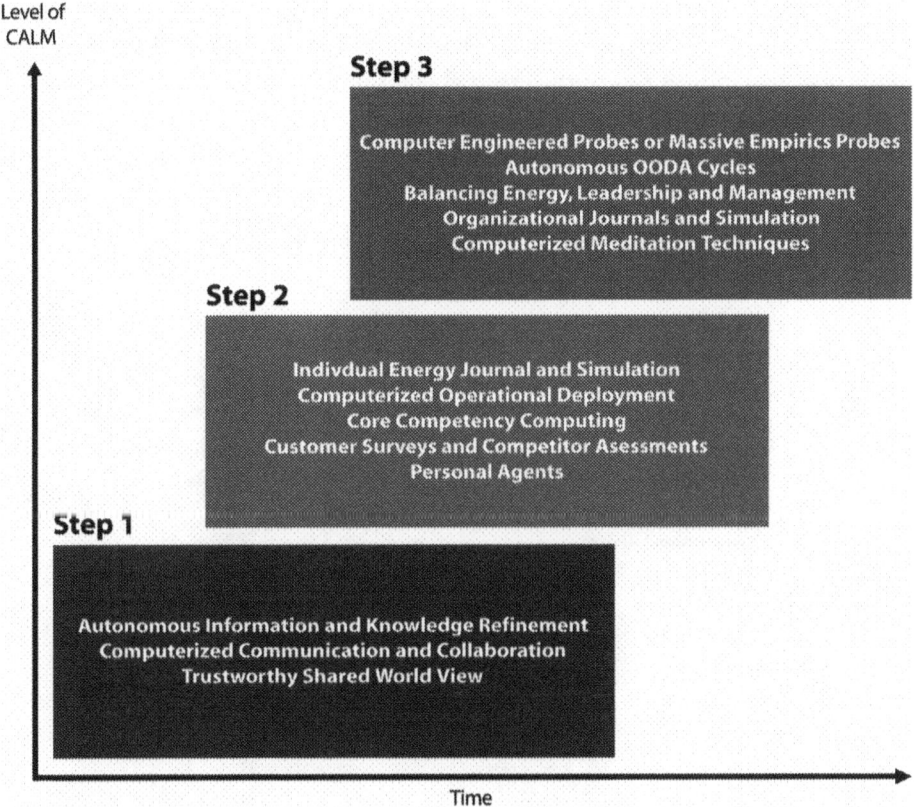

Figure 9.2 Three Steps to CALM

In my personal experience of having dealt with hundreds of organizations in the field of business intelligence, I have found that contemporary organizations are primarily striving to reach step 1. This can also be confirmed by industry analysts[121] in the market who deemed business intelligence the fastest-growing subsector in application software in May 2004. The statement is based on research primarily involving vendors of the tools that are intended to create a trustworthy shared world view based on the existing investments made in organizations' infrastructure.

The trend within organizations is for the focus to shift from analysis of financial figures only to sensing their external environment and understanding their core competencies. This was confirmed by a survey involving 355 participants from organizations ranging from small to large. The participants ranked the types of analysis they conduct today compared to what they think they should do three years from now.[122] As seen in figure 9.3, the overall trend is toward measurements that give indications of the external environment as well as internal knowledge about employee satisfaction and core competencies, as opposed to traditional factual financial figures. I would not argue that these facts are going to be used less in the future, but they are taken for granted and therefore are not expected to be of independent competitive importance.

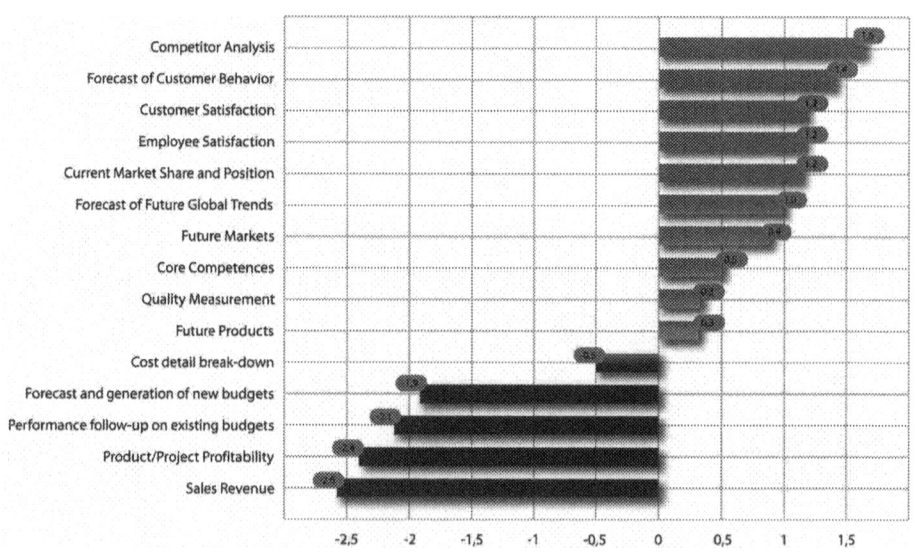

Figure 9.3 Findings from the Business Intelligence in the Future Study

In a deeper analysis, it was found that the larger the organization, the stronger the trend toward a wish to look at "customer satisfaction" and "future markets." Similarly, I found that the smaller the organization, the stronger the trend to look at "competitor analysis." Such trends could indicate that larger organizations that already operate on a global scale are relying more on their own ability to exercise core competency in terms of what they want to be for their customers and which markets they want to be in, rather than attempting to guesstimate the competitors' next move. This could indicate that larger organizations are leaning toward a hedgehog strategy in the hyper-volatile environment over the next couple of years. This is also an indication that the larger organizations envision themselves as being somewhere in between step 1 and 2 in the next three years.

From my experience in business intelligence over the past decade, it seems more than likely that smaller organizations will be doing tomorrow what large organizations are doing today. This is simply a consequence of the various computing technologies becoming more accessible in terms of pricing as well as more intelligent so that the smaller organizations can benefit from them without significant expenses in additional staff or training. The smaller organizations' need to be competitive with the larger ones in order to grow will make them more willing to accept the new technologies.

With these arguments, I believe it is fair to say that most organizations today are still striving to reach step 1 but are definitely willing to proceed at least to step 2. In theory, increased competition and the hyper-volatile environment will force them to evolve to step 3. In this context, it is important to note that we already have the computing technology to reach all three steps, so we do not need any new breakthroughs in technology to reach the full level of CALM. However, once the new inevitable breakthroughs come, the mindset of CALM will automatically absorb them since CALM is a continuous process of balancing and optimizing human and computer potential. The new breakthroughs will simply mean more potential, and markets will be won or lost through the leaders' ability to absorb this potential and turn it into action. The ability to harness the power of the latest breakthroughs will define the winners from an evolutionary perspective, and the best way to stay on top of the food chain is by continuing to practice CALM. We do not need to know very much about future technology, since our "feel" for the environment at the highest level of CALM will automatically let us take advantage of relevant technologies as they are probed and absorbed. However, let us now spend a few words reviewing at least some of the areas in which we can anticipate a few breakthroughs that will have a direct impact on the CALM concept.

The CALM Evolution

Having established the scope of the CALM concept, let us now turn to the trends in computing that will have direct impact over the next decade. Research into the societal learning curve suggests that new technology is not widely adopted in less than a decade, meaning that a new breakthrough technology that emerged today would probably not be widely available for one or two decades.[123] Depending on the definition, we could of course consider different meanings of *breakthrough technology* and *widely available*, using the examples below.

Space travel was a breakthrough in the 1960s, but it is hardly widely available today. The Internet has redefined the world as we know it in less than a decade, but its technology has been available since the 1970s.

The "Manhattan Project" to beat the Nazis to development of the first nuclear bomb commenced in 1942, based on a technology that emerged in 1938.[124] Three years later it changed history for the coming decades when the Cold War began. One could of course speculate that this radical development and application life cycle does not concern a technology that is broadly available, but indeed the fact that a breakthrough technology can mean significant changes in our world in less than a decade still stands.

However, in general, I believe that the technologies that will influence our lives during the next decade have already been conceived. Therefore this section is dedicated to the trends that are within the existing CALM components that I mentioned earlier. In the next chapter I will speculate further into the future, and history will tell whether some of these technologies should have been included in this section. The only certainty in the hyper-volatile environment is that things move at an increasing pace, but we should bear in mind that the adoption of new computing methods and other technologies is a human issue—at least for the time being. Therefore the pace with which we adopt these methods and technologies will perhaps tend to be unchanged even though the movement of potential is picking up speed.

With these arguments, let us consider the most plausible potential technological impacts during the next decade on the CALM components I have identified.

Transparency

The user interface will become increasingly transparent as computers becoming faster and both graphics and sound improve dramatically. In a more distant future we will be able to work with three-dimensional virtual environments that will improve the visibility of either analytical findings or simulated situations. The communication lines of these computers will allow us to have virtual face-to-face meetings regardless of the physical distance. All these factors will give us a sense of proximity and a closer relationship with the computer content. We will have better use of the data analysis in these environments, and thereby eliminate fear and shorten OODA cycles in the CALM organization. We will also be able to create more realistic simulations and virtual presence, both of which will enhance individual and organizational learning and communications abilities and even increase the interpersonal synergy in the organization.

The future capacity of computers will also be widely used to create interfaces that can communicate with speech, facilitating hands-free computer applications. Another idea is to capture some of the creativity that goes on outside the work-space. According to Mihaly Csikszentmihalyi, the most creative thinkers almost never come up with their ideas seated in front of the computer. Creativity comes to them at all sorts of times when inspiration hits, but perhaps future computers will allow us to capture these moments without the distraction of having to sit at a keyboard. Even better, perhaps the computer will not simply record the idea but also intelligently ping-pong with us to refine the idea.[125] A third option is to have computers translate speech on the fly, overcoming language barriers and enabling us to communicate multinationally. Although we might not be able to understand a culture simply by understanding what is said, this is the first step in doing so. All in all, there are a number of different uses of true-speech interfaces that will increase personal potential as well as communication and understanding of intent, even across language and cultural barriers.

In general, the speech, sound, and graphical environment will improve for computers, and they will become better at mimicking human behavior. Transparency of what we know today will be a natural consequence, but perhaps the ultimate application of this transparency is on the artistic level where computers will be able to create artwork in both picture and sound. Their artwork would have different meanings and could be either objects for relaxation or active communication. Computerized technology in this form has an interesting ability to communicate with humans on more than just the traditional mental level. The computer will eventually be able to address us on the emotional and perhaps even spiritual level as well. Granted, the first applications of this kind will not be able to create art forms like those of the humans they will be mimicking, but the ability to use the registers of communication will be there. During my work with R&D in the field of business intelligence, we at TARGIT have already conducted two successful experiments, one that generated computerized art based on the employee satisfaction in an organization, and one where music in a production facility changed according to the success or failure of the operation. These tests are only at the pioneering stage, and in the short term we would have human artists create artwork that has multiple emotional, mental, and spiritual layers that the computers could select among in the application. To evolve from this step, we would have to have human artists teach the computers how to create the layers autonomously. The computerized artist AARON, developed by Harold Cohen, has created paintings for nearly two decades, and it could perhaps serve as inspiration as well as knowledge that the reality of these things is much closer than we think. Such computing would take the availability of computer assistance to an entirely new level.

In summary, computers will evolve along the current trend in computing power, but interestingly the new applications arising from these possibilities will be able to expand and meet us as humans in entirely new situations and across a broader spectrum of human activities. Computers will be better at "playing ball with us," and stimulate the development of our potential.

Personal Synergies

The increase in processing power is inversely proportional to the size of computers. This means that we will be able to increase the processing power per cubic centimeter or, perhaps an even more appropriate measure, the cubic nanometer. Whatever the choice of measurement, it means that a world of better body-integrated computer applications will emerge because computers can be carried easily and almost invisibly. This means that from a personal perspective the computer will become ubiquitous, omnipresent, and therefore a whole new world of applications will become possible, as the computer will be able to assist us everywhere in physical space, and in a number of ways in the mental space.

The applications will evolve in three directions. First we will see traditional hand-held PDAs and cell phones merging into rich devices with unprecedented processing power, closely followed by new, more human-focused and experimental applications. In Tour de France, the worlds hardest bicycle race, the human physique is optimized by computer applications that monitor and manage the diet, heart rate, pedaling style, and power output of the racer.[126] Similar applications will emerge to assist people outside the elite sports arena to improve their physical condition. These applications span stress relief to general performance improvement for amateur fitness training.

One could anticipate that these computer applications will evolve into more than informative applications and directly interact with or even be integrated into our bodies; such applications already exist, but are not presently widely accepted. Perhaps we will find new inventive applications as a result of the acupuncture and meditation research already being conducted in the field of fMRI and EEG brain scans. Other areas in which we can expect additional development would be within the exercising equipment that massages and trains our muscles electronically. These techniques are becoming broadly available, but are still fighting for acceptance.

In general one could speculate that the most obvious places where we would seek to have the closest body integration would be to compensate for weaknesses and defects in our bodies, for example to assist people with disabilities. Much like plastic surgery that was initially intended for war victims, these techniques will be used and made broadly available to people who are seeking improvements to turn an average attribute into a strength. Perhaps the most interesting applications will emerge when we build computer and human synergies to improve strengths rather than compensate for weaknesses.

The development in human and computer interaction will be stimulated by the fact that not only computing, but also the tools needed to conduct research in the field will be less costly; and therefore breakthrough technologies that we cannot even begin to think of will probably emerge, since more people will be able to carry out the research. With more people researching and massive empirics becoming cheaper, interesting new breakthroughs in the human/computer integration are likely in this decade. Think about the broad availability of brain scanners and the tools needed to conduct research in the field of our mind. The broad availability of these applications is less likely to be influenced by the societal learning curve. However, these breakthroughs may very well be the "palms in the desert" for CALM leaders and managers.

Stress

As mentioned in the previous section, stress relief as a personal treatment is a very likely option as computing evolves. However as stress is becoming more and more the plague of the Western world, perhaps it is needed at more than a personal level. The evolution toward less stressful environments can be stimulated by computing, as we learned in Chapter 4, by coupling processes more loosely in order to have different people's performances peak at their own times. Bill Gates always claims e-mail is one of the single most important things to improve business processes;[127] and from a perspective of electronic global telepathy and the possibility of globally cooperation in less stressful environments, I would have to agree. But in this context the technology is really not the facilitator; humans are. If we use technology as a messenger, with the global society bursting in the door at all times, we are in fact doing quite the opposite. Simply the fact that the hyper-volatile environment will generate more and more traffic will make it increasingly important for humans to be selective and focus their energies. E-mail and other tools that don't provide global communications in real time, but allow for the individual's own priorities and timing, are effective tools to cope with this.

CALM practitioners should consider Stephen Covey's suggestion that the fourth generation of time management is about the things that are important, but not urgent.[128] Too much time has been dedicated to focusing on important and urgent issues; but perhaps this approach has the potential for losing the long-term opportunities and, even worse, ourselves. The issues in the important-but-not-urgent category are typically inspirational, personal, and interpersonal issues, all of which fuel our energies and eliminate fear. If we dedicate all our time to urgency, the stress level will go up, and we will be deprived of energy and synergic cooperation to find a cure for the urgency, remaining stuck in a personally stressed environment of continuous urgent problems.

Autonomy

The degree of autonomy in computing will be highly influenced by the fact that computer systems will be able to process more and more. Systems will become autonomous, working in real time instead of taking hours or days to analyze information and present findings. This means that they will be unable to work effectively unless people interconnect directly with the computer in the execution of a given task. Computing autonomy will also be driven by the emergence of new areas of computing that interrelate directly with humans on physical, emotional, mental, or perhaps even spiritual levels, sharing the same autonomic characteristics as our own nervous system, that is, making decisions without detailed instructions. At the organizational level there will also be processes that are either too costly or trivial to merit the commitment of human resources.

The techniques that computing will employ to gain autonomy in the next decade are the ones that we already know, so the only real difference between what we know as artificial intelligence, AI, today and what it will evolve into is that the systems will have much more computing power. The breakthrough technologies in the field will undoubtedly come, but they will not be able to make any significant impact in the next decade and therefore won't influence CALM significantly.

It should be noted that computer autonomy could also be fairly simple—many self-service applications are already available to us on the Internet. Many of these Web sites attempt to perform a better service through personalized offerings, many of which are based on simulation and artificial intelligence. The Amazon.com bookstore is one of the pioneers in this field. Interestingly, focus groups in the Danish telecommunications industry actually deemed the self-service applications to be a higher level of service than their human alternative, in that computers provided customers with faster responses and lower cost.[129] So in this case, not only do the autonomous OODA cycles service faster, they are actually in some cases also superior in service to humans!

The technologies we should be looking into are the traditional recurrent problem-solving methods: neural networks, fuzzy logic, and evolutionary algorithms that have already been around for decades. However, the potential for applying these techniques with computers, as their capacity evolves in terms of power and microscopic size, should not be underestimated. The autonomous completion of OODA cycles that seem to require human interaction should be scrutinized to understand which parts of the human energies are used in practice. If in fact no emotional or spiritual energy is involved, chances are that advanced computers can be trained to undertake the task. Another way to look at this is to investigate whether a computer is able to simulate the environment. We can benefit from training humans better and faster to complete the OODA cycle, but we could also have the computer train itself in the simulator and compare its performance to that of the human, and then assess the adequacy of the AI. The simulator will benefit us in both scenarios.

There will undoubtedly be many OODA cycles that can be successfully undertaken by autonomous computers as they become capable of processing massive inputs in real time at a level that matches the human head brain. Using simple forecasting of the current technological trends, this possibility will exist by 2020.[130] We should of course be wise about the implementation of such systems, as computers may very well displace human capacity in terms of some tasks that require mental energy, but on the other hand, none of these technologies will have anything that remotely resembles people's emotional and spiritual energy. In the next couple of decades, a computer will perhaps be able to mimic these human attributes by being trained by a human, but I will have to agree with Neil Postman, author of *Technopoly: The Surrender of Culture to Technology*, that the existing AI technologies do not enable computers to be programmed or train themselves to mimic or acquire these energies.[131]

Similarly to the OODA cycles, the massive empirics will be able to create new opportunities in terms of the time it takes to investigate problems. However, in this field the computer will have an alternative approach to the investigation, and thereby be able to do things that would normally require the spiritual energy of inspiration: the ability to intuitively improvise to uncover answers and solutions. This is actually quite an interesting phenomenon, since this is not a computer displacement of human skills and energy but a reengineering of the thought process. Such reengineering can perhaps also be done in some OODA cycles where it makes sense to have computers operating autonomously.

Although not covered by the CALM concept at this time, I can't help mentioning that of course nanoengineering and robotics will be able to create even more radical solutions to the operational and personal autonomy of computing. Intelligent materials that adapt to circumstances, such as for instance paint that rejects dirt, are already emerging; over time these fields will evolve into intelligent materials that are in fact made up of billions of microscopic computers. The uses of such materials are many, and from a CALM perspective there is no alternative to autonomous computing in such materials, since the micromanagement of each unit would be virtually impossible. What would the decision and action processes of a medical drug, which is really a number of nanoengineered robots operating on cell or even DNA level, look like if they were not autonomous? So in other words, if we want to benefit from the future prospects of nanoengineering, we might as well accept the autonomy of some processes in our operational environment today.

The Role of Leaders and Managers

Future leaders and managers will be the servants and the catalysts who apply computing wisely to organizations. The ability to create true human synergies with computing power will arise from the elimination of fear of computers as well as an understanding of the benefit or mere necessity of computerization in an organization. CALM leaders and managers will have to understand exactly where the sweet spot between human and computer cooperation is; to have this wisdom requires insight into both human and computer potential. In particular, the understanding of the strengths and weaknesses of both humans and computers is the key. Strengths must be built on to achieve the fullest potential cooperation. Leaders and managers should not fight the computers that will gradually displace some of the mental space that is currently occupied by humans. Fighting is unproductive energy since the evolutionary forces in the hyper-volatile environment will mean that competition will eventually be able to benefit from this. Organizations most fit for this environment are those with the wit to exploit and unleash the full potential of both humans and computing. If we free the energy that is used to occupy a niche that computers can fill, we might find that there is plenty of space in other areas of our human mind that is much more interesting; after all, our insight into our minds is the youngest science in the medical faculty.

In conclusion, let me simply note that the evolution of technology within the next decade will support the CALM concept, and it will absorb these technologies easily and convert it into energized organizations that are fit for survival and success in the Hyper-Volatile World of the tomorrows to come.

The Hypothesis Revisited

We now revert to the hypothesis from which we started and reflect on the findings and arguments so far in order to see if it can pass the test.

The evolution of man and computers has, in combination, rendered our world in a hyper-volatile state. This means, on one hand, that great achievements can be accomplished with little effort through the use of computers, while on the other hand it means that threats can "travel" effortlessly and rapidly toward us and strike at a pace that appears random. In essence, we perceive the Hyper-Volatile World as chaos.

With the arguments from Chapters 1 and 2, I find it hard not to accept the fact that the world is indeed hyper-volatile. The impact of the Hyper-Volatile World is indeed that we feel the pace picking up; in addition to this, there is not a single piece of evidence that suggests the opposite. The nomination of the human and computer combination as the main culprit in creating the hyper-volatile environment is in my mind also fairly well justified by the fact that the pace of global communication has been significantly increased by the Internet. It has given us unprecedented ability to share knowledge, and it has allowed this knowledge to take more diverse multimedia forms. This multiplication of global communication again fuels the hyper-volatility of the world. Finally, since we do not have the full picture, we as societies and organizations are continuously influenced by the hyper-volatile environment, and the technical definition of chaos from chaos theory is also fulfilled. Therefore, I do not believe there are any arguments in this part that suggest we should reject the hypothesis.

In the next section we explore the change in organizational energizing and strategizing as discussed in Chapters 3 through 8.

For an organization to succeed in the Hyper-Volatile World, the traditional strategies and long-term planning cycles are inferior to tactics that seek to seize the moment. The reason for this is that time is more important than the other traditional limiting resources: people and finance. In addition, it will be virtually impossible to predict action and reaction, which is the key to strategy formulation. If an organization accepts its environment as unpredictable, it can start working constructively with all its strength and energy and continuously strive toward survival and success.

The strategizing process is specifically discussed in Chapter 7, in which we concluded that the ability to probe and sense the environment appears to be an appropriate alternative to more long-term strategy formulation. The agility of an energized organization is discussed in Chapters 5 and 6. It appears obvious that organizations with the combined energy for survival through an interconnected set of more or less autonomous OODA cycles in combination with a strategizing process that takes the unpredictability of the hyper-volatile environment into account, will be superior to practically anything else. As there is no immediate alternative to such an organization, there is not any evidence to suggest that this part of the hypothesis should be rejected either.

Finally, we turn to the redefinition of the role of leadership and management of these energized organizations.

If we break the organization into its components in order to ensure the maximum effect in any given situation, we find that there is some inherent unused potential in the utilization of both individual human capacity and computer capacity. In addition, this unused potential can be accumulated and used by an organization. It is the challenge for leaders and managers today and in the future to understand their environment and apply the unused potential of their organizations to get the energy needed for survival and success.

The human and computer potential that is available is not the same as most organizations apply, as discussed in Chapter 2. Therefore leaders and managers should seek this potential actively. The idea of breaking the organization into multiple OODA cycles is simply a matter of unleashing this combined potential without creating an organizational managerial bottleneck. This also makes sense even if we consider how organisms in general cope with the environment that shaped their evolutionary lines. So the world will shape the organization: the winning organizations will allow themselves to be shaped and will harvest the opportunities offered by the environment. Computers are accelerating the environmental change process to hyper-volatility; therefore computers are probably the best choice for creating the organizational flexibility needed to evolve.

The computerization of tasks enables the organization to survive by adapting to, and being shaped by, the environment. The organization can even be energized on a new level of potential, a potential that can create victories and successes in the hyper-volatile environment. The wisdom of leaders and managers in computerizing the organization to increase energy, as discussed in Chapters 3 through 6, as well as the leaders' and managers' ability to exercise computer aided leadership and management, CALM, will lead to the benefits of full use of potential, as discussed in Chapter 7 and forward. Since computing builds and liberates the potential, CALM will be the most vital generic leadership and management component in the next decade. Adopting the CALM concept will also ensure that the organization continuously upgrades itself to exploit new technological as well as market opportunities. It is not a specific system, but a mindset in the collective synergic mind of the organization.

With these arguments, I find that the hypothesis stands, and I hope that you as the reader will agree with me in accepting this hypothesis.

In the following chapter, I will share with you some ideas that have arisen from researching and writing the book this far. The ideas are merely speculations, since they deal with the longer-term future of CALM. However, they are anchored in the trends and findings so far. Therefore I hope you will excuse me and accept the risk profile of venturing into the more distant future with me in the next chapter.

10

CALM Speculations

Synergic Evolution

I have always found it fascinating to speculate on where my skepticism would limit my thoughts and conclude that some things would not be technologically possible. Think back a few generations to our grandparents and further to their parents. To them, a little more than a century ago, flight may have seemed impossible, but today the idea that a plane can fly is not disputed at all. How about their perception of a trip in space to the Moon, or missions to Mars? Such suggestions might have been even worse, unless of course they were visionaries. Then think about the Internet: in reality it is teleportation of electronic thoughts, a world in which we are wirelessly and globally connected. Would such an abstract thought have even occurred to them, or even myself two decades ago? My point is that there are two limitations to thought: one is whether we think something is possible, and even if we do not have this limitation, the mere thought might not even be present as it is too far out of reach from where we stand today.

In Edwin A. Abbott's novel *Flatland*, written in 1884, there is a humorous lesson in geometry, which at the same time teaches lessons of higher dimensions as well as psychological closed-mindedness. A citizen from the two-dimensional world called Flatland encounters a sphere from the three dimensional world, Spaceland. Having great difficulty understanding the concept of space, he is finally led to be aware of a third dimension, and suddenly he realizes the emptiness of having not had this dimension. The notion of the third dimension then allows him to venture even further into a Thoughtworld in which fourth, fifth, and more dimensions become conceivable and therefore possible—at least in thought.[132] The idea of a presence of things that are simply beyond our reach physically is, in my mind, conceivable, but reading Abbott's novel intuitively poses the question of whether or not this also limits our thoughts. However, if we follow the path through Flatland to Spaceland, this first step is able to trigger even deeper ventures physically, mentally, and spiritually. In other words, if we are willing to take the first step, the result might be even more openness and ability to think. Perhaps the developments in the past century have already provided this platform of openness? It seems hard—at least to me—to see a boundary that we can be certain will not be pushed through over the years.

Another way of looking at possibilities is to consider what we can actually say will definitely not become a reality. The very nature of evolution means we have indeed ended up where we are today simply because nature found a way. When we think about the ultimate challenge of evolution—life—what is in fact logical about some single-celled organisms in the sea emerging into a life form that eventually became humans who, at this stage of our evolution, can now discuss whether we are the only beings that have a state of mind, the ability to choose our reaction to a stimuli, the ability to travel from our planet, and so on? If we consider our own evolutionary stages during the past millions of years through contemporary science, would we have thought our lives today possible?

In my mind there is only one certainty: the things we can dream will happen, and the things that we do not dream of today will be the dreams of tomorrow. Sure, we might overestimate the short-term effects and underestimate the long-term effects. That is a classic problem for most visionaries,[133] but things will happen! That is, in reality, the only certainty we have.

From this perspective let us now consider the evolutionary paths ahead, and consider that the evolution of the computer is a fragment of human evolution. What is in reality the logic of computers not developing a sense of intelligence that is much more advanced than what we call artificial intelligence today? At what point would we call it "real intelligence," and finally a spirit? Obviously, the technology would have to go through some rather salient events from where it is today, but so did the human evolutionary chain. At the point we are at today, I believe we should not consider "if"; we should consider "when." Ray Kurzweil's writings suggest that by 2029 we should expect that adding computer enhancements to our brains will be possible, and by 2099 it will be impossible to participate in the global debate unless we have them. Computer-aided human brains will at that point be a matter of social survivability; those who do not survive socially will eventually become extinct or form another evolutionary line.

Another interesting point in Kurzweil's suggestions is that in 2029, not only will humans debate whether computers are truly intelligent, but computers them-selves will participate actively in the debate.[134] To me, these thoughts might very well be wrong in time, but they are not wrong as dreams. Hence, they will all become part of a future reality; all that is left for now is the position of this future in time.

There are two perspectives in these dreams. One is the human and computer evo-lutionary chains becoming interrelated, and another is the evolutionary chain of computers alone. The latter will be discussed later in this chapter, but let us for now consider the perspectives of a synergic evolution between humans and com-puters.

The idea that computers will be able to tap into our brains, or that we will be able to tap into the computer through our brains, is not that far ahead. My guess is that the initial research will be able to reconstruct an image from the human mind in less than twenty years; successful experiments in which the classic com-puter game Pong was guided by two players using a brain scanner each have already been conducted. Additionally, the visual cortex, which controls our per-ception of sight, has been very well researched already, and it is also pretty linear to map, since it is possible to identify the individual areas of our eye all the way to the visual cortex. It is even possible to distinguish the different ways we perceive sight in terms of color, depth, and so on. It is therefore not unlikely that in a short time it will be possible to generate a visual computer image of what the eyes of a person see.[135] Such ability could easily evolve into the construction of a human eye or an alternative thereto, and, much like plastic surgery that was ini-tially intended for victims of war, the initial goal of this technology will most likely be a cure for blindness and age-related eye disabilities. However, much like the way plastic surgery evolved to become a tool for people seeking beauty, this technology could perhaps become a way for people who want vision that is beyond the normal human potential. The first computerized step in evolution would then be considering a battlefield in which an enemy was engaged by humans with night vision or thermal vision, or perhaps even X-ray vision. My guess is that in warfare such an evolution would mean that those who did not master this evolutionary step would eventually become extinct.

This technology has even more promising propositions for more peaceful appli-cations. There is still some way to go before we can see an actual thought; the

Pong experiment was indeed mind-guided computing in a primitive form, but the computer was guided using different thoughts and concentration that activated neurons in either the left or the right side of the brain. In other words, thinking of mathematics would move the cursor one way, and thinking of love experiences would move it the other.[136] Research like this, in combination with the fact that the visual cortex is probably the best-mapped part of our brain so far, could promise that in a not-so-distant future a computer could be guided by a human mind simply by imagining in the visual center what we would like to see or happen.

Even more interesting, to my mind, is the recent research conducted by the leading Danish neuroscience institute that concluded that the part of the brain that is activated when working with active sight is also activated during sleep.[137] Such findings suggest that perhaps further research into this field as well as the field of technologically enhanced sight will be able to create a digitally rendered image from the brain. Such technological findings along with technological application could possibly evolve into the display of dreams, at least during some of the sleep stages. Exploration of the visual cortex is just the beginning, as more parts of our brain will be researched and understood to the extent that we can tap into them as well; this will most likely allow a much more holistic application of computing where all three brains deliver input and perhaps receive stimuli, as opposed to just the one in the head. Such a technology would be able to read thoughts more broadly than simply from the visual spectrum; it would also be able to read emotions and spiritual energy levels. Effectively, the more we know about the workings of our brains, the better we will be able to create the hardware and software needed to read, repair, or enhance our brains. It does not seem unlikely that in the future we will be able to understand the synaptic energies sufficiently well to at least repair and enhance the brain with computer technology. Further down the road we might be able to use computers to read the actual content of a brain.

I would hesitate, though, to say that this development will be available in two decades, but to my mind it will most likely be in its infancy by then.

It is interesting to note that, much like the evolutionary steps that can be generated by the computer-aided mapping of the genome, it will not be possible to do the research to influence the evolution of computers into our mind without using computers. So computers are not only on the verge of becoming part of our evolutionary path, they are also aiding it in becoming so. One of the approaches in this process could very well be techniques like massive empirics; and an interesting perspective for the research that computers can assist in is perhaps in the fields that we already intuitively have an expectation of, but do not have significant empirics to back up our intuitive ideas. Although this approach does not necessarily cover the unthought of ideas mentioned earlier, it is a way to reach an understanding of the heritage our ancestors left us, and perhaps unleash the potential that we somehow lost in the era of enlightenment by modern science.

I have always wondered what we would find if we applied modern computing in the areas of the mystics and the occult. Perhaps we might be able to view them in an entirely new light. I do not think we will find exact knowledge of our soul through this path, but the spice of a mindset from ancient times could leverage our science to another level. In this context, consider the field of astrology; for centuries we have used it to try to predict the future. However, we do not need to adopt a fatalistic approach to use such methods. When I was researching in this field I had the opportunity to discuss the relevance of astrology with some professional astrologers, and one of them described the idea that all planets send out a vibration or energy that varies in strength at different times according to the planets' position in relation to earth; each of these energies will influence us to be more disposed to certain moods and perhaps actions. We know for instance that the Sun can influence our mood, and that the Moon has a visible influence on the tidal water and on some people's ability to sleep, and certainly on some people's psychological stability. All planets in our solar system are in between the distance of the Moon and the Sun, so why would we think that they had no influence at all? We can of course fight against these energies, but that requires more energy than if we followed the flow. Perhaps astrology is simply another way of describing the psychological phases or biorhythms, and as such there is no causal effect from the planets on the individual; the astrology simply works as a universal clock. But whatever the findings may be, the facts that our ancestors practiced such disciplines since what appears to be the dawn of our time should at least make us curious enough to apply the latest computing powers to investigate their relevance rather than dismissing it as irrational or illogical.

My reason for suggesting astrology, in particular, is that if it proves to be relevant, computers could easily support it, as much of astrological prediction is done using pure mathematics. Therefore astrology has a short-term potential for becoming the best approximation to a human-computer interface in which the computers that already exist today could start "sensing," or rather simulating the sensing, of the human mind and moods.

Moving forward into the computers that in a few decades will perhaps be able to see our thoughts, how about working with dreams and even the visions of people with clairvoyant abilities? In the sci-fi movie *Minority Report* a system consisting of three clairvoyant individuals, joining forces in a computer system that read and displayed their thoughts, was used to fight crime before it happened. The term "minority report" was used when the clairvoyants did not see the same thing; in this case the system was less reliable. Again, it is not up to me to argue whether or not seeing into the future is possible for any human, but the idea of the human mind seeing images of great visions would at least give us inspiration and fuel new dreams, and at best allow us to get new insight into ourselves, our minds, and perhaps even our souls.

In my mind there is no doubt that synergic evolution is the most likely scenario for the future, simply because computers will aid us in unleashing human potential. What alleys of inspiration we will choose remains to be seen, but why not at least have the curiosity to investigate what some of our ancestors considered wisdom; isn't this the courtesy to history that we would like future generations to exercise with our contemporary knowledge and wisdom?

The Ghost in the Machine

If we turn now to the computer evolution alone, I found myself inspired by Hans Moravec's *Robot: Mere Machine to Transcendent Mind*, and through a linear mindset it is not hard to imagine that future generations of robots will surpass anything we know today in terms of computing power per size and price unit. In a slightly deeper future, one would also be anticipating nanoscale engineering and quantum computing. Moravec theorizes on the potential of artificial intelligence in the sense of what one would normally refer to as the mind or soul. Moravec supports the idea that "a ghost in the machine" could be shaped by evolution just as much as by humans. This opens up a whole world of opportunities in itself.[138] Consider the fact that it takes one life of development to foster the brain children of humans, that is, children that not only take over our form but also our knowledge and behavior. The mind children of intelligent robots could be born at the speed of download; at the current pace of technological trends, computers will have the same potential for brain power as humans by 2020, so surely we must expect new technological breakthroughs to bridge the gap from the current level of artificial to "real" Intelligence for a new breed of mind children to evolve, but the idea that computers themselves will evolve to at least the extent possible through in massive empirics is hardly unexpected.

If this seems radical, consider this: the current stage of our research into time travel is in its infancy, yet theories like Einstein's General Theory of Relativity suggest that the speed of light as well as infinite matter should come into play if one considers traveling in time—or should we say beyond physical laws as we define them today? Whatever the definition, it seems easier to think of systems at nano-or quantum-scale traveling or working at the speed of light or beyond, perhaps simply by encoding a message in light and allowing the data to travel. Thinking about such exotic systems suddenly opens the possibility of creating output at the same time the input is present, or even faster than the input is present! How would we label such systems? Intelligent, because they would be matching the reaction and stimuli patterns of a human and even be able to outperform them in many tasks, based on superiority in time.

If you have worked with programming, you are probably familiar with the simple program "Hello World," the entire purpose of which is basically a dialogue that says the name of the program. At the time of writing, the most likely potential traveler in time is perhaps the "Hello Future" program, which in my mind would be similar to "Hello World," but would include a timestamp and be transmitted at a speed greater than the speed of light into the future. This simple thought experiment would not require any more computing than we have today; we would simply need the super-light-speed cabling to transmit our virtual traveler.

It is hard to imagine the practical methods that are needed for time travel to become a reality, and perhaps it never will. But the idea that something travels from one place to another in less time than other things is in itself a relative time travel. Computers have that ability and advantage over humans. Whatever we would call an intelligence that actively exploits this is irrelevant; what is relevant is that it would surpass anything we know today even if we do not succeed in moving through time.

Another provocative example is the idea of wiring a computer into a human brain or even more brains, effectively making a fluent interface between humans and computers. Since we start with an entire human and a computer, few would dispute that in fact there is a soul or at least an intelligence present. But what would happen if we then started removing parts? At what level would we draw the line and say that we are not dealing with a soul but merely a computer? And would it matter if it told us what it was? Vice versa, would we consider a person with an artificial heart and a brain prosthesis a human or a computer? These thought experiments only go to show that it is hard to determine specifically where the mind and the soul resides, and where our human energies originate. Our contemporary science really only offers us a binary life/no-life answer, but in reality life and evolution is much more complex.

Life and Computers

An unexamined life is not worth living

—Socrates

I predict that in the future the evolution of humans and computers will be integrated in the sense that we as human beings will become more and more dependent on computers, most likely to the same extent that computers are now dependent on us. Therefore I have deliberately integrated the two into one line of evolution. Some may be reluctant to accept this perspective, and argue that an evolutionary process is a biological process that happens to one species, but what relevance does this have if the very life of one species is dependent on the parallel evolution of another "species"? We should consider a process evolutionary to the extent that it is not only reproductive in a biological sense, but it is the mind children that are the key as knowledge and wisdom in the Hyper-Volatile World becomes more and more important. Therefore the interdependency of people and computing is becoming stronger, and our mind children will be partially human and partially computers; our thoughts will reside in both.

The life of humans will be inseparable from computers, and perhaps it will even be hard to distinguish when the actual magic of life originates in one or the other, as mentioned in the AI examples earlier. The boundaries between computers and humans will not be easy to define once they start sharing the same life of an individual.

To me, the human benefits are far greater than the disadvantages, therefore we should not think of this as a hostile takeover of our lives by computers; we should consider them our allies in life. Future developments in life-saving medicines, food technologies, energy sources, planetary protection from natural disasters, and much more will be possible only through the power of the computer. Nothing will move forward faster than a mutual relationship in trust, which will be able to facilitate the win-wins to move the relationship further. As explained by Bill Joy in "Why the Future Doesn't Need Us," this is also the case; we voluntarily swap jobs with computers and thereby gradually turn over the world to the computers in exchange for lives of leisure and prosperity. Therefore Joy looks at the globe from an existence perspective and rationalizes that it does not need us.

In my mind this is not a likely scenario; humans will gradually turn over some human tasks to computers, even tasks we do not dream of today, but we will have an inherent longing for meaning and an even deeper exploration of life. The life that will emerge from the excessive computing powers combined with human wisdom will pose more new questions than we will get answers. When working with business intelligence and analytics we usually say, as a rule of thumb, that one answer generates five new questions on another level. I believe this is indeed the truth for the exploration of the boundaries of life as well. If we look into the history of the latest discoveries in the field of psychology and neuroscience, we cannot but wonder what would happen if we managed to free up time with the help of unprecedented computing power in other areas to start exploring these short-lived historical findings fully. Surely computers will displace some of the tasks and knowledge domains of humans, but my guess is that this displacement will simply allow humans to evolve to another level in areas that at any given time will give meaning to and be highly relevant for the evolution of life on this globe and other places. If this is the case, then humans are in for an interesting acceleration of the evolutionary process of our own species, because we will be accelerating our mind children in accordance with computing power, which, at least from what we know today, will be evolving exponentially.

What we will find in such a future will be a mystery for any human living today, but it is interesting to note that the periods between incidents of evolutionary progress in intelligence and culture are getting shorter and shorter. This means that at any moment we could be on the verge of new and exciting breakthroughs. On the other hand, having worked with decision making and statistics for quite a while, I find it grotesque that our arrogance causes us as humans to fail to see the possibilities that arise from the fact that the human era is just a short breath in the life of the universe. What, apart from our inherent fear of change, makes us reject the possibility of life on other planets in other solar systems? Wouldn't no life be less probable from a pure statistical perspective? Or how about another culture on this planet that reached a very high cultural and technological level long before the culture we know today emerged? Even in the era of *Homo sapiens* there should be sufficient time for such an incident, its doom just needed to be more than 5,000 years old. There would have been sufficient time, since a culture can emerge and disappear in less than 60,000 years according to our own interpretations of prehistory; at least that was what happened to the Neanderthals.[139]

Obviously, some or perhaps all of these questions will remain unanswered for perhaps centuries or even millennia, but in the mystery of life there should at least be room for both humans and computers to unleash their full potential to their mutual benefit—there is plenty of wisdom to be found in areas that are still unexamined today, and there most certainly will be in the future as well.

Concluding Remarks

This book has been my summary of personal and researched perspectives of utilizing the full human potential through the use of computers. The term CALM is not just an acronym for the Computer Aided Leadership and Management; it is just as much a word that summarizes my perspective on the future in a part of my life where I can say that I have been engaged with computers for more years than I have not. From this perspective I see a future where humans can be more at peace, where computers can relieve us of some of the fear that wears us down, both personally and interpersonally. Such a world would, to my mind, allow us to lead our lives more calmly. In many ways the Hyper-Volatile World can sound fierce and scary, but it is simply a world in which dreams are becoming realities with less effort. Intuitively I would think that the only species that will become extinct in such a world are those who oppose people thinking and dreaming freely: for those types of regimes, the exponential countdown to extinction is on from the simple fact that the hyper-volatility of the world can not be stopped or contained, and it is a catalyst in the transition from thoughts to reality.

As my personal inspiration for computers has been the ability to create the best possible human and computer interface, I have also enjoyed reading the works of the Danish-born Guru in Usability, Jakob Nielsen; perhaps his perspective on computing in 2034 really sums up the optimism that I also find significantly justified: "*If we keep human needs in mind and harness the increased computer power appropriately, there will be great and exciting things ahead in our field.*"[140]

If we buckle up for the exciting times ahead and are willing to change with the world as it changes us, then it is hard not to be optimistic. And although it is hard to predict—especially about the future, as the Danish humorist Robert Storm Pedersen stated—at least from a statistical standpoint we can conclude that if our species is offered the same global hospitality as were the dinosaurs that walked the earth for about 135 million years compared to humans having only accounted for about half a million years so far, it seems fair to say that our time appears to be far from the end. This is merely the beginning.

Endnotes

1. Ray Kurzweil, *The Age of Spiritual Machines: When Computers Exceed Human Intelligence* (Penguin Putnam, 2000), 67–68.

2. Bill Joy, "Why the Future Doesn't Need Us," *Wired Magazine*, April 2000, http://www.wired.com/wired/archive/8.04/joy.html.

3. Dan Jensen, "Joint Strike Fighter rammer Danmark (Joint Strike Fighter hits Denmark)," *Computer World On-Line*, April 2004, http://www. computerworld.dk/default.asp?Mode=2&ArticleID=23740.

4. G. E. Moore, *Electronics* 38, no. 8, (19 April 1965).

5. Jakob Nielsen, "Global Web: Driving the International Network Economy," personal Web site, 1998, http://www.useit.com/alertbox/980419.html.

6. Rich Evans, "META Report: Room at the Data Center?" *EarthWeb*, August 2001, http://itmanagement.earthweb.com/datbus/article.php/858901.

7. Ray Kurzweil, *The Age of Spiritual Machines: When Computers Exceed Human Intelligence* (Penguin Putnam, 2000), 280.

8. Peter F. Drucker, *The Effective Executive* (HarperCollins Publishers, 1993).

9. Neil Postman, *Technopoly: The Surrender of Culture to Technology* (Vintage Books USA, 1993), 34–35.

10. "Nash Equilibrium," *Wikipedia*, free encyclopedia on the Web, http://en.wikipedia.org/wiki/Nash_equilibrium.

11. Garnett P. Williams, *Chaos Theory Tamed* (National Academy Press, 1997), 218.

12. Eric K. Clemons and Jason A. Santamaria, "Maneuver Warfare: Can Modern Military Strategy Lead You to Victory?" *Harvard Business Review*, April 2002.

13. Richard Florida, *The Rise of the Creative Class* (New York: Basic Books, 2002), 44, 47.

14. Age of the universe found at NASA Web site, www.nasa.gov. http://imagine.gsfc.nasa.gov/docs/science/mysteries_l1/age.html.

15. Age of Earth found at U.S. Geological Survey Web site, www.usgs.gov. http://pubs.usgs.gov/gip/geotime/age.html.

16. Marcus Buckingham and Curt Coffman, *First, Break All the Rules: What the World's Greatest Managers Do Differently* (Simon & Schuster, 1999), 80.

17. Dr. C. George Boeree, "Sigmund Freud," http://www.ship.edu/~cgboeree/freud.html.

18. Robert K. Cooper, *The Other 90%: How to Unlock Your Vast Untapped Potential for Leadership and Life* (New York: Crown Publishing Group, 2001), xvi.

19. Stephen M. Edelson, "Autistic Savant," Center for the Study of Autism, Salem, Oregon, 1995, http://www.autism.org/savant.html.

20. Kenneth Sylvan Guthrie, Diogenes Laertius, and Joscelyn Godwin, *The Pythagorean Sourcebook and Library: An Anthology of Ancient Writings Which Relate to Pythagoras and Pythagorean Philosophy* (Phanes Press, 1987), 19.

21. JOC/EFR, "René Descartes," School of Mathematics and Statistics, University of St. Andrews, Scotland, 1997, http://www-gap.dcs.st-and.ac.uk/~history/Mathematicians/Descartes.html.

22. S. S. Yoo, E. K. Teh, R. A. Blinder, and F. A. Jolesz, "Modulation of Cerebellar Activities by Acupuncture Stimulation: Evidence from fMRI Study," Department of Radiology, Brigham and Women's Hospital, Harvard Medical School, Boston, MA 02115, USA.

23. S. W. Lazar, G. Bush, R. L. Gollub, G. L. Fricchione, G. Khalsa, and H. Benson, "Functional Brain Mapping of the Relaxation Response and Meditation," Department of Psychiatry, Harvard Medical School, Massachusetts General Hospital-East, NMR Center, Charlestown 02129, USA.

24. fMRI stands for "functional magnetic resonance imaging." It is a process in which the blood and oxygen levels in the brain can be monitored; these

levels vary with the levels of neuron activity, and changes in them are therefore indications of neuron activity.

25. Edutainment is a term used for combined education and entertainment software applications.

26. Jim Collins, *Good to Great: Why Some Companies Make the Leap and Others Don't* (HarperBusiness, 2001).

27. Peter F. Drucker, *The Effective Executive* (HarperCollins Publishers, 1993).

28. Stephen R. Covey, *Seven Habits Of Highly Effective People* (Free Press, 1990), 68–70.

29. James A. Lovell, "Houston, We've Had a Problem," chapter 13 of online book *Apollo Expeditions to the Moon* (NASA, 1975), www.nasa.gov.

30. Sjak Svenstorp, "Frømandskorpset (Frogman's Corps)," MeMeMedia, 2000, www.mememedia.dk, 109–110.

31. Robert K. Cooper, *The Other 90%: How to Unlock Your Vast Untapped Potential for Leadership and Life* (New York: Crown Publishing Group, 2001), 16–19. Describes the three brains and their respective functions in the gut, heart, and head. The term brain is used based on the impact they each have on bodily functions.

32. Stephen R. Covey, *Seven Habits Of Highly Effective People* (Free Press, 1990), 47–48.

33. Kevin Craine, "The Cycle of Change," *The Data Administration Newsletter*, 2000, http://www.tdan.com/i014fe02.htm.

34. Stephen R. Covey, *Seven Habits Of Highly Effective People* (Free Press, 1990), 270.

35. "Game theory," *Wikipedia*, free encyclopedia on the Web, http://en.wikipedia.org/wiki/Game_theory.

36. Marcus Buckingham and Donald O. Clifton, *Now, Discover Your Strengths* (Simon & Schuster, 2001), 6.

37. Laurence J. Peter, *The Peter Principle* (William Morrow & Co, 1969).

38. Marcus Buckingham and Curt Coffman, *First, Break All the Rules: What the World's Greatest Managers Do Differently* (Simon & Schuster, 1999), 177–181.

39. Anthony Stevens, *Jung: A Very Short Introduction* (Oxford University Press, 2001), 86–87.

40. Stevens, *Jung: A Very Short Introduction*, 87.

41. Stevens, *Jung: A Very Short Introduction*, 89–90.

42. Peter Urs Bender, *Gutfeeling: Instinct & Spirituality @ Work* (Achievement Group, 2002), 197–198.

43. Roderick M. Kramer, "When Paranoia Makes Sense," *Harvard Business Review*, July 2002.

44. Patrick J. Robinson, "Research Update #88: Progressive Organizational & Personal Learning," *Journal of Consumer Research*, March 1996, Robinson Consulting Inc.

45. Marcus Buckingham and Curt Coffman, *First, Break All the Rules: What the World's Greatest Managers Do Differently* (Simon & Schuster, 1999), 56–57.

46. Morten Middelfart, "Business Analytics: From Chosen Few to Common World View," personal Web site, December 2002, http://www.morton.dk/articles/bastudy.shtml.

47. Investment Prospectus, "Ambient Devices," May 2004, www.ambientdevices.com.

48. Tony Foster, *The Bush Pilots: A Pictorial History of a North American Phenomenon* (Authors Choice Press, 2000), 21–33.

49. Mihaly Csikszentmihalyi, *Flow: The Psychology of Optimal Experience* (New York: Harper & Row Publishers, 1990), 39.

50. Spencer Johnson, *Who Moved My Cheese? An Amazing Way to Deal with Change in Your Work and in Your Life* (Putnam, 1998).

51. Marcus Buckingham and Donald O. Clifton, *Now, Discover Your Strengths* (Simon & Schuster, 2001), 41–61.

52. Robert K. Cooper, *The Other 90%: How to Unlock Your Vast Untapped Potential for Leadership and Life* (New York: Crown Publishing Group, 2001), 98.

53. According to Rap Dictionary, www.rapdict.org: It is probably Jamaican, in which case it comes from the TV game shows, Master of Ceremonies (although the term existed before TV). It was the only person at a gather-

ing that was allowed to use the microphone. "The term, MC, stands for Master of Ceremonies"—A Tribe Called Quest (Midnight Marauders, 1993).

54. Erwin Rommel, *Infantry Attacks* (1937; repr., London: Greenhill Books, 1990).

55. William S. Lind, *Maneuver Warfare Handbook* (Boulder, CO: Westview Press, 1985), 4–5.

56. Eric K. Clemons and Jason A. Santamaria, "Maneuver Warfare: Can Modern Military Strategy Lead You to Victory?" *Harvard Business Review*, April 2002.

57. Marcus Buckingham and Curt Coffman, *First, Break All the Rules: What the World's Greatest Managers Do Differently* (Simon & Schuster, 1999), 115.

58. Rober Slater, *29 Leadership Secrets from Jack Welch* (McGraw-Hill, 2003), 19.

59. Bill Gates, *Business @ the Speed of Thought* (New York: Warner Books, 2000), 15.

60. Gary Hamel and C. K. Prahalad, *Competing for the Future* (Boston, MA: Harvard Business School Press, 1994), 30.

61. Vivek Ranadivé, *The Power of Now: How Winning Companies Sense & Respond to Change Using Real-Time Technology* (McGraw-Hill, 1999)

62. S. C. Mednick, K. Nakayama, J. L. Cantero, M. Atienza, A. A. Levin, N. Pathak, and R. Stickgold, "The Restorative Effect of Naps on Perceptual Deterioration," *Nature Neuroscience* 5, no. 7 (July 2002): 677–681.

63. Alison Motluk, "Power Naps Boost Work Performance," *NewScientist*, May 2002, http://www.newscientist.com/news/news.jsp?id=ns99992328.

64. Hemi-Sync® Audio Technology from the Monroe Institue, www.monroeinstitute.org, is a product of such research in meditation stimuli, http://www.monroeinstitute.org/research/hemisync/hemi-sync.html.

65. Diane L. Coutu, "Business on the Brain," *Harvard Business Review*, February 2004, 16–17.

66. EEG stands for electroencephalography.

67. MEG stands for magnetoencephalography.

68. Larry Bossidy and Ram Charan, *Execution: The Discipline of Getting Things Done* (Crown Business, 2002), 46–48.

69. Ralph Kimball, *The Data Webhouse Toolkit* (John Wiley & Sons, 2000), 233.

70. Bill Inmon and others, *Corporate Information Factory* (Wiley, 2000), 169–187.

71. Masaaki Imai, "Kaizen, the Key to Japan's Competitive Success." According to Mr. Masaaki Imai, Kaizen means improvement. Moreover, Kaizen means continuing improvement in personal life, home life, social life, and working life. When applied to the workplace Kaizen means continuing improvement involving everyone—managers and workers alike. Reference found at http://www.kaizen-institute. com/knowkaizen/knowkaizen.html.

72. Equilibrium also justified by both James Martin, *An Information Systems Manifesto* (Prentice Hall, 1984), 44; and Bill Inmon and others, *Corporate Information Factory* (Wiley, 2000), 237.

73. ActiveViews, www.activeviews.com, is one example of vendors that see an 80/20 distribution between standard reports and analysis, http://www.activeviews.com/products.

74. James Martin, *An Information Systems Manifesto* (Prentice Hall, 1984), 46. Suggests that management does not know what they want until they see it.

75. Robert S. Kaplan and David P. Norton, *The Balanced Scorecard: Translating Strategy into Action* (Harvard Business School Press, 1996), 10–12.

76. Nils-Göran Olve and Anna Sjöstrand, *The Balanced Scorecard* (Capstone Publishing, 2002), 67.

77. Abraham Zaleznik, "Managers and Leaders: Are they Different?" *Harvard Business Review*, January 2004, 74–81.

78. Max DePree, *Leadership is an Art* (New York: Dell Publishing, 1989), 11–22.

79. Marcus Buckingham and Curt Coffman, *First, Break All the Rules: What the World's Greatest Managers Do Differently* (Simon & Schuster, 1999), 67.

80. Buckingham and Coffman, *First, Break All the Rules*, 57.

81. Stephen R. Covey, *Seven Habits Of Highly Effective People* (Free Press, 1990), 68–70.

82. Marcus Buckingham and Donald O. Clifton, *Now, Discover Your Strengths* (Simon & Schuster, 2001), 138.

83. Cpl. Robert W. Wynkoop, "Heart of Samurai Still Beats Strong," *Marine Corps News*, Marine Corps Air Station Iwakuni, Japan, 20 February 2004, story identification number: 200422011619.

84. James Clark, "Way of the Warrior," Pacific University, 1996, http://mcel.pacificu.edu/as/students/bushido/bindex.html.

85. Eckhart Tolle, *The Power of Now: A Guide to Spiritual Enlightenment* (New World Library, 1999).

86. Stephen R. Covey, *Seven Habits Of Highly Effective People* (Free Press, 1990), 130–135, 95–44.

87. Napoleon Hill, *Think and Grow Rich* (New York: Ballantine Publishing Group, 1983), xvi.

88. Hill, *Think and Grow Rich*, 1–13.

89. Samuel B. Griffith, *The Art of War* (Oxford University Press, 1971), 96, 90–101.

90. Gary Hamel and C. K. Prahalad, *Competing for the Future* (Boston, MA: Harvard Business School Press, 1994), 139–161.

91. Bill Gates, *Business @ the Speed of Thought* (New York: Warner Books, 2000), 171.

92. Rita Shor, "Managed Innovation: 3M's Latest Model for New Products," *Manufacturing & Technology News*, 2000, http://www.manufacturingnews.com/news/editorials/shor.html.

93. Igor Ansoff, "Strategies for Diversification." *Harvard Business Review*, September-October 1957, 113–124.

94. Dr. C. George Boeree, "General Psychology: The Emotional Nervous System," Shippensburg University of Pennsylvania, 2002, http://www.ship.edu/~cgboeree/limbicsystem.html.

95. Marcus Buckingham and Curt Coffman, *First, Break All the Rules: What the World's Greatest Managers Do Differently* (Simon & Schuster, 1999), 71–104.

96. Buckingham and Coffman, *First, Break All the Rules*, 153. Suggests focusing on the best employees by spending the most time with them.

97. Mihaly Csikszentmihalyi, *Flow: The Psychology of Optimal Experience* (New York: Harper & Row Publishers, 1990), 74.

98. Csikszentmihalyi, *Flow*, 39–41. Suggests that optimal performance of an individual takes place by working in a continuous process where we are competing against ourselves, a state of flow.

99. Marcus Buckingham and Curt Coffman, *First, Break All the Rules: What the World's Greatest Managers Do Differently* (Simon & Schuster, 1999), 151. Suggests that excelling should be done by competing against oneself.

100. Albert E. N. Gray, "The Common Denominator of Success," references from Web sites, http://www.zaadz.com/inspiration/the_common_denominator_of_success.html and http://www.thinkarete.com/wisdom/works/essays/1462/.

101. Stephen R. Covey, *Seven Habits Of Highly Effective People* (Free Press, 1990), 149.

102. Based on interview with Siegfried W. Andersen's partner Ulrik Villadsen from management consulting company Villadsen.biz, www.villadsen.biz.

103. Marcus Buckingham and Donald O. Clifton, *Now, Discover Your Strengths* (Simon & Schuster, 2001), 155–159.

104. Stephen R. Covey, *Seven Habits Of Highly Effective People* (Free Press, 1990), 151.

105. Bill Gates, *Business @ the Speed of Thought* (New York: Warner Books, 2000), 174.

106. Mihaly Csikszentmihalyi, *Flow: The Psychology of Optimal Experience* (New York: Harper & Row Publishers, 1990), 39.

107. Richard Florida, *The Rise of the Creative Class* (New York: Basic Books, 2002), 44, 47.

108. CAD stands for computer aided design.

109. John Seely Brown, "Research that Reinvents the Corporation," *Harvard Business Review*, August 2002, 105–114.

110. Axel Michaelowa, "Phasing out Lead in Gasoline: How Developing Countries Can Learn from the Experiences of the Industrialized World,"

World Development Aid and Joint Venture Finance 1997/98, London, 1997, 268—272, http://www.hwwa.de/PersHome/Michaelowa_A/Lead.htm.

111. "The Monkey Shakespeare Simulator" is an example of a computerized approach to this saying, http://user.tninet.se/~ecf599g/aardasnails/java/Monkey/webpages/.

112. Jesper Stein Sandal, "Universiteter og erhverv sammen om grid (Universities and Enterprises Join Forces on Grid)," *Computer World On-Line*, http://www.computerworld.dk/default.asp?Mode=2&ArticleID=23109.

113. SETI@home is a scientific experiment that uses Internet-connected computers in the Search for Extraterrestrial Intelligence. See more on http://setiathome.ssl.berkeley.edu.

114. Edward N. Luttwak, *Coup d'État* (Penguin, 1969).

115. Based on interview, 22 June 2004, with brain researcher, engineer, and Ph.D. student Torben E. Lund, Hvidovre Hospital, MR Department, Denmark.

116. Ballistic Missile Defense Organization, "2001 Technology Application Report," 2001, 16, http://www.acq.osd.mil/bmdo/bmdolink/pdf/2001tar.pdf.

117. Paul E. Green, Patrich Robinson, and Peter T. Fitzroy, *Experiments on the Value of Information in Simulated Marketing Environments* (Boston: Allyn and Bacon, 1967), 26–43.

118. Marcus Buckingham and Donald O. Clifton, *Now, Discover Your Strengths* (Simon & Schuster, 2001), 76–80.

119. Stephen R. Covey, *Seven Habits Of Highly Effective People* (Free Press, 1990), 185. Covey suggests that reaching personal victory is a prerequisite to reaching public victory.

120. "PlanPlus" from FranklinCovey, www.franklincovey.com, is a product that allows personal value and goal identification and monitoring. Effectively this product is an early stage of what is referred to as an "individual energy journal," http://www.franklincovey.com/planplus/index.html.

121. Equity Research, "Dawn of the Performance Enterprise," Banc of America Securities, Software Industry Overview, May 2004.

122. The research was conducted via a web survey conducted from June 2002 to May 2004 in which 355 volunteers participated.

123. Allan Hammond, *Which World: Scenarios for the 21st Century: Global Destinies, Regional Choices* (Shearwater Books, 2000), 82–85.

124. History taken from the Atomic Museum, www.atomicmuseum.com, 2003, http://www.atomicmuseum.com/tour/manhattanproject.cfm.

125. Mihaly Csikszentmihalyi, *Creativity* (HarperCollins Publishers, 1997), 144–147.

126. Dan Lee, "Tour de Tech: Latest Innovations Help Cyclist Train for Race," *The Mercury News*, 28 June 2004, http://www.mercurynews.com/mld/mercurynews/9030077.htm?1c.

127. Bill Gates, *Business @ the Speed of Thought* (New York: Warner Books, 2000), 176–177.

128. Stephen R. Covey, *Seven Habits Of Highly Effective People* (Free Press, 1990), 159–171.

129. Based on interview with Jakob Algreen-Ussing from the company Wavetech, www.wavetech.com. His source for knowledge is focus groups on Danish telecom services "Club Blah Blah" and "Selvhenter."

130. Hans Moravec, *Robot: Mere Machine to Transcendent Mind* (Oxford University Press, 1999), 60. 2020 computers match human brain power.

131. Neil Postman, *Technopoly: The Surrender of Culture to Technology* (Vintage Books USA, 1993), 110–122.

132. Edwin A. Abbott, *Flatland: A Parable of Spiritual Dimensions* (1884; repr., Oneworld Publications, 1994).

133. Jakob Nielsen, *Designing Web Usability: The Practice of Simplicity* (Indianapolis, IN: New Riders Publishing, 2000), 348.

134. Ray Kurzweil, *The Age of Spiritual Machines: When Computers Exceed Human Intelligence* (Penguin Putnam, 2000), 279–280.

135. Based on interview, 22 June 2004, with brain researcher, engineer, and Ph.D. student Torben E. Lund, Hvidovre Hospital, MR Department, Denmark.

136. Based on interview, 22 June 2004, with brain researcher, engineer, and Ph.D. student Torben E. Lund, Hvidovre Hospital, MR Department,

Denmark. See perhaps also prof. Paul Sajda, "A Brain-Computer Interface for Playing Pong," January 2003, http://www.bme.columbia.edu/ ~sajda/bme3910/sajda.html.

137. Based on interview, 22 June 2004, with brain researcher, engineer, and Ph.D. student Torben E. Lund, Hvidovre Hospital, MR Department, Denmark.

138. Hans Moravec, *Robot: Mere Machine to Transcendent Mind* (Oxford University Press, 1999), 163–212.

139. Ray Kurzweil, *The Age of Spiritual Machines: When Computers Exceed Human Intelligence* (Penguin Putnam, 2000), 14–15.

140. Jakob Nielsen, "Thirty Years With Computers," personal Web site, 24 May 2004, http://www.useit.com/alertbox/20040524.html.

0-595-32991-8